INSIDE

MICROSOFT
EXCHANGE SERVER

BRUCE HALLBERG

KATHY IVENS

New Riders

New Riders Publishing, Indianapolis, Indiana

Inside Microsoft Exchange Server

By Bruce Hallberg and Kathy Ivens

Published by:
New Riders Publishing
201 West 103rd Street
Indianapolis, IN 46290 USA

Printed in the United States of America 1 2 3 4 5 6 7 8 9 0

Library of Congress Cataloging-in-Publication Data

Hallberg, Bruce A., 1964-

      Inside Microsoft Exchange Server/ Bruce
      Hallberg, Kathy Ivens.
                    p. cm.
            Includes index.
            ISBN 1-56205-570-4
            1. Microsoft Exchange. 2. Client/server
      computing. I. Ivens, Kathy. II. Title.
      QA76.9.C55H35 1996
      005.7'1369--dc20
      96-3258
      CIP

Warning and Disclaimer

This book is designed to provide information about the Microsoft Exchange Server computer program. Every effort has been made to make this book as complete and as accurate as possible, but no warranty or fitness is implied.

The information is provided on an "as is" basis. The author(s) and New Riders Publishing shall have neither liability nor responsibility to any person or entity with respect to any loss or damages arising from the information contained in this book or from the use of the disks or programs that may accompany it.

Publisher	*Don Fowley*
Publishing Manager	*Emmett Dulaney*
Marketing Manager	*Mary Foote*
Managing Editor	*Carla Hall*

Development Editor
  Becky Campbell

Project Editors
  Nancy Albright
  Amy Bezek

Copy Editor
  Nancy Albright

Technical Editor
  Dan Hodges

Associate Marketing Manager
  Tamara Apple

Acquisitions Coordinator
  Stacia Mellinger

Publisher's Assistant
  Karen Opal

Cover Designer
  Sandra Schroeder

Cover Production
  Aren Howell

Book Designer
  Sandra Schroeder

Production Manager
  Kelly Dobbs

Production Team Supervisor
  Laurie Casey

Graphics Image Specialists
  Stephen Adams
  Daniel Harris
  Clint Lahnen
  Ryan Oldfather
  Casey Price
  Laura Robbins
  Jeff Yesh

Production Analysts
  Jason Hand
  Bobbi Satterfield

Production Team
  Angela Calvert
  Daniel Caparo
  Kim Cofer
  Tricia Flodder
  Aleata Howard
  Beth Rago
  Erich Richter

Indexer
  Tim Tate

About the Authors

Bruce Hallberg is the Director of Information Systems for Genelabs Technologies, Inc., a biotechnology company located in Redwood City, California. He has been heavily involved with PCs since 1980, and has specialized in accounting and business control systems for the past seven years. He has consulted with a large number of local and national companies in a variety of areas and has expertise in networking, programming, and system implementations. He works with a wide variety of PC computing platforms, including DOS, Windows, OS/2, UNIX, and Macintosh.

Kathy Ivens has been a computer consultant and management consultant in private practice since 1984. Operating as Ivens Consulting, Inc., her company specializes in accounting applications for micro and mini computers, network design and installation, database design and development, word processing training, and operating system training.

Ms. Ivens has taught diverse computer subjects at a variety of institutions and has authored several books on computer subjects: *Porting Applications to OS/2* (Simon & Schuster), *The Virus Handbook* (McGraw-Hill), *OS/2 Inside & Out* (McGraw-Hill), *Byte Magazine's OS/2 Programmer's Cookbook* (McGraw-Hill), *WordPerfect 6 for DOS Made Easy* (McGraw-Hill), *WordPerfect 6 for Windows Made Easy* (McGraw-Hill).

She is a frequent contributor to national magazines on computer topics and has been the computer columnist for several regional publications in the Delaware Valley area. She is certified for CPA training (CPE courses) in Pennsylvania and New Jersey. She leads the Philadelphia WordPerfect Users Group under the aegis of the Philadelphia Area Computer Society and is also the instructor for DOS classes for that organization.

Trademark Acknowledgments

All terms mentioned in this book that are known to be trademarks or service marks have been appropriately capitalized. New Riders Publishing cannot attest to the accuracy of this information. Use of a term in this book should not be regarded as affecting the validity of any trademark or service mark. Exchange Server is a registered trademark of Microsoft Corporation.

Acknowledgments

The people at New Riders Publishing are always fun to work with, and their professional skills are a wondergul asset for us to lean on. We extend warm thanks to Emmett Dulaney, who, as always, provided guidance amd humor and the warm cozy feeling of working with a team that cares; kudos to Becky Campbell, who gave us constructive feedback in addition to constant help with every aspect of this book's development; appreciation to Nancy Albright for making our language skills look good with her editing abilities and logical mind; thanks to Stacia Mellinger for keeping everything organized with great skill and aplomb; gratitude to Amy Bezek for juggling details and providing a level of organization we're not capable of; gratefulness to Dan Hodges, for technical editing that probably saved us from a great deal of embarrassment.

Contents at a Glance

Table of Contents

2   Mastering the Concepts   27

Part II: Planning Your Microsoft Exchange Server System   61

3 Ascertaining Needs   63

Introduction

Microsoft entered the PC electronic messaging arena with its purchase of an e-mail product called Network Courier about five years ago. The product, which enjoyed a substantial portion of the market, was quickly renamed Microsoft Mail for PC Networks and has done very well. Since then, MS Mail has evolved in bits and spurts, but basically has remained fairly static. The reason MS Mail hasn't been improved much over the years is that Microsoft has been working on building an entirely new messaging system: Microsoft Exchange Server.

Microsoft Exchange Server bears no resemblance to Microsoft Mail for PC Networks. Although Exchange Server can interface with existing MS Mail post offices, it is an entirely new product, built from the ground up—and one that is light-years ahead of MS Mail.

In this book, you learn about Microsoft Exchange Server—how to install and configure it, how to administer it on a day-to-day basis, and how to develop powerful messaging applications for your organization that make use of Exchange Server's power.

Client-Server Messaging

The biggest problem with MS Mail is that it's built as a file-based messaging product, where all the messages are stored in a directory structure located on a network file server. All users of the MS Mail e-mail system need full access to that directory structure. Although the message files are encrypted to prevent unauthorized reading of messages, it's relatively easy for users to browse around the file structure, potentially deleting files that can bring the entire e-mail system down. Of course, people could copy those encrypted message files and break their encryption. Clearly, with companies relying on e-mail systems for more and more crucial information, this is unacceptable. It's also pretty clumsy, particularly for larger companies that have much more sophisticated messaging needs.

Another problem with file-based approaches is that they are more difficult to scale up to meet increased demands. It also becomes much more complicated to extend the system beyond its original design specification. The situation is similar to the old-fashioned shared file-based accounting systems. Although the approach works, it runs out of steam when you try to grow the system beyond a certain point.

Exchange Server, on the other hand, is a client-server messaging system. The Exchange Server software runs on a computer running Windows NT Server. Users log into the server, after which their client software (Exchange Client) can log into the Exchange Server software running on that server. This is a fundamentally better and more robust system for almost any need.

Generally, client-server systems are more secure, more scalable, and easier to administer. They are more flexible as well. Exchange Server brings a new architecture to the table that can be configured to meet almost any need. It's a revolutionary product.

Understanding Exchange Server Features

Many features are built into Exchange Server that make it very well-suited to organizations of any size. These features include the following:

◆ **Server Redundancy.** You can run multiple servers in a given site, both to balance heavy messaging loads and to provide some level of redundancy for users, so that key messaging applications keep running, even if a particular server is down.

◆ **Automatic Directory Replication.** All the Exchange Server computers can be set up so that they automatically update each other on changes to the messaging directories. Administrators don't have to update changes manually from one server to another or from one site to another.

◆ **Connectors to Foreign Systems.** A variety of connectors are available for Exchange Server that enable you to connect it to other messaging systems running in your organization. Because Exchange Server has a modular design, additional connectors can be developed and then "plugged in" to Exchange Server to extend its capabilities.

◆ **Industry Standard Connectivity.** Exchange Server can connect to X.400 messaging backbones and to the Internet using SMTP.

◆ **Seamless Integration with Windows NT Server.** Exchange Server's integration with Windows NT eases the burden of administering the system. Often, actions that would otherwise involve changes to both the Windows NT Server software and to Exchange Server (such as adding a new user mailbox and account) are now accomplished at the same time. Exchange Server also makes use of other Windows NT Server services, such as its built-in backup program and the Event Viewer. Because Exchange Server is built specifically to run on Windows NT Server, Exchange Server also inherits many of Windows NT Server's capabilities, such as those for managing server disk drives and building disk arrays easily.

◆ **Many Ways to Connect Sites.** You can connect your far-flung sites by using a variety of methods, ranging from modems over standard dial-up telephone lines all the way to multimegabit bandwidth solutions. Exchange Server can use any underlying WAN connectivity that can carry TCP/IP, IPX/SPX, or NetBEUI traffic. You also can configure Exchange Server to use Windows NT Server's Remote Access Services (RAS) to provide remote connections for traveling users or people located in small offices who don't warrant their own messaging server.

◆ **Public Folders.** Exchange Server's public folders enable users to share information more easily than ever before. Security built into the public folders enables the administrator to control who has access to them, preserving company security.

◆ **Electronic Forms.** Built into Exchange Server, this feature enables you to develop your own custom forms that make use of the messaging system. These forms can automate many paper-based systems in most companies, such as purchase orders, check requests, time allocation sheets, vacation requests, and much more. Exchange Server comes with Forms Designer, an application designed for easy form creation. Forms Designer generates forms using Visual Basic code, so you can bring the power of Visual Basic to bear on more thorny automation problems when needed. A variety of useful sample form applications comes with Exchange Server, and these forms can be used as-is or they can easily be modified to suit your company.

◆ **Advanced Security.** Not only does Exchange Server make use of Windows NT Server's security tools to restrict access to resources in the messaging system, it also includes capabilities that enable your users to encrypt messages by using public keys. These security tools mean that you can develop and deploy applications that require a high degree of trust.

◆ **Client Software.** Exchange Client, first included with Windows 95, is a powerful end-user messaging tool. Versions are available to support DOS, Windows 3.1, Windows 95, and Windows NT desktops. A Macintosh client is not available at the first shipping of Exchange Server, but it will be available sometime in the middle of 1996.

Kathy Ivens and Bruce Hallberg are always interested in hearing your ideas for improvements to future editions of this book. If you have any suggestions, please feel free to contact them directly. Bruce can be reached at the following e-mail address:

76376.515@compuserve.com

Send e-mail to Kathy at this address:

74020.42@compuserve.com

New Riders Publishing

The staff of New Riders Publishing is committed to bringing you the very best in computer reference material. Each New Riders book is the result of months of work by authors and staff who research and refine the information contained within its covers.

As part of this commitment to you, the NRP reader, New Riders invites your input. Please let us know if you enjoy this book, if you have trouble with the information and examples presented, or if you have a suggestion for the next edition.

Please note, though: New Riders staff, or the authors, cannot serve as a technical resource for Microsoft Exchange Server or for questions about software- or hardware-related problems. Please refer to the documentation that accompanies Exchange Server or to the applications' Help systems.

If you have a question or comment about any New Riders book, there are several ways to contact New Riders Publishing. We will respond to as many readers as we can. Your name, address, or phone number will never become part of a mailing list or be used for any purpose other than to help us continue to bring you the best books possible. You can write us at the following address:

New Riders Publishing
Attn: Publisher
201 W. 103rd Street
Indianapolis, IN 46290

If you prefer, you can fax New Riders Publishing at (317) 581-4670.

You can also send electronic mail to New Riders at the following Internet address:

`edulaney@newriders.mcp.com`

NRP is an imprint of Macmillan Computer Publishing. To obtain a catalog or information, or to purchase any Macmillan Computer Publishing book, call (800) 428-
5331.

Thank you for selecting *Inside Microsoft Exchange Server*!

PART I

Introducing Microsoft Exchange Server

CHAPTER 1

Introducing Microsoft Exchange Server

Microsoft Exchange Server is a LAN-based electronic messaging application that has powers and features most companies will find useful, such as the following:

◆ E-mail—internal and external

◆ File transfer—internal and external

◆ Access to shared information in files and folders

◆ Scheduling (an additional, optional application)

◆ A modular client/server environment

◆ Built-in tools for designing applications that work with the messaging features

Multiple LANs, WANs, and MANs within an organization can be linked in Microsoft Exchange Server to bring the software's features to all users.

Microsoft Exchange Server consists of two major components:

- ◆ *Server components* that run on each Microsoft Exchange Server computer

- ◆ *Client components* that run on each user's computer

There are many functional elements within each major component, and they all work together to accomplish tasks across a network or a group of networks.

In order to operate on various scales of size and breadth, Microsoft Exchange Server runs with a hierarchical structure. As a result, a one-server company with a small number of users is configured similarly to a large, international company with multiple LANs in many locations.

Microsoft Exchange Server runs on Windows NT Server. This gives the system many features that are built into Windows NT:

- ◆ Centralized client management

- ◆ Connectivity to other servers and to clients running a variety of operating systems

- ◆ Interoperability with a variety of networking and messaging systems

The client software for Microsoft Exchange Server runs on a number of operating systems:

- ◆ MS-DOS 5.0 or later

- ◆ Windows 3.1

- ◆ Windows NT 3.51 Workstation

- ◆ Windows for Workgroups 3.11

- ◆ Windows 95

Defining the Terms

To use Microsoft Exchange Server efficiently, you need to understand the terminology as well as its structure. Some of the terms you will find as you install and administer Microsoft Exchange Server are self-explanatory, but others require some explanation.

Defining the Organization

Microsoft Exchange Server is structured on a hierarchy of organizations and sites within organizations. Most companies configure Microsoft Exchange Server as one organization. The word "organization" can be confusing because most people think of that term as a definition of their corporation or conglomerate. This book uses the term the way it is defined for Microsoft Exchange Server and uses *enterprise* to refer to a corporate organization. Your enterprise can have one organization (everything running from the top down on one Microsoft Exchange Server system) or several organizations.

An *organization* is one or more Microsoft Exchange Servers that are linked in order to provide services for a whole group. It is the highest-level administrative unit for Microsoft Exchange Server. Think of it as a service provider that sits at the top of a company's organizational chart. Although it is logical to visualize the top of the organizational chart as a single unit, because of special features in Microsoft Exchange Server, you can actually duplicate that top unit to make managing a large enterprise easier.

 Don't think of the organization as a computer; it is a concept representing the enterprise (the corporation). In terms of function, it is the service provider for the enterprise. It can provide its services from a single computer or multiple computers.

For example, if you install Microsoft Exchange Server for a company contained in a single building where all the computers are directly connected, a single server runs Microsoft Exchange Server as the organization and handles all the work for the entire enterprise. Figure 1.1 shows a diagram of a typical company and its configuration.

Figure 1.1

All the computers are connected, and the organization is administered by a single server.

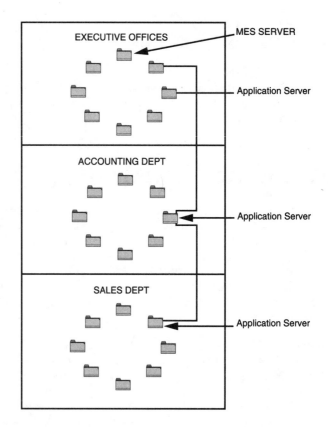

If the company has multiple offices in different geographical locations, a server in each location can represent the organization (see fig. 1.2).

Even if you have multiple locations, you can choose to have one organization server for the enterprise. It is usually more expedient, however, to configure one server at each location to hold the mailboxes for the local users. Figure 1.3 illustrates a simple way to accomplish this.

If the locations have a large number of users, you might want to have a mailbox container in each division of the location, as seen in figure 1.4.

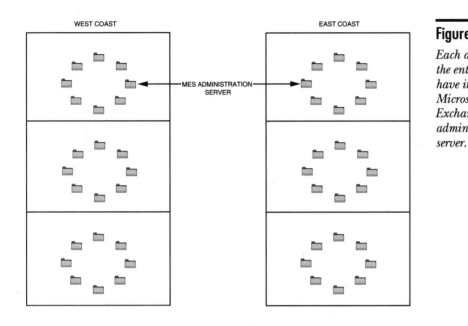

Figure 1.2

Each division of the enterprise can have its own Microsoft Exchange Server administration server.

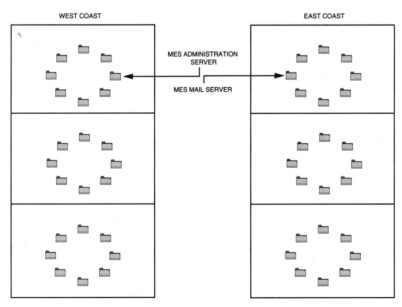

Figure 1.3

You can administer the organization from one server, even if there are multiple locations.

Figure 1.4

Local mailboxes (by floor or department) make it easier and faster to distribute and collect mail—you can still administer the other site functions from one main server in another location.

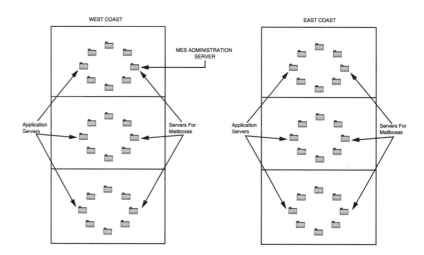

Note Remember—the servers handling Microsoft Exchange Server duties must be running on NT. Other servers, such as those that hold applications accessed by local users, can run on other network operating systems.

In order to make everything more manageable (and split the work load efficiently), an extremely large and scattered company can have several servers in various sites. Regardless of how they interact with each other (perhaps splitting tasks between servers) or how they connect with the users and each other, servers that provide Microsoft Exchange Server services represent the organization.

Understanding the Organization's Divisions

Services provided by Microsoft Exchange Server throughout the organization are sent through a series of divisions of the organization. If you are using Microsoft Exchange Server in a small company, some divisions will overlap, but for large organizations, the divisions provide a structure that makes administration easier.

Site

A *site* is a server, or a group of servers that can communicate with each other, that uses the same directory information and the same Microsoft Exchange Server structure. Directory changes to any server in a site are automatically replicated to all other servers in the site. To qualify as a site, some conditions must exist:

◆ The network link must be permanent, with no temporary dial-up connections between any computers within the site.

◆ All servers within the site must be part of the same Windows NT domain (or be domains that trust each other—see the section on domains and trusts later in this chapter).

Usually, a site is a single geographic location. It might be an organization's only location, a divisional office, the headquarters of a subsidiary company, or the warehouse of a company with executive headquarters in another place. You also can declare multiple geographic locations that are connected to be a site if it makes sense in terms of administering Microsoft Exchange Server.

Creating sites within Microsoft Exchange Server makes managing the administration of Microsoft Exchange Server easier, but you need to do some careful planning before you set up the sites for your system. Changing the configuration of sites is a very complicated process.

 You can configure Microsoft Exchange Server so that you can administer your own site as well as all the other sites in the organization from your computer.

Domain

A domain is a Windows NT concept that Microsoft Exchange Server uses for rights, permissions, and general security issues. A *domain* is a group of computers that are connected together. The computers in a domain are administered as a group, and the domain can have multiple servers. These servers, which run Windows NT, are responsible for authenticating logon requests and are called *domain controllers*.

All computers (clients and servers) in a domain are connected to a Windows NT server that is designated as the *Primary Domain Controller* (PDC). This PDC stores the security database for the entire domain, and any maintenance of that database must be performed on this computer. You cannot have multiple PDCs in a domain.

The PDC can be set up to replicate its data automatically to the other domain controllers, and this can make recovering from a PDC crash a fairly easy procedure— any of the other domain controllers can be configured to take over the PDC tasks.

Domains are named (see the section on naming conventions later in this chapter), and the names and properties of domains are set by an administrator with the appropriate permissions and rights.

For many companies, domains and sites are overlapping organizational units; the entire site is one domain, and another site becomes its own domain.

Domain Trust Relationships

A *trust relationship* is a special link between two domains. The link means that a user who has an account in one domain can access resources in another domain.

For instance, domain One has a trust relationship with domain Two. This means domain One trusts domain Two. Domain One is the trusting domain and domain Two is the trusted domain. Domain One gives access to the list of groups and the user information it owns to domain Two.

Once the trust is established, users from the trusted domain (domain Two) are given rights to objects in the trusting domain (domain One) with the same result as if they were members of domain One.

Domain Models

Your Windows NT operating system offers four domain models to choose from when you set up your NT system. If you are installing Microsoft Exchange Server on an existing NT system, you have to determine the model that is being used. If you have to change it, be prepared to reinstall Windows NT.

Single Domain Model

The single domain model is the simplest one because your NT network has only one domain. You can create all your users in one place, and you don't have to worry about trust relationships.

You can have as many as 22,000 users in a single domain. If you do have thousands of users, however, you will probably see a performance level deterioration. In addition, because you can link domains to multiple servers, there could be some performance problems when this single domain has to search multiple servers to gather information.

Complete Trust Domain Model

The complete trust domain model is useful for decentralizing the management tasks on your system without having to build varying levels of security. You can split users and domains into manageable groups and know that each domain trusts the others.

You can have up to 22,000 users in each domain, which could be an unwieldy number to administer, regardless of the technical capabilities of Windows NT.

Because each domain keeps control over its own user accounts, this model is good for organizations that have definitive departments or divisions that are managed by individuals assigned to them rather than a central IS Director. It's the best of two worlds—security levels and permissions are global, administrative tasks are split.

Master Domain Model

The master domain model is useful when your network has to be divided into domains to make administration easier. This usually occurs when the organization's structure is such that it is logical to split the Windows NT and Microsoft Exchange Server administration in a way that matches that structure.

The master domain model has two levels: the master domain itself is on the first level, all the other domains are on the second level. The following characteristics apply to this model:

◆ The master domain contains all user accounts and can accommodate up to 22,000 users.

◆ The second level domains (meaning all the domains except the master domain) trust the master domain.

◆ None of the second level domains trust each other.

◆ The master domain does not trust any of the second level domains.

Using this model means that each defined group in your organization administers its own resources—everything, that is, except user accounts and global groups, which are administered in the master domain.

In effect, this model provides centralized administration of user accounts and decentralized administration of everything else.

Multiple Master Domain Model

This domain model is useful for organizations that want or need decentralized administration, because they are arranged into groups, divisions, or locations (or all three).

The multiple master domain model is organized into levels, following the same pattern as the master domain model.

The first level is the master domain, and the second level is comprised of all the individual domains that are established throughout the organization's division.

The following characteristics apply to this model:

◆ The master domains trust each other.

◆ The second level domains trust the master domains.

◆ The second level domains do not trust each other.

◆ The master domains do not trust the second level domains.

This is an attractive model for a very large organization because one copy of each user account is set up on the master domain that makes the most sense for that particular user. After all, the master domains all trust each other, so having a user in one domain is the same as having the user in every domain. The administrative tasks that are needed to maintain a larger number of users are split, so no administrator or administrative department is responsible for keeping up with the entire user list.

Don't underestimate the amount of work involved in this model, however. This is a busy system to maintain, with lots of work involved in defining, configuring, and maintaining all the local and global groups involved with the second-level domains.

Mapping Domains and Sites

Sites and domains can be related (mapped) to each other. Mapping connects the service/user accounts in a site to a domain. There are a number of ways to establish your mappings:

◆ You can map one site to one domain, which is a fairly easy concept to understand and administer.

◆ You can map multiple sites to one domain.

◆ A site can map to multiple domains, but the domains must trust each other so that the servers in the site can authenticate each other's users.

◆ Mapping has nothing to do with the domain model chosen.

Servers

Computers that are established for the purpose of exercising some authority over other, connected computers are called *servers*. Servers also hold files that connected computers use to perform the work of the organization.

The servers that implement the core services for Microsoft Exchange Server must run on Windows NT, but they can connect and communicate with servers that use other operating systems.

If you have a very large enterprise, you might find it more productive to split the administration of individual programs and features in Microsoft Exchange Server among multiple servers. All the servers and workstations that use a particular Microsoft Exchange Server computer as a "home base" computer are called *server recipients*.

Clients

Clients (users) are the computers that do the work that keeps a company running. In addition, they use Microsoft Exchange Server programs and features to communicate with each other, communicate with the outside world, and share certain files.

In order to use Microsoft Exchange Server features, clients must have the client software installed. If you have a large enterprise, don't worry; you do not have to walk to each client workstation and perform an installation. There is a way to install the client software from an attached server, even if the server is not an NT server. (See Chapter 6, "Installing Exchange Server," for detailed information.)

 The DOS Client software does not support the Schedule + module of Microsoft Exchange Server.

Understanding Naming Conventions

Spend some time planning the names for all the parts of your organization. If the names make sense in terms of the way you divide your organization, it will be easier to administer the system. Geographical locations, department names, division names, and so forth can be included in your naming schemes.

You should consider the name of your organization, the sites, and the servers as being permanent, because making changes will involve a reinstallation.

To avoid serious stress when you are administering e-mail, remember that addresses include parts of your system's names (servers, directories). The syntax for a user's mail address in Microsoft Exchange Server is the following:

o / ou / cn / cn

where

- ◆ *o* is the enterprise name (the organization).

- ◆ *ou* is the site name.

- ◆ *cn* is the recipient's container (the directory that holds the mailboxes).

- ◆ *cn* is the recipient's mailbox name.

An address that contains all these elements, the labels, and the data, is called the *distinguished name.*

Here is a distinguished name for Beverly T who works for Calliope, Inc. in the East Coast office (which has a site name of East):

```
o=CALLIOPE/ou=East/cn=recipients/cn=BeverlyT
```

In its own naming conventions, however, Microsoft Exchange Server abbreviates the name by eliminating the labels. For the same employee, Microsoft Exchange Server uses this name:

```
calliope/east/recipients/BeverlyT
```

In both the distinguished name and the Microsoft Exchange Server name, you can see the resemblance to a path name.

Organization Name

Part of the setup task is to name your organization. You should choose a name that is descriptive of your company, because you can use the name when you configure e-mail addresses. There are a few other things to be aware of about organization names:

◆ Once you name your organization, you can't change it (unless you're prepared to reinstall everything).

◆ Because you probably want to use the organization name in your e-mail addresses, do not use any characters that are forbidden in any e-mail software or service you encounter.

◆ The organization name is a part of the directory names for user-accessed directory objects, such as mailboxes and public folders.

◆ You can use up to 64 characters for your organization name.

Site Names

Every site in your organization needs a unique name. You can use whatever naming convention makes sense to you, using geographical locations and departments, or perhaps using a name that reflects the function.

Remember that the site name is part of the e-mail address, so do not use any characters that are not allowed in any of your e-mail software or outside e-mail services. Up to 64 characters are permitted.

Server Names

Server names must be unique, and up to 15 characters are permitted.

 Do not use any spaces in the names of servers that act as domain controllers, because the name will not be interpreted correctly in login scripts.

Mailbox Names

You have to devise a name for each mailbox in your organization. Apart from the name that is displayed in your administrator's window and in e-mail address books, other information is attached to the mailbox name record. Creating the mailbox is covered in the installation and configuration chapters (Chapters 6 and 7, respectively) of this book.

Understanding Message and File Exchange

The primary function of Microsoft Exchange Server is to handle messages within an organization and outside the organization. In addition, files and folders can be established that are public, open to users in the organization.

Messages

The term *messages*, unlike some of the other terminology discussed, can be used literally, the way you use it in plain English. Of course, the world of computers usually uses the word e-mail to indicate messages sent and received via computer.

The messaging power of Microsoft Exchange Server gives you the capability of sending messages throughout your organization, even to users on computers with different operating system platforms.

In order to accomplish all this you need to configure your system down through the hierarchy, from the organization to the individual mailboxes that hold the messages.

Foreign E-Mail

In addition to your internal e-mail system, you can have messaging services with individuals outside your organization. E-mail has to reach your organization's users from these individuals, and there has to be a way to send e-mail from your organization's users to them.

To exchange e-mail with non-Exchange Server systems, you have to create internal e-mail addresses in a format that can be read by those foreign e-mail systems. In order to send e-mail to foreign systems, you have to create a system for storing those e-mail addresses on your system. When that is done, users in your organization can send and receive e-mail everywhere, without having to worry about special conventions and formats.

Individuals who are on foreign e-mail systems, and who have addresses residing in address books within your organization, are called *custom recipients.*

As you establish the protocols, conventions, and formats in the course of setting up e-mail addresses, Microsoft Exchange Server will generate X.400 and Internet addresses for custom recipients. You need to establish e-mail addresses for all the e-mail systems that are accessed by the users in your organization (PROFS, SNADS, and so forth).

All the information and instructions for establishing and maintaining e-mail services are found throughout this book.

Public Folders

The concept of public folders is an important part of Microsoft Exchange Server. *Public folders* are folders located on Microsoft Exchange Server computers that store information that can be accessed by all users.

A public folder is one of the four recipients in Microsoft Exchange Server (the other three are mailboxes, distribution lists, and custom recipients).

Do not confuse this concept with folders to which many users have access, permission, and rights, such as folders that hold application software. The public folder is like a public mailbox. Most organizations use it as a repository for items of substantial size that all users, or a specific group of users, should see. Placing the information in the public folder is a superior method of distribution, compared to copying the information to each user's mailbox.

In many organizations, the public folders receive the company newsletter, copies of articles or studies that are relevant to the recipient users, and other, similar information. Users can move files from their computers to the public folders; in fact, users who run Microsoft Windows can use File Manager or Windows Explorer to drag documents between their computers and the public folders.

You can also use public folders for online discussions and conferences.

Replication

You can establish public folders on multiple servers. Microsoft Exchange Server supports bidirectional replication, which ensures that files in each public folder are identical. When changes are made, the changed document is sent to all the public folders in the system.

 Public folders do not have to be placed on the same server as the user mailboxes. In a multi-server network with multiple public folders, Microsoft Exchange Server automatically finds the nearest public folder when a user needs to access information. Because there is automatic replication of data in multiple public folders, users are sure to get the current copy of any file.

Understanding the Client/Server Architecture

Microsoft Exchange Server is a modular client/server system. It is modular because it contains a number of components that can be plugged in wherever they are needed (or where you think they fit for your particular organization). It is client/server-based because processing tasks take place at both the client and the server (which is called *distributed processing*).

When a client sends a request to a server, if the completion of the task requires a server-based process, the server will proceed with the task, returning the results (if there are results) to the client. For example, the client might ask the server to send a message or to receive a file and place it in a public folder.

If it is a request for information for a local process, such as retrieving information from a public folder, the data is sent to the client for processing locally.

Components

There are two major components to this client/server architecture model, which Microsoft Exchange Server calls the front-end and the back-end.

The *front-end* is the part of the system that the user at the client computer sees and uses. In Microsoft Exchange Server, the front-end consists of those components that provide access to e-mail, sharing information, and scheduling (if it is installed). The application design component is also a front-end procedure.

The *back-end* consists of core components running on a Windows NT computer that has Microsoft Exchange Server installed on it. In addition to the core components, any optional server components you choose to add to your system are back-end components.

The back-end provides the messaging services, transfer and delivery of messages, storage of messages, and other server/administrative tasks, such as directory services.

Communication

Each time there is a client/server communication process, it is handled by a Remote Procedure Call (RPC). RPC is a protocol used specifically for client/server communication between cabled computers and is unconnected to any of the network protocols used. The independence of RPC is significant because it is not related to the network protocols; it can permit communication between servers and clients running different protocols.

Note When an RPC routine is working, the computer that called the routine operates as if all the processes in the routine—all the subroutines that are called to complete the task—are running locally. The calling computer also believes that any data accessed was found locally.

This occurs because the client computers have RPC runtime processes that transfer the functions to the server. The runtime looks for a server on the system that will respond to the RPC call (a server that has a runtime module that matches the needs of the RPC call), and when it finds it, the function (and any data) are moved to the server.

The server calls whatever library is needed, creates the structure that is needed, and runs the function. Then, when the process is completed, it returns information back to the client by using RPCs.

The front-end and back-end fit together and accomplish tasks through the use of Microsoft's Messaging Application Programming Interface (MAPI). The clients use MAPI to access the server components.

MAPI is a collection of application programming interfaces (APIs) that are used specifically for messaging services. In effect, Microsoft Exchange Server is a group of

MAPI applications (the components installed on the client are an example) and MAPI services (the address book is an example).

You can think of MAPI as a set of drivers, and these drivers enable messaging the way hardware drivers enable access to hardware.

The Client Architecture

One of the most important features of the Microsoft Exchange Server architecture for the client side is the fact that there is a modular approach to its installation and use.

Users (or administrators) can choose the modules they want to install, and the information about those selections is kept in a user profile.

Choices include the type of messaging service (for example, a user might have Microsoft Mail operating through Microsoft Exchange Server), the directory that will be accessed for information (global and personal address books), and the type and location of information storage (public folders and personal folders).

The modular installation for a client can include more than one type of service (perhaps the client needs access to two or three different messaging services). Each client can mix and match the modular choices and end up with more than one profile. When the client software for Microsoft Exchange Server is started, the appropriate profile for the session can be selected.

The Server Architecture

The most significant aspect of the Microsoft Exchange Server architecture for the server side is its use of the capabilities inherent in Windows NT, particularly the multi-tasking power built into the operating system.

Windows NT offers, and Microsoft Exchange Server uses, multi-tasking to permit multiple processes to run at the same time, and also permit multiple instances of a specific process to run at the same time.

The server component of Exchange Server uses Windows NT capabilities for a variety of basic services:

◆ Creates a structure for maintaining information that can be sent and retrieved by clients

◆ Establishes rights and permissions to control access to information

◆ Establishes rights and permissions to control changes to information

◆ Provides services that transfer messages throughout the organization

◆ Provides services to transport messages in both directions, from foreign e-mail systems

◆ Monitors all servers and connections on the system

The Microsoft Exchange Server components handle all the messaging, scheduling, and application development processes:

◆ Directory Services provide all the organization's resources in a display that can be replicated to every server.

◆ The information stores, located on the servers, hold mailboxes, public folders, and private folders. The public information store keeps data that resides in public folders. The private information store maintains personal mailboxes and messages.

◆ The Message Transfer Agent (MTA) routes messages.

◆ The System Attendant provides ongoing maintenance of the system—checking connections between servers, tracking messages, and keeping an eye on systemwide services.

Servers as Clients

Many times, servers act as if they are clients. When a server communicates with another server, the calling server is initiating a process as if it were a client.

You also can use a server as if it were a workstation to send and receive mail and perform other client chores.

Plenty of processes on a typical Microsoft Exchange Server installation involve servers talking to servers. Details about these functions are found throughout this book, but the following are some examples:

◆ A server on one site requesting replication services from a server on another site

◆ A server requesting a directory display from another server

◆ A server finding an address or a mailbox on another server

Clients are always clients, they never perform any server functions.

CHAPTER 2

Mastering the Concepts

Microsoft Exchange Server offers an easy administration interface through graphical presentation of the system's components. Some of the graphical elements might be new to you, such as objects and containers.

This chapter takes a look at these elements to present an overview; later chapters in this book refer to their use as you explore the configuration and administration of your Microsoft Exchange Server system.

Understanding Exchange Objects

An *object* is a record in the Microsoft Exchange Server directory. For example, a site, a server, a mailbox, a folder, and a file are all objects. When you view your system hierarchy, the objects are displayed (see fig. 2.1).

Figure 2.1

The display of your Microsoft Exchange Server system is a series of objects that you can manipulate and configure. It resembles the two-pane system familiar from Windows File Manager and Windows 95 Explorer.

You can configure the properties of an object with the Properties dialog box for that object. The properties vary depending upon the object type, and can include permissions, object names, and choices about object behavior.

Details about setting properties and configuring objects are found throughout this book.

Containers

A *container* is a Microsoft Exchange Server object that holds other objects. All the mailbox objects, for example, are usually placed in a recipient's object, making the recipient's object a container.

Containers and the objects within them have a parent-child hierarchical structure that controls permissions. *Permissions* are the rules that determine which users can access the object and what manipulations they can perform upon it.

Parent objects are any objects that are superior to another object (the child object). A container object is a parent to all the objects within it (which could include other containers that become parents to the objects they contain). Permissions granted to the parent object are automatically inherited by every child object.

Child objects are any objects that are subordinate to another object (the parent). Objects in a container are child objects because they are subordinate to the container itself. The permissions granted to each child object are inherited from its parent.

Connectors

A *connector* is an object that sets the properties for a particular connection. Each type of connection you establish has connectors (see fig. 2.2). Connectors also exist for directory exchanges (used to update addresses and other recipient information), and you can establish connectors between sites.

Figure 2.2

Click on the Connections object to see the connectors installed on a server.

Object Types

Your Microsoft Exchange Server system has a variety of object types, and configuration options vary by object type. Here are some of the object types you will encounter:

◆ Site (container object)

◆ Connections (container object)

◆ Connectors

◆ Monitors (container object)

◆ Recipients (container object)

◆ Mailboxes

◆ Messages

◆ Distribution Lists

◆ Public Folders

◆ Servers (container object)

Understanding Server Components

Each server you establish in your system runs components of Microsoft Exchange Server. The specific services run by a specific server vary depending upon the installation and configuration choices you make. Recall that the server components are also referred to as the back-end components (the client components are the front-end components).

Microsoft Exchange Server has both core services and optional services. *Core services* are the directory and messaging services. *Optional services* enhance the power and flexibility of your system by adding connectivity as well as directory exchange with other systems. Most of the optional components are provided with your Microsoft Exchange Server disks. Some optional services, however, need to be purchased separately.

Directory

A server's *directory* holds information about the organization's resources and users, such as servers, mailboxes, public folders, and distribution lists. It is automatically replicated to all servers in the same site, and you can configure your system to replicate the server's directory to servers in other sites.

Information Stores

Recall that the information stores hold the data that moves through your system via Microsoft Exchange Server's messaging functions. The public information store and the private information store are the components of the information stores. The information stores also maintain and enforce data security.

The public information store holds public folders, which can contain files or public messages. The public folder can be replicated on multiple servers. Microsoft Exchange Server ensures that the replication is ongoing so that whenever a public folder changes, the changes are replicated on every selected server. The private information store holds mailboxes and individual, personal messages.

Information Store Databases

The *public database* and the *private database* are databases that track the information in your public information stores and private information stores. The databases are part of the information store structure.

When an item is placed in a public folder, it is analogous to adding a record in a database. If it changes, the database record changes accordingly. To keep performance at an optimum level, Microsoft Exchange Server keeps a separate transaction log to record additions, deletions, and changes in the database. Everything is recorded in the transaction log and periodically saved to the database.

Message Transfer Agent (MTA)

The Message Transfer Agent (MTA) is your Microsoft Exchange Server postal service. MTA routes messages throughout your system and to gateways that connect to outside e-mail systems. When necessary, it handles the conversion of message formats and addresses for external systems.

The MTA is an object in a server container, and it moves messages from one server to another in order to deposit them in the correct mailbox or gateway location (using each server's MTA).

You can set the properties for an MTA object to limit the size of messages, enable log files, and rebuild the routing tables. Specific information about configuring and administering the MTA is found throughout this book.

The MTA engine uses three Microsoft Exchange Server core components to route and transfer data to other servers (or to foreign e-mail systems):

◆ Microsoft Exchange Server site connector

◆ Remote Access Service (RAS) connector

◆ X.400 connector

Site Connector

A *site connector* connects two sites using remote procedure calls (RPCs). The sites must be linked with permanent connections. Site connectors are easy to set up and configure because using RPCs means you do not need to worry about configuring a network transport—the connector uses the existing transport. This transparency means you can use multiple network platforms in your system.

RAS Connector

The *Remote Access Service* (RAS) connector also is a site connector, except it is used between sites where you do not have a permanent connection. It is an asynchronous communications connector that you can configure for regular, automatic initiation of the connection process.

X.400 Connector

You usually use the X.400 connector because you want to do the following:

◆ Connect sites that have low-bandwidth network connections.

◆ Take advantage of an existing X.400 backbone.

◆ Access a public X.400 system.

The connector can be configured to match your needs. You are able to schedule the times for initiating connections, control the size of messages that use the connector, and control the routes messages take.

Microsoft Exchange Server supports X.400 over the following OSI transports:

◆ Transport Protocol, Class 0 (TP0)/X.25

◆ Transport Protocol, Class 4 (TP4)/Connectionless Network Protocol (CLNP)

◆ TP0/RFC 1006 to Transmission Control Protocol/Internet Protocol (TCP/IP)

The X.400 connector supports all the standard binary message body parts (such as ASCII text, fax image, or a spreadsheet attachment) so that embedding and transferring binary data is supported for most messaging needs.

Other Connectors

Other connectors are built into Microsoft Exchange Server so that users have a wide variety of message targets:

◆ The Internet Mail Connector permits users to communicate with Internet users through the Simple Mail Transfer Protocol (SMTP). Because this connector is built into Microsoft Exchange Server, messages received from an Internet system are indistinguishable from internal messages.

◆ The Microsoft Mail connector gives users seamless connectivity to Microsoft Mail for PC Networks, Microsoft Mail for PC Networks gateways, and Microsoft Mail for AppleTalk Networks.

System Attendant

The *System Attendant* is an ongoing service that runs in the background, but it must be running in order for the Microsoft Exchange Server messaging processes to run.

The System Attendant performs several basic, important functions that enable messaging:

◆ It monitors the connections between servers to make sure that messages sent from one server are received at the target server.

◆ It runs any monitor tools you establish in the system (you can create monitors to check specific links between servers or to monitor specific server functions).

◆ It generates e-mail addresses for new message recipients so that mail gets to the right mailbox on the right server.

◆ It logs the information needed to track messages, if you opt to enable the message tracking features.

The System Attendant also communicates with other components of Microsoft Exchange Server to perform some of its functions. Communication with the Directory is established by the System Attendant for the following:

◆ Looking up addresses

◆ Building routing tables

◆ Checking the uniformity of directory replication

Communication with the Key Management Component is established by the System Attendant to manage digital signatures and encryption information for mailboxes.

Communication with the System Attendant is initiated by the MTA when there is a message sent or received between a site and another site or system. The System Attendant logs the event in order to track the messaging activities.

The information store initiates communication with the System Attendant to notify the SA when the messaging is local.

Learning about Optional Components

Optional components are included in your Microsoft Exchange Server system that you can install on an as-needed basis. Some optional components, however, need to be purchased separately.

Directory Synchronization

The *directory synchronization component* exchanges directory information between Exchange Server and Microsoft Mail 3.*x*, as well as other messaging systems that use the Mail 3.*x* protocol.

The directory synchronization component works with the Directory (to add, modify, or delete custom recipients) and the MTA (to deliver directory-related messages bound for foreign e-mail systems). There is no communication between this component and any other components of Microsoft Exchange Server.

Key Management

The *Key Management component* manages all the security information that is used for digitally signing and sealing messages with Microsoft Exchange Server.

It sends communications to the Directory in order to store digital signatures and encryption information. It receives communication from the Administrator Program and the System Attendant to set up and manage the digital signatures and encryptions for mailboxes.

Microsoft Schedule+ Free/Busy Connector

The optional Schedule+ Free/Busy connector is used if the Schedule+ program is installed. It is the vehicle through which Microsoft Exchange Server exchanges Microsoft Schedule+ free and busy information with Microsoft Mail for PC Networks. It is actually an extension to the Microsoft Mail connector.

Free and busy information is collected in order to facilitate group scheduling. Schedule+ users are able to view each other's free and busy times in order to ascertain the most productive schedules for meetings (picking a time when all or most of the attendees are free).

The Schedule+ Free/Busy connector communicates with other components of Microsoft Exchange Server:

◆ It initiates communication to the Microsoft Mail connector in order to send information about free/busy times to post offices on Microsoft Mail for PC Networks.

◆ It initiates communication to the information store to send data about free/busy times for Microsoft Mail for PC Networks users. Once the data is in the information store, it can be accessed by Microsoft Exchange users.

◆ It initiates communication to the Directory in order to get address book information.

The Schedule+ Free/Busy connector is not on the receiving end of any communication from any other Microsoft Exchange Server components.

Third-Party Gateways

An optional, separate purchase, the Third Party Gateways component is used to exchange messages to foreign e-mail systems such as IBM's Professional Office System (PROFS) and System Network Architecture Distribution Services (SNADS). This component performs message translation in both directions so that users have no difficulty using the system.

Understanding Client Components

The Microsoft Exchange client components, which are installed on the workstations, comprise the front end of your Microsoft Exchange Server software:

◆ Microsoft Exchange component, which provides the messaging services to users

◆ Forms Designer component, which permits users to develop forms for messaging in a graphical environment

◆ Schedule+ component, which manages users' schedules and to-do lists, and provides a personal information manager

The detailed instructions for installation are found in Chapter 6, "Installing Exchange Server." For now, let's look at the concepts and issues that have to be considered before deciding what to install. This should give you an edge in your planning.

In order to install the Microsoft Exchange client software, you must already have set up Windows NT user accounts and Microsoft Exchange Server mailboxes for users. An NT user account is configured with all the information that creates a user for Windows NT, including a name and password. For Microsoft Exchange Server, all users must have an NT user account in order to access a mailbox.

Client Components Options

You should consider two major decisions before you begin installation of the client components:

◆ The method of installation

◆ The location of the client files

Client Components Installation Methods

You can install the client components on client workstations directly from the Microsoft Exchange Server disks or CD-ROM.

You also can install the client components directly from the server once a workstation is connected to the server. In order to accomplish this, you must make sure you install the client software when you install Microsoft Exchange Server. The client software will be placed in a subdirectory called Clients, and there will be subdirectories named DOS, Ntx86, Win16, and Win95upg.

Each workstation will install the appropriate client files from the server as if they were connected to a CD-ROM.

Figure 2.3 shows the opening screen for installation via the network for a Windows for Workgroups client. Figure 2.4 is the opening screen for the same process being run on a Windows 95 client. Note that for Windows 95, this is an installation upgrade, because Exchange is an application included in Windows 95.

Figure 2.3

A Windows for Workgroups Client is installing the client components after logging on to the NT server.

Figure 2.4

A Windows 95 client is upgrading Exchange from the NT server.

Using an Installation Point on a Different Server

By default, when the Clients directory is installed on an NT server, it is a shared directory and becomes an installation point for client machines. Clients can access the installation point and begin the installation of the client software.

As an alternative, you can copy the client files to another server, even a server that is not running NT, and use that server as the installation point for the client components. You must make sure that user access and permissions for the directory are established appropriately.

Exchange Software Location

You can configure Microsoft Exchange Server so that the client components run from either local hard drives or from the network. After you establish a shared directory, the Setup program for client components can designate the directory as the target drive and path.

User Profiles

Users can establish profiles that contain the configuration for their Microsoft Exchange sessions. In fact, they can have multiple profiles and direct the software to ask for a profile when Microsoft Exchange is launched. Multiple user profiles are useful for companies where users might find themselves at different computers occasionally.

Mobile Users

Mobile users who dial in to get their mail and messages need a bit of special handling, but all the necessary functions are available. The dial-in protocols differ by platform:

◆ MS-DOS clients can use ShivaRemote, which is included in Microsoft Exchange Server.

◆ WIN 3.*x* clients can also use ShivaRemote.

◆ Windows 95 clients use Microsoft Dial-Up Networking, which is included in Windows 95.

◆ Windows NT clients use Remote Access Service (RAS), which is included in Windows NT (Server and Workstation).

 During installation of the client components, the Setup program provides an option to copy the ShivaRemote files to the \EXCHANGE\SHIVA directory on the local disk. Once the files are copied to the client computer, the ShivaRemote Setup program must be run to finish the installation and configuration of ShivaRemote.

After installation and configuration, MS-DOS clients using ShivaRemote have to connect to the network, launch the software, and then disconnect from the network. For all other platforms, invoking the software makes connection and disconnection an automatic process.

If your users have dial-up software that they prefer to use to access Microsoft Exchange Server to pick up their mail and messages, it is likely that the software is supported (almost all of them are). The connection and disconnection, however, must be made manually; the third-party software will not process the instructions needed to log on, get through the password processes, and reach the mailbox. Once there is a third-party connection, all the steps to open the Inbox, fetch any received messages, and so on, are taken one at a time as if the user were in front of the client workstation.

The Microsoft Exchange Server Setup Editor

One of the handy tools you will find in your Microsoft Exchange Server software is the Setup Editor (see fig. 2.5). You can use this program to establish default setup conditions for various platforms. Each platform can have specific configuration information regarding the location of files, how the notification of mail arrival is handled, and so forth.

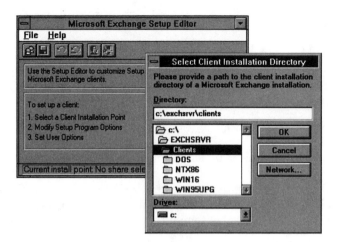

Figure 2.5

The Setup Editor enables you to program the configuration for each of the client installation points.

To jump-start your grey cells when considering the use of the Setup Editor, consider the following scenario.

You have several hundred users and most of them work in your company's office, some are on the road most of the time, and some work from home. The office workstations are running various platforms:

◆ The accounting department is connected to two servers, one runs NetWare and contains the accounting software, the other is an NT server running Microsoft Exchange Server and has each user's mailbox. All users are running DOS machines, to get the speed and productivity they want from their text-based accounting programs.

◆ The executive suite and clerical staff are using computers that are running Windows of varying flavors. They are connected to NT server for their mail, and specific individuals are also connected to specific servers (some NetWare, some NT, maybe even some peer-to-peer) for software access.

◆ Salespeople are working from laptops as they rove the world servicing customers. The laptops run various operating systems, depending upon the comfort level of the individual users.

◆ The public relations people work from home, and their computers run whatever platform they find comfortable (or their children demand).

You need to decide how they will access the NT server running Microsoft Exchange Server to get their mail. You have several options for configuring all these client workstations:

- ◆ Software installed on local drives for every machine

- ◆ Software installed on local drives for the in-office machines only

- ◆ Software installed on local drives for mobile laptop users only

- ◆ Software installed on local drives for home users only

- ◆ Software installed on the server for every platform

- ◆ Repeat choices on local drives here, substituting server for local drives

You can remove all the installation choices except the one you want from any setup file. For example, you can create a setup file for your mobile users so that the only choice they see is the setup for a portable computer.

You also have to set up a mail notification system:

- ◆ Do you want individuals in the office to be notified every time messages arrive in their mailboxes?

- ◆ Do you want individuals in the office to learn about their mail when they log on to check their mailboxes?

- ◆ For the remote users, do you want to notify somebody in the office every time mail is placed in the mailbox so a telephone call can be made to the remote user?

Okay, that last suggestion is silly, but this is just an example of the decisions you will have to make. You can control these options by using the features available in the Setup Editor.

 The Setup Editor creates default configurations, and you can use them as the basis of specific configurations if an individual user's needs do not match the original defaults. Nothing is etched in cement.

Understanding Mail Component Concepts

The Exchange component for clients is used for e-mail and information sharing. It is available for the following client platforms:

- ◆ Windows 3.x

- ◆ Windows for Workgroups 3.11

- ◆ Windows NT Workstation 3.51 and higher

- ◆ Windows NT Server 3.51 and higher

- ◆ Windows 95

- ◆ MS-DOS 5.0 and higher

Note that at the time of this writing, the Macintosh and Unix client software had not yet been released.

The messages and shared files that are sent and received by the client users all pass through the public and private folders located on a server running Microsoft Exchange Server. During your planning and installation, be sure that all users have a connection to the nearest, easiest-to-access server.

The Inbox

The client Inbox holds mail, messages, files, and whatever else has been sent to the client. It is a universal container that saves clients the trouble of fetching mail and then switching to another container to retrieve other items.

The Inbox appears as a folder in the graphical hierarchy of the client's mailbox configuration (see fig. 2.6). Users can arrange, sort, select, design, and otherwise customize their view of the Inbox.

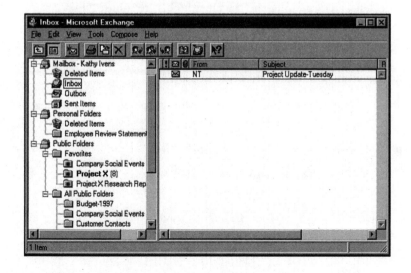

Figure 2.6

When a user checks mail on the server, the graphical display is easy to use, and there are lots of ways to customize the display and use of the mailbox.

Client Mail Assistants

Intelligent Mail Assistants can be established by each user on the server so that certain procedures are implemented even when the user is not logged in. The design and configuration of these Assistants are executed easily by using dialog boxes, and no programming or other special computer skills are necessary in order to get the full power of the Mail Assistants.

With the Inbox Assistant, users can configure their Inboxes so that the contents are reported back with a priority and selection scheme suiting each user. Incoming messages can be sorted and filed in specific folders automatically, so when a user does check the Inbox, everything is set up conveniently.

Users can establish procedures for being notified when a message arrives in the Inbox, or, when circumstances require it, set up an Out Of Office Assistant to handle mail while the user is away on vacation or a business trip, or is otherwise unavailable. This could be implemented either as forcing an immediate response to messages by generating an automatic reply to the sender (such as I'm away on vacation, will return on Monday), or forwarding the mail to someone else.

E-Mail with Personality

The Microsoft Exchange client Mail Component supports rich text formatting (RTF) and provides a full range of editing features. The message environment is identical across all the supported platforms. RTF is preserved only across graphical platforms, however, and if a message is sent to an e-mail application that can't use RTF, it is converted to regular ASCII text. Note that this conversion to regular text may leave behind unreadable characters where the formatting codes were.

When e-mail is created, the formatting and document tools are robust. There are toolbars and formatting bars (see fig. 2.7), making the following elements available:

◆ Fonts that are installed and supported by the underlying operating system

◆ Paragraph alignment: left, right, and centered

◆ Bullets, which can be inserted automatically, giving the paragraph a hanging indent

◆ Character formatting, including bold, italic, underline, and color

◆ Tool tips, which are just like those in Microsoft Office—pointing the mouse at a button produces a tool tip that tells you that button's function

◆ AutoText, which enables you to store frequently used text, formatting, graphics, or messages for quick retrieval

◆ Drag and drop editing, including elements from other applications (spreadsheets and graphics)

◆ Spelling checker

Figure 2.7

The window used to create a message is similar to that used by word processing applications, with plenty of configuration options, tools, and application features.

The Microsoft Exchange client mail component also supports incorporation of files as attachments. The attachments are in the form of icons, which can be placed in the body of a message (the icons include the file names). The message body supports object linking and embedding (OLE) 2.0, so users can edit any attached and embedded files they receive.

Understanding Form Designer Concepts

Sometimes it might be convenient or more productive to create a specific form to use when sending messages of a certain type. A predesigned form for all those messages that say "let's meet for lunch" or "where shall we meet for lunch" makes sending such messages faster. A department head who likes to call meetings could create a form that requires very little data entry to complete.

Throughout the enterprise, forms for administration of the company can be designed for quick distribution—a vacation schedule form, announcements of the annual company picnic, and so on.

Once the Forms Designer is installed, it can be accessed during an Exchange session. Just choose Application **D**esign, **F**orms Designer from the **T**ools menu. When the program launches, you see the window shown in figure 2.8.

Figure 2.8

To create a new form, you can use the wizard for step-by-step help, or open a form as the starting point to creating a new custom form.

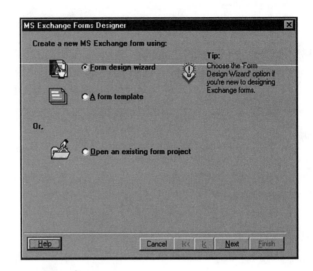

The Form Designer Wizard

Using the wizard is a simple process of answering questions about the type of form you want to create and the way you want it to look. You can create forms for messages (e-mail sent to one or more users) or for postings (items that are placed in folders for public access through the enterprise).

The process includes the capability of designing the method used to display your form to users (see fig. 2.9). You can change the fields that are displayed so that one set of fields is available during message creation and a different set displays when a user reads the data in the form.

Using Templates

If you choose to use an existing template to design a form, the Select Form Template dialog box displays a list of all the existing form templates (see fig. 2.10).

Design Elements

Once you create the basic layout for your form through the wizard, or by choosing a template, you can customize the form.

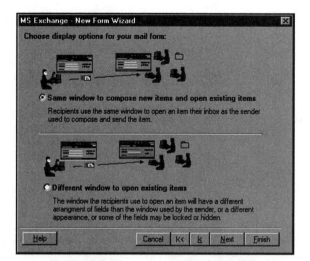

Figure 2.9

You can decide to have two formats for your new form, one for entering the data and a different one for reading it.

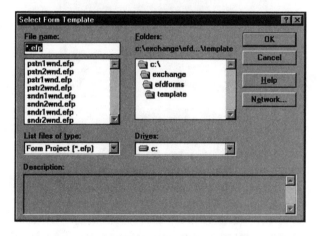

Figure 2.10

You can choose a form that approximates the form you want to create as a starting point for your design.

On the left side of your workspace is a toolbar that lists the fields that generally go into a message header (From, To, Date, and so on) as well as buttons that enable you to create other fields as needed. You can add any of the following field types and label them as you wish:

◆ Text entry field

◆ Check box field

◆ Option button field

◆ List box or combo box field

◆ Group box field (used for holding multiple options and selection buttons)

◆ Tabbed panel field (choices on separate windows, accessed by clicking on tabs)

◆ Picture field, in which you can insert a graphic

Field Properties

Once you drag a field to your form and position it where you want it, double-click on it to bring up its Properties dialog box (see fig. 2.11) and configure the way the field is used and displayed.

Figure 2.11

Once you insert a field in a form, you get to write the rules about its use.

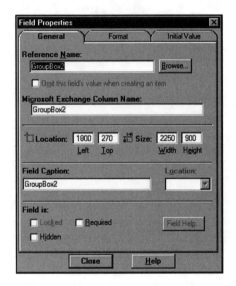

You can format the location, size, font, alignment, and attributes for each field. If appropriate, you can also enter an initial value for certain fields.

Saving and Installing the Form

When you are happy with the new form, you can save it by choosing **S**ave or Save **A**s from the File menu. This saves the contents of the window as if you were saving a document, and, in effect, you have a new template.

Installing a form is a separate step. The form is compiled (it is a Visual Basic program that is so easy to use, you don't need to have any programming experience), then is placed in a Form Registry (see fig. 2.12) for use.

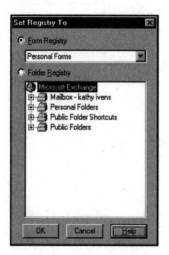

Figure 2.12

You can install a form into a registry or a folder so it can be used by you or everyone in your organization.

A *Form Registry* is a container for forms that can be used by you (if it is a Personal Registry) or everyone (if it is a Global Registry).

A *Folder Registry* is a folder that contains forms and is usually a public folder dedicated to a particular topic. All the files and forms in the folder are connected to the topic. You might have a Personnel Policy folder, for instance, that contains memos, the company's employee policy handbook, and various forms for employees to fill out.

 You cannot install a form in the Global Registry unless you have the appropriate permissions on the network.

Before it is sent to the registry, the form's properties have to be established (see fig. 2.13).

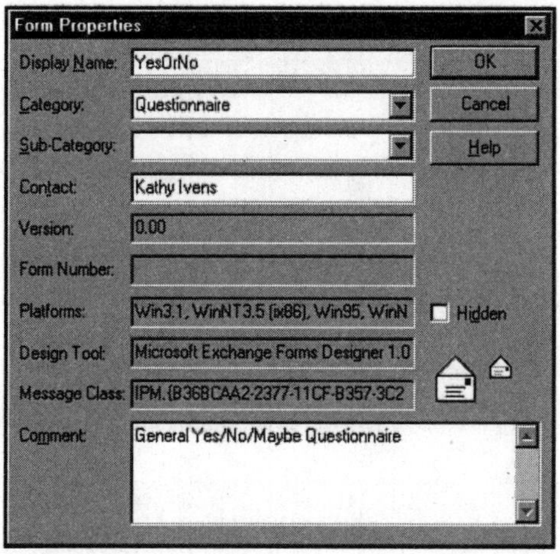

Figure 2.13

As with all objects in Microsoft Exchange Server, your form has to have Properties.

Application Design

Once a form has been designed, compiled, and put into general use, it is really an application. In fact, there is an executable file on your system that is the compiled runtime program you wrote. It has the same information in its Properties as any other executable file in your system.

Besides the ability to design the way the form looks, you can program the form's behavior. For instance, you can cause specific instructions (written by you) to appear any time Help is clicked. Your custom Help statements can be about the form or any specific field in the form.

You can cause specific actions to occur as a result of the data that is placed in the form. This means you can define an event (or a series of events) that should take place in response to an entry. The response might be that a new form is opened or some data is sent to a folder.

Your Microsoft Exchange Server client component has a number of sample applications you can use to help you understand how all this power can be used.

Although you can use all the features and power of Microsoft Exchange Server application design without any knowledge of programming, if you are comfortable with programming in Visual Basic, you can expand and strengthen the scope of your applications. You could, for example, create a form, have it automatically sent to specified recipients, make sure the replies are received, gather the replies, and create some sort of new file format from the data. More information about programming for Microsoft Exchange Server is found in Chapter 21, "Using Visual Basic."

Understanding Schedule+ Concepts

Schedule+ is a dual-purpose program—it provides tools for individuals and also provides important services for the entire organization.

For an individual user, it is an easy-to-use application that helps you manage your time and provides the functions available in a personal information manager.

You can use Schedule+ to do the following:

◆ Display your schedule in a variety of formats (daily, weekly, monthly, or yearly).

◆ Track your projects with a task list.

◆ Combine your appointments and your task list to see everything you need to do in a specific day, week, or month.

◆ Keep a list of all your contacts.

For the organization, each individual user's schedule can be centrally collected in order to provide group scheduling:

◆ Choose a meeting time by determining the availability of the attendees.

◆ Send a notice to all the necessary people, and collect their responses.

You also can schedule resources such as conference rooms and factor in their availability when you are scheduling events.

To understand the concepts and features in Schedule+, take a brief look at its functions. Examine the configuration options to get an idea of their breadth and explore some of the functional parts and how they work.

The Schedule+ Window

When you launch Schedule+, the window that displays is chock-full of information (see fig. 2.14).

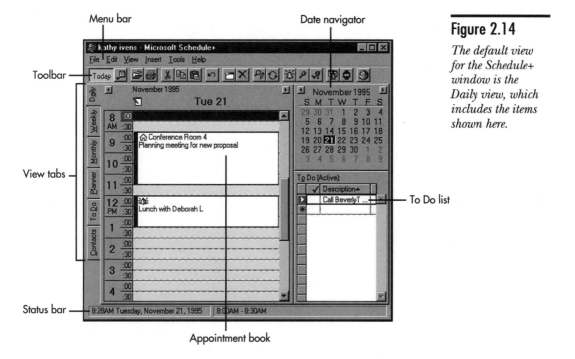

Figure 2.14

The default view for the Schedule+ window is the Daily view, which includes the items shown here.

Appointment book

Configuring Schedule+

The appearance and settings of Schedule+ can be configured to match your work habits. Most of the configuration options are controlled through the dialog box that displays when you choose **O**ptions from the **T**ools menu (see fig. 2.15).

Figure 2.15

Having a wide choice of configuration options makes it easy to use Schedule+ in a way that exactly matches your needs.

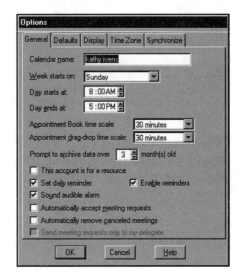

Setting General Options

Take a brief look at the variations available, starting with the General tab:

◆ Calendar **n**ame sets the active appointment book—you can have multiple appointment books.

◆ **W**eek starts on enables you to decide which day is the first day of the week (usually a choice between Sunday and Monday).

◆ D**a**y starts at specifies the hour that displays at the top of the appointment book.

◆ Day **e**nds at specifies the last hour that displays. Hours later than that time are still available for entry—but they are shaded.

◆ A**p**pointment Book time scale specifies the size of the time block in which you want to work. For example, some people prefer 15-minute blocks, others prefer 30-minute blocks.

◆ Appointment **d**rag-drop time scale specifies the time duration that changes when you drag the handles of an appointment block. For instance, if you choose 15 minutes, as you drag an appointment block to make it longer, the appointment becomes 15 minutes longer, then 30 minutes longer, and so forth. To change an appointment to a duration that does not match these multiples, you have to enter data instead of using drag and drop.

◆ Prompt to a**r**chive data over specifies the number of months that will elapse before you are prompted to archive the information in your schedule. Archiving removes the data from the current files and saves it in special archive files. This keeps your file sizes manageable, and you can still answer a question about where you were a year ago last Thursday.

◆ This acc**o**unt is for a resource, if selected, indicates that you are tracking the use of a room or another resource rather than a person.

◆ Set dai**l**y reminder, if selected, causes your To Do list for the current day to display when you first launch Schedule+ (see fig. 2.16).

◆ Ena**b**le reminders specifies that a pop-up appears to remind you about some task, event, or appointment that is imminent (see fig. 2.17).

◆ So**u**nd audible alarm, when selected, causes a noise to be sounded when a Reminder pops up.

◆ Automatically accept **m**eeting requests specifies that when any meeting request form comes to your mailbox, an acceptance is sent back and the meeting is scheduled in your appointment book.

◆ Automatically remove **c**anceled meetings causes meetings to be deleted from your appointment book when a cancellation notice is received in your mailbox.

◆ Send meeting requests only to my delegate, when selected, diverts meeting requests to another user who is acting as your delegate (usually an administrative assistant).

Understanding Access Permissions

If the Send Meeting Requests Only to my Delegate checkbox is greyed out, it means you have not created any delegates.

Figure 2.16

You can configure Schedule+ so that when you start the software at the beginning of your work day, today's list of things to do appears automatically.

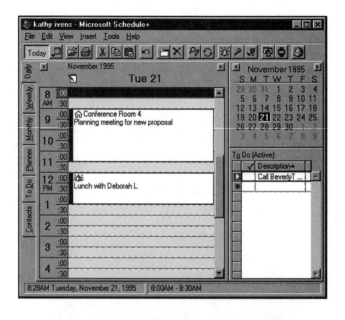

Figure 2.17

It's almost lunch time and you've been reminded of your lunch appointment. You can ask to be notified again in a specified number of minutes, ask to be notified at a certain interval before the actual date, or choose not to be reminded again.

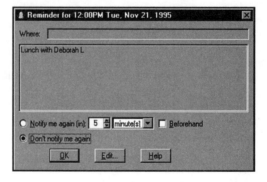

Besides assigning a delegate, you can establish permissions for access to your schedule, giving others the right to change or add items. The sender does not need to be notified whether someone else is receiving your meeting notifications, because your configuration options cause this to happen automatically. (Don't worry, you can restrict people with access from seeing your private appointments and notes.)

To give other users specific access to your schedule, follow these steps:

1. From the **T**ools menu, choose Set A**c**cess Permissions.

2. To give a user permissions in your schedule, choose **A**dd to bring up the Add Users dialog box.

3. Click on the arrow to the right of the box labeled **S**how Names from the: to select the source of a users list (see fig. 2.18).

4. Highlight each user to whom you want to give access to your data, then choose **U**sers to move the name to the right panel. You can select multiple users. Click on OK when you finish selecting users.

5. From the Users tab of the dialog box, highlight a user name and click on the arrow next to the User role: text box to choose a role for this user (see fig. 2.19).

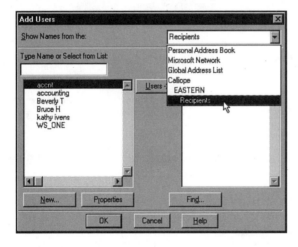

Figure 2.18

Because your mail comes to your Domain Server, you can choose a name from the users who have mailboxes and access to that Domain.

The user roles are connected to the four item types shown on the dialog box (see fig. 2.20). Each of the user roles has specific permissions for the four item types (except Custom, in which you can select permissions for each item type). The following are the available user roles:

◆ Read, which gives the user read-only access to all items except those you've marked as private.

◆ Create, which permits the user to read all items not marked private and to create new items.

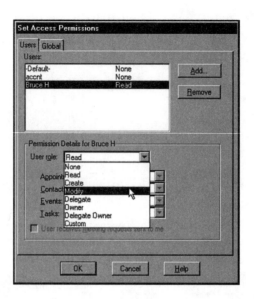

Figure 2.19

Giving another user permission to access or change your schedule data is a one-click operation.

◆ Modify, which enables the user to read and modify all items except those classified as private.

◆ Delegate, which permits the user to read and modify items. Private items are included in these permissions. A Delegate can also receive meeting requests sent to you.

◆ Owner, which enables the user to read and modify all items, including private items.

◆ Delegate Owner, which permits the user to read and modify all items and also receive and send meeting messages for you.

◆ Custom, which enables you to specify access for each particular item type.

Setting Defaults

The Defaults tab of the Options dialog box is where you set the default specifications for the events, tasks, and appointments you enter. Items such as priorities, reminder intervals, and so on, are configurable.

Configuring Display and Time Zone

Use the Display tab to control the colors and features of your Schedule+ windows. Then move to the Time Zone tab to choose a primary time zone and secondary time zone (to keep track of an office in a different time zone, or for your own schedule if you travel a lot).

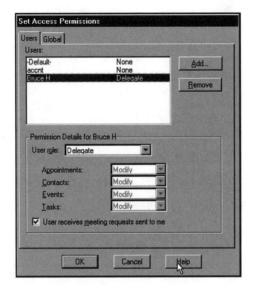

Figure 2.20

*The level of access
to each of the four
types of items in
your schedule is
determined by the
role of the user to
whom you're
giving
permissions.*

Synchronizing Schedules

Because you can keep multiple files in Schedule+, perhaps establishing a personal schedule and a business schedule, you can set up the configuration for synchronizing the items on the schedules. This helps you avoid scheduling yourself in two places at the same time.

Understanding Tab Views

Each tab view has a particular display configuration, and you can switch views as you need to. In addition, you can invent your own tab views and add them to your Schedule+ window.

The following are the default tab views:

◆ Daily, which displays a single day's appointments, the Date Navigator, and any active tasks in your To Do List

◆ Weekly, which displays the Appointment Book for a week (or as many days as you want it to) and the Date Navigator

◆ Monthly, which displays a monthly calendar with your appointments showing

◆ Planner, which shows your free/busy times

◆ To Do, which displays the To Do List

◆ Contacts, which shows a list of contacts and a business card display of those contacts

Changing Tabs

You can remove, edit, or create tabs to suit yourself:

1. Choose Tab Gallery from the View menu to see the Tab Gallery dialog box (see fig. 2.21).

2. To remove a current tab, highlight it and select Remove.

3. To change the position of a tab, highlight it and then choose Move Up or Move Down.

4. To add a new tab, select it and choose Add. You can change the title of the tab if you wish.

Figure 2.21

The Tab Gallery shows all available tabs in the left pane and the tabs currently being used in the right pane.

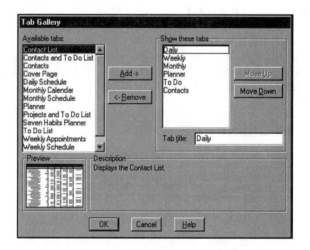

Putting Items into Your Schedule+ System

After you configure the look and settings of your Schedule+ software, it is time to enter items. All the items are available from the Insert menu.

Appointments

Choose **A**ppointment to place an item into your calendar. The Appointment dialog box offers a host of options and places in which to store reference information (see fig. 2.22).

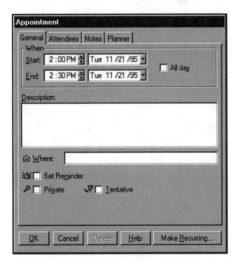

Figure 2.22

Set up an appointment, make it private if you wish, and decide whether you need a reminder.

The Attendees tab displays the names of the other people expected to attend this appointment. You can issue an invitation to other users by choosing **I**nvite Others. This displays a dialog box into which you can insert names from any user list (see fig. 2.23).

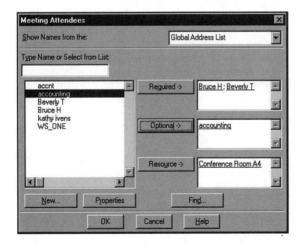

Figure 2.23

When you invite people to attend a meeting, their schedules are compared to yours. If there's a conflict with a required attendee, one schedule has to be changed.

The Notes tab is a place for you to make notes to yourself about this appointment.

The Planner tab displays a graphical indication of the meeting time, and it indicates the current status of responses from the other attendees (see fig. 2.24).

Figure 2.24

The meeting time is blocked on the calendar, and the attendees' status shows they have not yet responded.

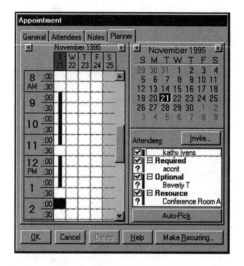

When you finish filling out the fields you need in the dialog box, choose OK. A Meeting Request form automatically appears so that you can send the meeting notice to the list of attendees.

Tasks

Choose **T**ask from the **I**nsert menu to enter a task in the To Do list:

◆ The General tab of the Task dialog box enables you to set a date range for the task and to specify whether you want to be reminded.

◆ The Status tab enables you to track the number of hours or days you have spent on the task (and reports back the percentage complete by using the number of estimated hours or days). The Status tab also provides fields for billing information.

◆ The Notes tab enables you to keep a diary of the progress or jot down any other kind of notes you'd like to amass about this task.

Projects

Choose **P**roject from the **I**nsert menu to establish a project in your system. A project is a way to link tasks that are related under one umbrella. Each project is named and given a priority. You can make a project private if you want.

After you create a project, when you insert any item, you can attach it to the project.

Contacts

In addition to handling your schedule and your list of things to do, Schedule+ has a built-in link to a personal information management system. Choose **C**ontact from the **I**nsert menu to begin (see fig. 2.25).

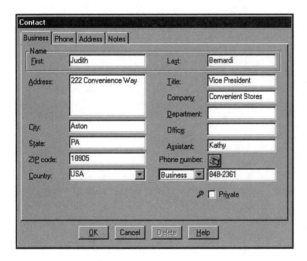

Figure 2.25

The Contact record holds information about people you want to keep track of— click on the telephone icon above the phone number to have Schedule+ dial the number.

Move to the Phone tab to insert additional telephone, fax, or pager numbers, and so forth.

Move to the Address tab to fill in a home address and other personal information (birthday, spouse's name, and so forth).

The Notes tab, of course, is for any comments or notes you want to keep on this contact.

Events

An event is something you want to remember to do or attend, but does not occupy any specific time block in your schedule. You might use the feature to track trade shows or conventions you'll probably want to attend and other miscellaneous reminders. When you choose **E**vent from the **I**nsert menu, the dialog box asks for an event day and start and end dates, and offers an opportunity to make the event private.

Permanent Items

You can also use Schedule+ to track permanent or recurring items. When you designate an item as recurring, you enter it only once. Schedule+ automatically fills in the future occurrences, and you can change or cancel any individual occurrence:

◆ Recurring appointments occur regularly (your Monday morning sales meeting, your monthly sales meeting). They are indicated in the appointment by a circular-arrow symbol.

◆ Recurring tasks are items for your To Do list that occur regularly.

◆ Annual events are events that occur every year on the same date, such as birthdays, anniversaries, and so forth.

This chapter is an overview to give you an idea of what to expect as you install and use Microsoft Exchange Server. The details you'll need for completing the installation and implementing the services are found throughout this book.

PART II

Planning Your Microsoft Exchange Server System

CHAPTER 3

Ascertaining Needs

Well before the actual implementation of your Microsoft Exchange Server system, there's a period of planning. You have to make decisions about hardware, connections, sites, domains, servers, and so on. This process of walking through the organization, the users, and the features they need, is called *needs ascertainment.*

There are three main considerations in this process of needs ascertainment:

◆ The features and tools needed by all the users in your company

◆ The way hardware needs to be deployed (or purchased) in order to fulfill the user needs

◆ The number of Microsoft Exchange Server licenses you have to purchase

Along the way, you have to consider details such as the networks already in place, the protocols being used in your network, the assignment of personnel to perform the administrative tasks, and the training required.

Planning for User Needs

There are two levels of user needs to consider:

◆ **General software application use and the method of accessing the software.** As you consider the way existing servers are used (and new servers may be installed) you have to consider the burden on those servers that provide access to software and also store application data.

◆ **Specific Microsoft Exchange Server options and the services needed by each user.** This includes designing a network layout that makes reaching mailboxes and public folders an easy, productive operation.

For general application use, take a careful look at all the servers in your organization and estimate future needs so that you don't get into storage space trouble as your Microsoft Exchange Server data grows.

Looking at the Tasks

Most of your planning and needs analysis are related to the way the users in your organization will use the services available in Microsoft Exchange Server.

One helpful step is to develop a report about your users. Determine who uses e-mail and to what extent, and who needs scheduling and other features. The following are some of the things to consider:

◆ E-mail messaging needs and patterns

◆ Scheduling needs and patterns

◆ Public folder implementation

◆ Private folder implementation

◆ Application design needs

◆ Permissions (allowing one user to read and send mail on behalf of another user)

◆ Rules about the way e-mail, scheduling and other features can be used, and by whom

◆ Hardware needs

◆ Administrative assignments

If your organization is large, some of these tasks require diagrams, plans, flow charts, or other reference materials in order to plan correctly.

You should come up with a planning form or questionnaire for the users who will be impacted by your Microsoft Exchange Server system. Then decide how you want to group your users.

If your company has clearly defined departments, with each department having a specific location, organize your planning form by department.

If departments aren't organized into specific physical locations, but there are clear groupings because of the layout of your LANs, you should organize your planning form by servers. Everyone connected to Server X would be considered a group, for example.

If there aren't any clear ways to group users, consider grouping the users by functions—for example, office salespersons, field salespersons, administrative personnel. Although they may be scattered all over the building (or all over the world), the odds are that their Microsoft Exchange Server needs are related to their functions.

Determining E-Mail Needs

The most popular service your Microsoft Exchange Server installation will provide is e-mail. You need to take a careful look at the current e-mail patterns if you have an existing system. If Microsoft Exchange Server is your first e-mail system, you need to discuss the features with users and administrators in an effort to get a handle on the proposed usage.

The way e-mail is used in your organization has a great deal of influence on many of the other decisions you have to make about servers, connections, sites, and disk space.

Most companies operate in departments, whether those departments are physically real or imaginary. A real department occupies a specific site, and every office in that part of the company's space is part of the department. An imaginary, or loosely defined, department is a concept that identifies those offices where certain types of work are done.

For example, depending upon the kind of organizing scheme a company has, saying "she's in accounting" can mean anything. In some companies, it means "she's on the third floor," where all the people who do accounting chores are situated. It could mean "she's situated somewhere in the Philadelphia office," where the company's accounting is done. It could mean that "she's in some office somewhere and does accounting-type stuff," and the other people who do accounting work may or may not be in close proximity to her.

Although it may seem trivial to delve this far into such definitions of company organization structures, it really isn't. If your accounting department is gathered in one large office space, with desks wedged close together, you'll find the e-mail traffic within the group isn't as heavy as it would be if these bookkeepers were spread around the building. (It's just easier to lean over and speak to someone than to open software in order to create e-mail.) It will also probably be easy to put all the people in the department onto the same server for mailboxes, public folders, and so forth.

As you plan your system, the needs of the users will be connected to the way your company is organized. There are several common messaging patterns for organizations:

◆ Messages are usually exchanged within a group or department.

◆ Messages are usually exchanged between specific groups or departments.

◆ Messages are exchanged on a predictable basis between sites (for example, there are regular reporting procedures between a remote site and a home office, perhaps weekly or monthly).

◆ Messages are exchanged with a foreign message service.

As you design your planning forms or questionnaires, you might want to provide these preconceived usage patterns and ask people to check off the most appropriate one or rank them. This is easier than asking users to write their own descriptions.

Planning Migration

If you have an e-mail system in place, you might be able to migrate it into Microsoft Exchange Server (depending on the system and its database structure). The migration requires some planning so that you don't interrupt the flow of messages around your organization.

You can migrate your old e-mail system all at once, or in increments. Take a careful look at the way your current system is configured in order to plan an incremental migration. There are a number of approaches to choose from and each should be examined:

◆ Migrate by location

◆ Migrate by site

◆ Migrate by department or division

◆ Migrate by job function

To make incremental migration even easier for some organizations, Microsoft Exchange Server supports some messaging applications so that you can continue to run them without having the double work of administering them and Microsoft Exchange Server at the same time:

◆ Microsoft Mail for PC Networks

◆ Microsoft Mail for AppleTalk Networks

◆ Microsoft Mail for PC Networks gateways

Information about migrating e-mail applications into Microsoft Exchange Server can be found in Chapter 5, "Planning for E-Mail Migration."

Foreign E-Mail Services

If you have a research department or a public relations department, those employees will likely need access to the Internet or other information sources.

If your company is in a joint venture with another company, you have to plan for frequent messaging between their e-mail system and yours, either via a remote access setup to CompuServe or other service provider or through the Internet.

A department (or the whole enterprise) may need access to PROFS or SNADS, which requires the purchase and installation of optional add-ons to Microsoft Exchange Server.

These needs involve considerations beyond the placement of mailboxes and public folders, because you have to plan for varying connectors. Gateways, remote connectivity software, X.400 connectors, Internet Mail Connectors, and TCP/IP are built in to Microsoft Exchange Server. However, implementation requires planning, installation, and configuration.

Dial-In Users

Another factor for some companies is the need to give access to a substantial number of users who spend a great deal of time in the field rather than in a company office. Planning for remote user support includes both the hardware considerations (modems, lines, and so forth) and the assignment of computers to handle this traffic.

Delegated Responsibilities

You should identify those users in your organization who will probably delegate the handling of a great many of their e-mail tasks to others.

Many executives want to give away responsibility for collecting and responding to e-mail that is not confidential or marked for the recipient only.

Outside sales people frequently send e-mail to arrange for services or correspondence to customers. Although the e-mail is addressed to a particular in-office individual, you may find that it's more productive to let any person on the sales support team access the mail.

Be sure to create a planning form/questionnaire that includes this possibility. Unless you're going to let users into the configuration options (not always a good idea), you have to do all the setup chores necessary for establishing multiple user access to certain mailboxes.

Mailbox Naming Conventions

Whatever mailbox naming scheme you decide on should make it easy to identify each user and find each mailbox. Remember that the mailbox name is the tail end of the e-mail address; you have the organization and site names built into the address in addition to the mailbox name.

You might want to use a naming convention that's based on the way your company keeps records for names and office phone numbers. Alternatively, you might want to take advantage of any existing naming scheme being used for Windows NT user accounts. If Microsoft Exchange Server is replacing an existing e-mail system, you might want to keep (or come close to) the naming system you employed with the old system.

If this is your first e-mail system, you can establish some conventions and then let users follow them as they select their own mailbox names. Questionnaires or planning forms for mailbox names should take into consideration all the information needed in creating a mailbox (see fig. 3.1):

- ◆ **F**irst is the first name of the mailbox user, and it can contain up to 32 characters.

- ◆ **L**ast is the last name of the mailbox user, and it can contain up to 64 characters.

- ◆ **D**isplay is the name that is shown in address books and also in the administrator's window. It can contain up to 256 characters. You can choose any scheme that makes sense to you (last name first, first name first, and so forth) but be consistent.

- ◆ **Al**ias is a name used to identify the mailbox user. The alias name is frequently used to generate the e-mail address for this user for external mail systems. Although this field can contain up to 64 characters, many foreign e-mail systems permit fewer characters. In fact PROFS and SNADS have an 8-character limit. You should set a character limit based on the external systems you expect to access.

◆ If you wish to track such information, you can enter data in the Address Information and Company Information sections of the dialog box.

◆ The Primary **W**indows NT Account field is the NT account that has mailbox owner permissions for this mailbox. You can assign administrative permissions to a mailbox to additional NT accounts on the Permissions tab.

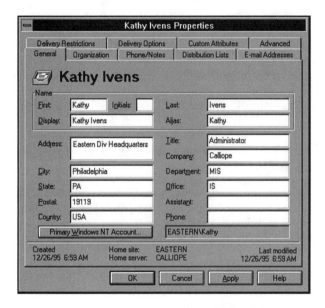

Figure 3.1

Some of the fields in the Mailbox dialog box are used in the creation of e-mail addresses, and there are rules about the data for each field.

You can also create mailboxes for entities in your organization that aren't users. You can have a mailbox for a department (with multiple users given permission to access it) or for company resources such as conference rooms.

Additional, specific information about establishing and configuring mailboxes is found in Chapter 12, "Mailbox Administration."

Mailbox Capacity

You can set limits for user mailboxes. You can limit the size of messages, and you can establish a maximum size of disk space allotted to each mailbox. Based on the information gathered in your ascertainment process, you can decide whether you want to impose any limits, and if so, what type and size.

Ascertaining Needs for Schedule+

There are a variety of schemes for establishing scheduling tasks, and your choice will depend upon the way your company is organized. If most scheduling needs are department-based, and your departments are each site-based, things will be relatively easy to plan and set up.

Remember, however, that the scheduling software does more than schedule meetings—it's also capable of keeping appointment books and contact lists for each user in your organization. You'll find that some users prefer to use paper for keeping track of appointments, or perhaps users have personal information management software that they've grown used to and prefer. No matter how carefully you plan, no matter how you simplify the use of Schedule+, no matter how many training sessions you hold to show users how easy and convenient your plan is, you'll probably find that there are some users who just don't want to use it. Therefore, make sure you get accurate and truthful information in your user ascertainment process so that you don't go to a lot of trouble establishing software configurations that aren't used.

Regardless of whether users keep their personal appointments in Schedule+, there are two things that Schedule+ does so well that it makes sense to insist on its use for scheduling meetings and tracking group projects.

Make sure your ascertainment process includes an overview of the number and type of meetings and projects that are common in your company. Then you have to design your software configuration and site configuration to make it easy to communicate with the users who commonly come together for these tasks.

Projects

When you establish the configuration for tracking projects, you have some choices about default sorting schemes, naming conventions, and so on. For example, you can view and report on projects sorted by the tasks involved (each task is linked to a project as it is entered into the system), the start date, the due date, billing codes, and other criteria.

Meetings

Users can request meetings, send notices about meetings to other users, view other users' schedules to see free and busy times, and schedule resources such as conference rooms and audiovisual equipment.

Each site server keeps a Free/Busy schedule to track individual user schedules (providing you make sure users cooperate by keeping their schedules current in the Microsoft Exchange Server system). It reads the user's schedule and transfers the information to the centralized Free/Busy schedule. This Free/Busy information can be replicated throughout the organization (it's a public folder).

You can configure your system so that individual users can control access between their own schedule and the central Free/Busy schedule.

To Do Lists

Users can keep lists of tasks and reminders, which can then be sorted by task, project, or date. This feature also provides a contact list with a variety of contact management features.

Determining Public Folder Needs

A public folder is a compartment of information that a group of users can access to share information. The following are some examples of public folder usage:

◆ Company newsletters

◆ Company announcements

◆ Departmental announcements

◆ Questionnaires or other requests for information from employees (for instance, vacation preferences)

◆ Work schedules

◆ Information connected to a specific project

◆ Internally developed white papers or informational files that are needed by specific users

◆ Information from an outside source that a user wants to share with other users

Depending upon the number of sites or the number of servers at a site, you can make choices and rules about how public folders are used. Remember that you can set up replication schedules to broaden the distribution of the data in the public folders to the other servers and public folders throughout your organization.

When you do replicate your public folders, the entire hierarchy of public folders can be replicated to any Microsoft Exchange Server computer that has had a public information store installed on it (see fig. 3.2).

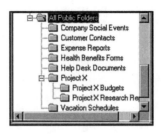

Figure 3.2

The display of the public folders objects is hierarchical—you can configure as many subfolders as you want.

Understanding the Display of Public Folders

The view of public folders that displays to a user is a nice, neat, logical, hierarchical view. That view is totally independent of the actual physical storage locations of the public folders. Different folders can reside on different servers, but those details are transparent to the users. If the user can connect to the server containing the public folder (or one of its replicas), it appears to the user as if the public folder is local.

For example, in the display of public folder objects shown in figure 3.2, the folders themselves are physically residing on any of three servers in the organization (see fig. 3.3).

  If the hierarchy and size of your organization make it feasible, you can dedicate a specific server to be the public folder repository to aid in ease of administration. This dedicated public folder server will be the place that all users go for access to all the public folders in the organization. In this case, the displayed folder hierarchy will match the physical storage of public folders.

The items in each public folder can vary—e-mail messages, forms, notes, enormous documents, graphic files, sound files, and so on. The items in a particular folder are stored on the same server on which the folder was created, but they can be copied and replicated throughout the organization.

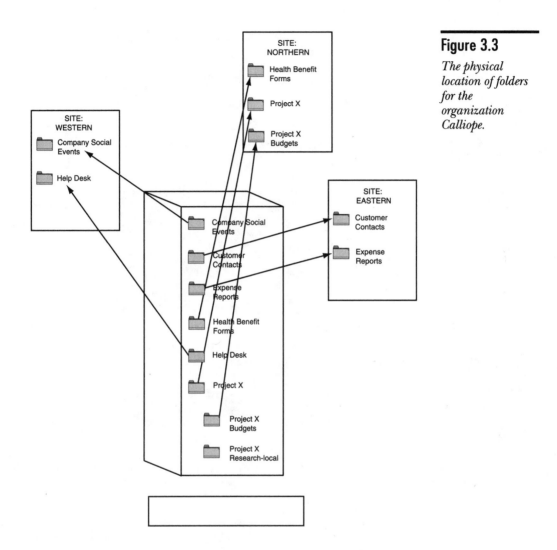

Figure 3.3

The physical location of folders for the organization Calliope.

Planning Public Folder Permissions

As you plan the number and location of public folders, you also need to give some thought to the permissions you give users for accessing and manipulating those folders. Detailed information about maintaining folders is found in Chapter 13, "Administering the Core Components." For the purpose of planning, let's look at a brief overview of the permissions features here.

Folders have property dialog boxes that include a tab for Permissions (see fig. 3.4).

Figure 3.4

You can establish user permissions for the public folders in your Microsoft Exchange Server system.

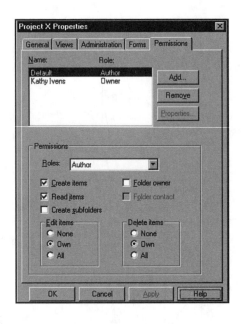

To assign permissions, first select the user name with which you want to work. Choose Add to see a list of all the users in the organization (see fig. 3.5).

Figure 3.5

By default, the names in the Global Address List display when you configure permissions for users for a public folder.

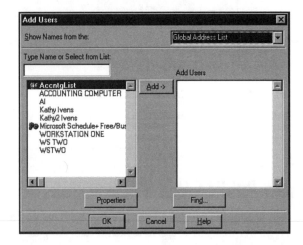

If you wish, you can choose a specific domain or server to see a list of the users attached thereon instead of using the Global Address List. Click on the arrow to the right of the **S**how Names From list box to see the available lists.

Once you choose a user or multiple users (to choose users, highlight the user name, then choose **A**dd), you can give permissions and assign roles.

The Permissions you can grant are the following:

◆ **C**reate items, which gives permission to place items into the folder.

◆ Read **i**tems, which gives permission to open any item contained in the folder.

◆ Create **s**ubfolders, which gives permission to create a public folder that will be a subfolder under this public folder.

◆ **F**older owner, which gives all permissions to manipulate the folder.

◆ F**o**lder contact, which gives a special status known as the Contact. Contacts get notifications from the folder when there are replication problems and also get requests from users who want changes made (such as additional permissions) in this folder.

◆ **E**dit items, which gives editing permissions for items in the folder. You can choose None, Own (a user can only edit items they put there), or All.

◆ De**l**ete items, which gives permission to delete items in the folder. You can choose None, Own, or All.

Roles

A variety of permutations and combinations of permissions have been put together as roles. If you select the combination that matches an existing role, that role is assigned. If your combination of permissions doesn't match any role, the user's role is called a Custom role.

Of course, it's usually faster to select a role for a user than to go through all the individual permissions and select the ones you want to give to the user you're creating permissions for (unless you're creating a custom role).

The roles are, for some reason, tied to the job titles found in the publishing world (which is quite comfortable for the authors of this book, of course). Table 3.1 shows the preconfigured roles and the permissions given for each.

TABLE 3.1
Permissions Given in Predefined Roles

Role	Permissions
Owner	All permissions
Publishing Editor	Create, read, edit, delete, create subfolders
Editor	Create, read, edit, delete
Author	Create, read, edit own, delete own
Reviewer	Read
Contributor	Create

 There is also a role called None, which has no permissions attached to it. You might want to use this as the default role/permission group so that only the users you specifically choose will have permissions in a public folder.

Using Forms in Public Folders

You can create a form for use in a particular public folder, which provides a structure for the way users enter and display information in that public folder. For instance, if the public folder is for the collection of vacation requests, the items placed in it by users can follow a form that is specifically designed for that purpose.

As you plan the use of public folders, make sure that you've planned the design of any forms that will be used in those folders. This generally makes public folders easier to use.

You can configure a public folder so that it accepts only items that follow the form you created for the folder.

Information about creating and using forms is found in Chapter 19, "Developing Forms."

Planning Age Limits for Public Folders

As you accumulate information about users, their needs, and the disk space available for public folders, you should bear in mind the fact that you can put age limits on the items in public folders. This automatically eliminates items in folders as they grow old (and presumably, outdated).

To set age limits for public folders, follow these steps:

1. From the Microsoft Exchange Server Administrative Window, highlight a server, then select its Public Information Store.

2. Choose **P**roperties from the **F**ile menu to see the Public Information Store Properties dialog box; then select the Age Limits tab (see fig. 3.6).

3. Highlight the folder you want to manipulate and select **M**odify (or double-click on it). This displays the Modify Age Limits dialog box (see fig. 3.7).

Figure 3.6

You can view, modify, and configure age limits for all the public folders in your Microsoft Exchange Server system.

Without going through all the specific steps and fields connected with this dialog box (see Chapter 19 for more information), the following are options this feature offers:

◆ You can set an age limit for a folder and a separate age limit for its replicas.

◆ You can establish an age limit for all public folders.

◆ If you establish an age limit for a specific folder, no matter where it is in the hierarchy, that limit overrides the limit for all folders.

◆ You can set an age limit for a specific replica, and the other replicas of the same folder can have different age limits. This means that administrators of sites with replicas can decide that the age limit should be changed on that site for some reason.

Figure 3.7

Setting age limits for items in public folders helps eliminate clutter and saves disk space.

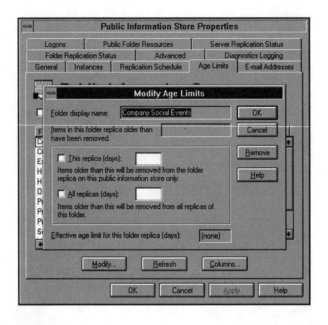

Planning Sites

Most of the site planning you need probably took place when you first installed your NT system. You had to create sites for geographic or divisional locations.

As you plan your Microsoft Exchange Server system, those sites may have to be rethought as you decide on the configuration of servers for your Exchange Server needs. To plan properly, consider the services you will be providing for users and then decide on the number of servers, the amount of disk space, and the variety of connections you need to accomplish that.

An Overview of Planning Needs

There are a number of considerations you have to think about as you plan your Microsoft Exchange Server site services:

◆ Planning servers that are on the same LAN segments as the users that will be creating traffic on the site eliminates some of the traffic across bridges and routers.

◆ If the site will be busy (many users, many public folders, and so forth), you may want to plan to have multiple servers on the site. You can split the work between servers, or split the users by logical function, perhaps by departments.

◆ If you need to support remote client access, you have to install the appropriate type of remote services and be able to support the volume the site will handle.

◆ If users in a site use a network operating system other than NT, you need software that supports the integration between that network software and Microsoft Exchange Server.

◆ For security, encryption, and digital signatures, you must choose the site for the location of the Key Management server (KM server). For information about installing and maintaining the KM server, see Chapter 14, "Installing and Maintaining the Key Management Server."

◆ When planning the strategy for routing messages around your organization and outside your organization, you need to plan the connections to other sites and systems.

◆ A replication plan for moving information between your sites must be established.

◆ A backup strategy for the site (and appropriate hardware) must be established. See Chapter 11, "Backing Up and Restoring," for detailed information about backing up Microsoft Exchange Server sites.

Planning the Layout of a Site

Because sites can be quite large, with multiple servers for Microsoft Exchange services, it's helpful to create a planning schematic to make sure you've considered all the important details.

The place to start is the network at the site and its connections. If the site is one LAN, it's fairly easy to draw a blueprint—just indicate the location of the server (or servers) and the peripherals, such as printers.

If the site has routers, be sure to indicate the protocols you'll need for each router.

If the site has network segments, perhaps spanning different floors of a building, or is segmented by departments that are separated, be sure to note any differences in protocols used by individual segments.

Tip   If you have multiple servers on a site, they can communicate with each other using different protocols than the ones they use for communicating with workstations. Of course, that means you have to install multiple protocols on the servers.

Planning Site Servers

After you decide how many servers you need on a site, where they will physically reside, and how client workstations will connect to them, you need to plan the services the servers will offer.

The permutations and combinations are almost infinite, of course, and the decisions are made by taking into consideration all the factors you've learned about in this chapter.

The primary service the server(s) provides is Microsoft Exchange Server and all the features built into it. However, the server also has to provide the communications protocols to make sure all clients have access to those features.

Interfacing with NetWare

A client running software that provides connection with NetWare can also connect to a Windows NT Server computer running Microsoft Exchange Server. Because the communication that takes place between servers and clients is conducted with remote procedure calls (independent of communication protocols such as TCP/IP), clients can be integrated to use both Microsoft Exchange Server and NetWare.

NetWare users can log on to Microsoft Exchange Server computers as long as they have been given Windows NT Server user accounts. Without that, of course, they cannot be authenticated in a Windows NT Server domain. To make this process easier, you can use the tools in Exchange Server that fetch user account information from the NetWare bindery and migrate the information into Windows NT Server.

 You cannot integrate Windows NT Server with NetWare unless you configure the NT server for NetBIOS.

Depending upon the operating system used by clients, you may have to make specific configuration adjustments on the workstations. Information on installing and config-uring connectors is found in Chapter 7, "Configuring Sites."

Windows 3.x, WFW, and DOS NetWare Clients

You can install services and drivers that permit these clients to access both servers, or, if necessary, you can use an Exchange Server site server as a gateway to the NetWare server for these workstations.

All the protocols for NetWare and Microsoft Networks are built into the operating system and can be installed in these workstations.

Planning Server Services

The major task in planning servers is to make decisions about the Microsoft Exchange Server services offered on a server and the resulting hardware and software needs.

The results of your needs ascertainment process with your users will determine the way you install services on your Microsoft Exchange Server site servers.

Again, this is one of those situations where the permutations and combinations are almost endless, but there are some things you can do to keep your system robust and productive.

For example, if the users on the site will generate heavy e-mail traffic and use numerous public folders in order to share large documents (or large numbers of documents), consider having two servers. You can place the mailboxes on one server and the public folders on the other.

If you cannot place multiple servers on the site, be sure to take advantage of the features in Microsoft Exchange Server that enable you to manage the size of mailboxes and public folders, as well as the automatic deletions available with establishing age limits for items in public folders.

 Most of the time it won't help productivity to enlarge the storage capacity of a server if there is a large quantity of mail and private folders. All the gigabytes you can cram into a server won't help the performance level, which can become sluggish simply because of the volume of user access.

If you have a substantial number of users, you'll get the most productivity by providing a server for each LAN segment. Users who access a connected (by cable) server directly work fastest. This productivity is usually enhanced even more if the connected users are members of the same department or division, because most companies find that the highest volume of e-mail is between users within a division. If it's financially feasible, consider breaking a large department or group into two or more units, giving each its own server.

 Connecting similar users to a single server also conserves the total amount of disk space your organization will use, because only one copy of a message will be stored. If a copy of a message must be sent to another server, you're using double the disk space to provide communication between two people.

Predicting E-Mail Patterns

You have a few methods to choose from for determining the volume of messaging to expect as you go through your needs ascertainment process. This information will help you plan the size and configuration of your site servers.

If you have a current e-mail system that you are planning to migrate into Microsoft Exchange Server, run whatever statistic reports are available.

If there aren't any reports that give you the information you need, devise a questionnaire and have users periodically note the number of messages in their mailboxes at a given moment.

If Microsoft Exchange Server is going to be your first e-mail system, you need to get information directly from users. Although you can ask them to estimate how many messages they expect to send (or receive) in a specific time frame, that's really asking users to guess, because they have no experience with e-mail. It might be better to ask them to keep a piece of paper near the computer for several days and make a tick mark every time they do something that they could do with e-mail:

◆ Every time a user sends a document (either a hard copy or on disk) to another user, there should be a tick mark.

◆ Every time a user picks up a phone to call another user for information that has to be written down (or asks that a document be sent), there should be a tick mark.

◆ Every time a department head sends out a memo to all users in the department, a tick mark should be recorded.

◆ Whenever company forms—such as expense reports, vacation requests, personal leave requests, and so forth—are delivered, more tick marks should appear.

Tip Encourage users to be forthright and realistic about their communication. Otherwise, they're not likely to tell you about all the interoffice telephone calls they make to do things such as arrange lunch. The fact is, making lunch plans by e-mail keeps productivity levels higher, because telephone calls made for that purpose tend to be long (involving other topics of conversation). E-mail that asks "where do you want to eat lunch" and triggers a response of "Joe's Diner at Noon" doesn't take up much disk space and takes a few seconds to accomplish.

Planning E-Mail Storage

You can configure your Microsoft Exchange Server system to store mail on the server, on the user's computer, or on a combination of both.

 It makes no difference to the users where you store e-mail. Users can't really tell where the mailbox objects are stored when they use the software. When a user sees the display of objects, such as Inbox, Outbox, Sent Items, and so on, there's no indication of the physical location of these Personal Folder items. A user whose mailbox is on the server has an identical display as a user whose mail is stored locally.

If disk space isn't a problem, storing all mail on the server ensures its safety, because you'll back up the server regularly. It isn't likely that all the workstations have backup equipment, and every administrator in the world knows that it's useless to insist on disk backups every night—it's just not going to happen.

Users who spend a lot of time out of the office and dial in from remote sites or portables must have server-based e-mail, of course.

Planning the Key Management Server

The advanced security features for your Microsoft Exchange Server system are handled by the Key Management Server (usually referred to as the KM Server). There is only one KM Server in an organization; this is not a feature that can be duplicated. Specific information about installing and maintaining the KM Server is found in Chapter 14.

The KM Server can be installed in any site in the organization. If you plan to put the KM Server in a location other than your own site, make sure you have RPC connection capabilities between yourself and the KM Server in order to administer it.

In addition, you should be aware of the following:

◆ The KM server should be in the domain that will be the central administrative point of your system.

◆ For the greatest level of security, you should install the Windows NT Server NTFS file system.

◆ The KM Server should be secured physically (not easy to get to) and should be backed up at least once a day.

Planning Site-to-Site Communication

Sites communicate with each other to exchange messages, public folders, and directory information. However, you can limit the information that is exchanged between sites, which can be especially necessary if the speed of the connection between two sites isn't terribly fast.

If you have multiple sites in your organization, at least one server at each site must connect with at least one other site. Part of your planning is to diagram the sites in order to make sure that, as you develop each site-to-site connection, you include all the sites in the organization.

An extremely important planning consideration is the connectors you'll use and the configuration of site servers so that messaging isn't interrupted in case of problems:

◆ Plan for redundant connections. A single server can be configured for multiple connectors—install an RAS connector as a backup to the primary connector for the server. Multiple servers can be configured so that in case of connector problems a backup server (with a choice of connectors installed) can take over.

◆ Take advantage of the speed and productivity you can achieve with a large bandwidth—you can have multiple connectors move messages.

Planning Pass-Through Routing

Messages passed by a specific site server to other sites for delivery to and from local users may not be the only burden that server carries. If you have multiple sites, a site server may have to act as a pass-through as one site sends messages to another site, using this site only to make the connection.

You can reduce this burden by planning alternatives if your multiple sites must have a "hop around" routing scheme:

◆ Consider having a specific, dedicated, bridgehead (a computer dedicated to collecting and moving data that's being routed off-site) server on sites that do a lot of pass-through routing. The cost of the extra hardware can easily be amortized by the time saved when the site server accessed by users is able to remain responsive (time is money).

◆ Consider having one server on the site for incoming traffic and a different server for outgoing, so that the system doesn't bog down with double-direction traffic.

Planning Routing Schemes

There are two routing schemes for organizations with multiple sites: routing messages throughout the site, and routing messages to other sites. The former is pretty much automatic and doesn't require a great deal of planning or work. The latter, however, is a major planning consideration, and the decisions you make will impact the messaging efficiency of the entire organization.

 If you set up a specific site for routing messages to a foreign system, total directory replication must be configured between that site and the other sites so that the foreign gateway site can resolve addresses.

Here are some of the considerations that should go into your planning:

◆ The financial impact. Not just the hardware budget needs to be considered, you also have to plan for the cost of communication links. If you configure multiple connectors, you might want to use certain connectors during specific parts of the day when rates are lower. This makes sense if your sites are scattered across time zones.

◆ Although you can use a single connector with one network connection for several sites, you'll have serious consequences if that network connection has a problem. Even if you plan for multiple connectors using the same network connection, that's safe only until the network connection has a problem.

On the other hand, if you have multiple connections with multiple network connections, the effort and cost of administration can be onerous.

In the end, depending upon the number of sites and the volume of traffic, you need to plan for a balance of efficiency and redundancy.

As you plan for direct and pass-through routing, you have to balance economics and efficiency of the hardware. If you have a low number of servers providing the routing, it's easy to upgrade them if you need to improve speed or storage space capacity. The administrative burden isn't too troublesome. If you distribute connectors to most or all of the servers, you have faster traffic throughput, but the cost of upgrading is expensive and the administrative burden may increase payroll costs. Again, this is a matter of finding the right balance.

Planning Administration

When you finish your needs ascertainment and have used the information to complete the plans for all the elements mentioned in this chapter, you have to figure out who's going to help keep it all running smoothly. Microsoft Exchange Server is a robust, complicated application and you have to plan for administrators on several levels (and don't forget to plan training time).

Monitoring the System

There are a number of administrative tasks involved in monitoring your Microsoft Exchange Server system—at the organization and site levels. You can run as many monitoring software applications as you wish on each site, but the more monitors you require, the more administrators you need. Although experience tells us that a little paranoia about hardware and software is probably healthy, don't go crazy. Try to approach the decision about site monitors intelligently—if the site is set up with some particular set of circumstances that requires special caretaking, you can run daily just the monitors that apply to the potential problem.

In this section, you take a brief look at the overview for monitoring your system. Chapter 15, "Monitoring Events," contains complete information about configuring and running the Microsoft Exchange Server monitors.

Most of the real work is done by the monitors; the administrators merely have to initiate the service. If there's a problem, of course, the administrator has to work to repair it. The following are monitors that administrators should run, either regularly or occasionally:

◆ The Link Monitor, which checks the links between servers. The servers can both be running Microsoft Exchange Server, or one can be a server or gateway in another system. The Link Monitor, established at both points, sends a message from one server to the other, sends a reply, measures the round-trip travel time, and reports if there's a delay exceeding a specified (by you) limit.

 When you run Link Monitor between an Exchange Server and an outside mail service you may be able to establish a way to get a reply; but if you can't, have the administrator send a message to a bad address (a nonexistent address) and measure the "undeliverable" bounce-back time.

◆ The Server Monitor, which checks all the processes on a server. The administrator can configure some automatic responses to problems or take action directly, depending upon the degree of severity.

The Server Monitor works in a Boolean fashion, recognizing only that a service is on or off. A service that is stalled, or hung up, isn't off and therefore won't be reported as being troublesome. The administrator has to be able to determine those things when the monitor fails to recognize these problems.

◆ The Performance Monitor, which displays statistics about the way a server is performing. Depending upon your configuration, you can see processor use, memory use, server throughput, the number of threads in use, the quantity of read/write operations in a given moment of time, and so on. You can set values for the various performances, then have the monitor alert you if the actual values are too high or too low.

Setting Permissions

You might want to have site or server administrators (depending on the traffic volume) who can modify permissions for mailboxes and public folders. Any permission changes or configurations that permit one user to access another user's mailbox should be made in concert with organization policy.

Backing Up

Every server in your organization has to be backed up regularly, and this should be one of the prime responsibilities of an administrator. Even if automatic, unattended backup is invoked, the administrator should check the backup logs for problems.

Client/User Administration

Besides the hand-holding and help-desk duties that an administrator spends time on, the ability to install, configure, or modify workstation software should also be limited to the administrator. This ensures that organization policies are always being met, to say nothing of avoiding the potential disasters that can occur when a user who knows just enough to be dangerous is let loose on a workstation.

CHAPTER 4

Deciding on Hardware

If your company is like many, you rely heavily on your e-mail system. In fact, in most companies, it can be difficult to find a single application that is used by more of your user base than your e-mail system. Nothing could be worse than to install a new e-mail system with significant new capabilities and then disappoint your users with inadequate performance. Implementations of systems such as Exchange Server have lots of lead time, during which your users will look forward to using the new features—and you don't want to disappoint them with inadequate performance. Not having sufficient horsepower for the new system adversely impacts the success of your implementation.

Microsoft Exchange Server is a client-server messaging system with considerable capabilities. To maximize productivity, you need to ensure that you install Exchange Server onto computer hardware with sufficient resources to handle your current and future needs. Selecting and configuring such hardware is not a difficult task. Following the guidelines set out in this chapter—coupled with an understanding of the key performance issues—will help cinch your installation and keep your users pleased with their new system.

Planning the Servers

Before selecting and configuring your Exchange Server hardware, you need a solid grasp of how you expect to configure your e-mail environment. Because Exchange Server is extremely flexible in how you configure it, there are many considerations you need to take into account as you plan your hardware needs. After reading the earlier chapters in this book, you should have some idea of how you expect to set up your Exchange Server environment. That knowledge is critical before you move forward and specify your server hardware.

Hardware Performance Considerations

Before selecting your server hardware, spend time reviewing the following information about overall hardware performance areas. Doing so will help you understand the relative tradeoffs involved as you choose the server hardware.

The following are the most important topics to consider in order to achieve the best possible performance with Exchange Server, *listed in order of importance*.

◆ **Disk I/O.** Fast disk I/O, such as that provided by local-bus Small Computer Systems Interface (SCSI) caching disk controllers, has the most impact on Exchange Server performance. Both of the popular local-bus implementations offer good performance; Peripheral Componenent Interconnect (PCI) and VESA local-bus (VLB) both perform better than either ISA- or EISA-based disk controllers.

Remember that server operating systems such as Windows NT receive additional performance benefits from SCSI disk subsystems as compared to those based on integral drive electronics (IDE) disk systems. Although this isn't necessarily true for most desktop operating systems, such as DOS or Windows 95, it is true for Windows NT.

◆ **Distributing files across hard disks.** Exchange Server is designed to enable you to locate key files onto different disk drives. Doing so reduces contention for a single drive's read/write head when many reads and writes are being rapidly performed on various Exchange Server files. In fact, a tool that ships with Exchange Server, called the Optimizer, can automatically test the performance of all the installed disks in a given server and can recommend the best location for each key Exchange Server file to achieve best possible performance. The Optimizer will then even take care of moving the files to the drives you select by using its results. Using the Optimizer is covered in Chapter 6, "Installing Exchange Server."

◆ **RAM.** If your server is utilizing the system swap file in order to run Exchange Server services, you can typically improve performance dramatically by increasing the RAM installed in your system. However, if another component in the system is causing a performance bottleneck, increasing RAM may have little or no impact on performance.

At a bare minimum, you need 32 MB of RAM on the Exchange server. Microsoft recommends 64 MB, and large installations (thousands of mailboxes) may need even more installed RAM. The key is to examine the change in utilization of the Windows NT Server's swap file as you start Exchange Server and it runs over time. You can see the swap file utilization with the Windows NT Performance Monitor. If the swap file utilization or size is growing during Exchange Server use, adding RAM may help performance. Look at how busy the disk drives are as the server is running. If they seem excessively busy, and examining the swap file reveals heavy usage, adding more RAM will help. If, on the other hand, there is little swap file usage even under heavy loads, adding more RAM will do little or no good.

◆ **Striping data.** Windows NT enables you to create a single virtual disk, called a disk array, which is made up of multiple hard disks. In this scenario, data is striped across the drives so that a file's data will be scattered sequentially across all the drives in the disk array. This striping property is automatic in various levels of RAID disk configurations. Further, most server-class computers have facilities within their disk controllers to build disk arrays supported directly by the controller. Using the disk controller to manage arrays generally offers better performance than creating them in the operating system software.

Exchange Server benefits from having its data files located on disk arrays.

Note | You should always let your swap file usage determine your need (or lack of need) for more RAM. Although running other applications on the same server that Exchange Server is using will increase RAM requirements, let the system's swap file utilization be your ultimate guide.

◆ **Processor.** If you have eliminated other bottlenecks in your system, you can make further performance improvements by using faster processors or by using multiple processors in the server. Because Exchange Server uses a multi-threaded multitasking model, it can easily dispatch different threads of the system to run on different processors in your server.

In general, new Exchange Server servers should be purchased with at least a Pentium processor running at 90 MHz. However, you should always purchase the fastest system you can within your budget. Exchange Server will need more and more resources over time as you expand your use of its features, and you will want to provide plenty of room for growth.

◆ **Network throughput.** Increasing the speed of the interface between the server and the network can improve performance. Poorly designed network interface cards (NICs) in the server will hamper performance, as will NICs that aren't really designed for server use. Try to stay with NICs that are PCI- or VLB-based. EISA NICs are the next-best bet; ISA-based NICs will generally be too slow to handle Exchange Server traffic.

 If your overall network architecture is poorly designed, client-server and server-server performance can be impacted. For instance, having too many clients on a single subnetwork can cause excessive collisions, worsening overall performance.

Scaling Performance

When selecting server hardware for Exchange Server, try to select hardware that can be easily expanded. Exchange Server brings many new capabilities to your messaging services, some of which you will not completely implement immediately, so you may not realize your full performance needs until you have been running Exchange Server for some time. Because you might not implement all the services immediately, try to leave yourself room to grow your server as easily as possible.

To maintain the ability to scale up the performance of a given server easily, make sure you can do the following:

◆ Add processors.

◆ Add RAM.

◆ Add disk drives, or replace existing hard disks with faster units.

◆ Reconfigure existing disks into drive arrays.

◆ Add new disk controllers.

◆ Add new network interface boards.

Remember that it's almost always less expensive in the long run to purchase server hardware that can be easily expanded rather than get yourself into a situation in which you have to replace your server with a faster unit.

Recommended Server Configurations

It is virtually impossible to predict the exact configuration needs accurately for your server for your Exchange Server installation. Because Exchange Server enables users to store not only text-based e-mail, but attachments that can be quite sizable, and also supports many different connection and security strategies (with varying load requirements), the actual server requirements can vary wildly from company to company, even with similar numbers of users and sites. The best strategy is to use a server that will enable you easily to add more capacity if needed. Then, keep a close eye on your server's performance and utilization as you implement Exchange Server, making changes as required. Optimally, you should be able to add more processors, RAM, and disks to your server easily.

As a general guideline, consider Microsoft's tested server configurations, shown in table 4.1.

TABLE 4.1
Recommended Server Configurations

Size	Users	Processor	RAM	Disk Configuration
Low-end	100–300+	Single Pentium	32 MB	Two 2 GB disks
Middle	250–600+	Single Pentium	64 MB	Five 2 GB disks
High-end	500–1000+	Three Pentiums	256 MB	Eight 2 GB disks

Backup

When planning your backup strategy, you first need to understand Exchange Server's backup features and capabilities. Provided with Exchange Server is an enhanced version of Windows NT backup designed to work with Exchange Server. Using this utility, you can do full (normal), copy, incremental, and differential backups. You can back up your Exchange Server to a locally attached tape drive, or to a tape drive on another Windows NT system across the network.

Note   A *full backup* (called a *normal backup* by Microsoft) backs up all data files and components of Exchange Server, marks them as being backed up, and deletes the transaction log files that contain data already committed to the database.

A *copy backup* backs up all data and components to the tape, but does not mark the files as being backed up, and does not affect the transaction log files. You use a copy backup when you don't want to disturb a sequence of incremental or differential backups.

continues

An *incremental backup* backs up only components of Exchange Server that have changed since the last full or incremental backup. Transaction logs with data that is already committed to the database are deleted after the backup. You cannot do incremental backups if you are using the circular logging feature of Exchange Server. Incremental backups reset the archive bit of the files backed up. *Circular logging* is a feature of Exchange Server that reuses the transaction log files as data is committed to the Exchange Server database.

A *differential backup* copies all the components changed since the last full backup. All new transaction logs are backed up, but none are deleted from the server. You cannot do differential backups if you are using the circular logging feature of Exchange Server. Differential backups do not reset the archive bit of the files backed up.

Exchange Server uses a sophisticated database that makes use of transaction log files. New data being written to the database is first written directly to the transaction log files. This provides the best performance possible for writing data immediately to disk. Then, when the server is less busy, data is copied (committed) from the transaction logs into the database itself. If at all possible, use the Optimizer utility to locate the Exchange Server transaction logs on a different disk drive from the database itself. By doing so, if you lose one of your disk drives, you can recover the maximum amount of data by using a combination of the previously backed up database and the transaction log files, or simply the current database if you lose the disk that contains the transaction logs.

 For best performance, the log files should be located on a disk that's formatted with the FAT file system. FAT-formatted disks give better performance than NTFS disks for sequential writes to files, such as the log files.

In choosing backup hardware, you not only have to consider the amount of data you will need to back up, but also the load on the server and your network. Locally connected backup devices back up and restore data fastest, but they make heavier demands on the server when running. Remote backups and restores to another computer running Windows NT cause less load on the server, but they take longer to perform and increase your network traffic.

When choosing backup hardware, consider these questions:

◆ Do you want to back up data to a tape drive or other device on the server itself, or to another backup device across the network?

◆ What backup rotation scheme do you plan to use (for example, Grandfather-Father-Son, Tower of Hanoi, or some other scheme)?

◆ How much data do you expect your server to hold in the next two or more years, and how much useful life do you want your investment in tape backup hardware to yield?

◆ Do you need backup media that can handle the entire size of the server contents so that tapes do not have to be changed during the backup, or is spanning (and changing) tapes acceptable in your site?

◆ How often will you back up the server; what combination of full, incremental, or differential backups will you use?

◆ Is there enough time when the server will not be busy, such as during the night, in which a full backup can be completed?

Generally, it's recommended that you install a local backup device onto the server computer, with backups being scheduled to happen when the system is not busy. If you have a 24-hour operation, however, consider using a backup device on a remote system, so that server performance is impacted as little as possible while the system is in use.

RAS Configuration Impact

If you will use Windows NT's RAS Server to provide remote connectivity to Exchange Server, each simultaneous RAS connection requires about 2 MHz of processor overhead and about 1 MB of RAM.

Connections between Sites

There are many technologies from which to choose to connect remote sites. Exchange Server supports many networking protocols, including IPX/SPX, TCP/IP, and Data Link Control (DLC).

When planning your site links, carefully weigh the costs and benefits of the different connection types available. Generally, the higher the bandwidth requirements between sites, the more expensive the link is to implement and maintain. For this reason, it's almost always wiser to locate servers in each physical site. This keeps internetwork traffic to a minimum, because only cross-site mail needs to be carried over the link. In some cases, however, you may have small remote offices that cannot justify their own servers and must rely on a server at a larger site to provide their e-mail needs. In cases such as this, you need to invest in some sort of connection model for those remote users, depending on how many you expect.

Table 4.2 lists possible remote network connections, their bandwidths, and their typical monthly costs (in U.S. dollars).

Note   Telecommunications costs are impossible to quantify here. However, you will want to get an estimate of your actual costs either from your internal telecommunications people or from the carrier of your network link. They should be able to work with you to determine an estimate based on the type of link you want to use, the times of day your connection will function, how many minutes it will be connected, and how distant the remote sites are.

TABLE 4.2
Network Connection Bandwidths and Costs

Network Type	Bandwidth	Avg. Cost/Month	Notes
Dial-up modems	Up to 28 Kbps	$100 to $1,000	Depends on distance and number of minutes
Leased line	Up to 64 Kbps	$150 to $1,000	Depends on distance; available 24 hours a day
ISDN	Up to 128 Kbps	$250 to $1,000	Depends on distance and number of minutes
T-1	1.544 Mbps	$1,000 to $3,000	Depends on distance and number of minutes
T-3	44.184 Mbps	$50,000 to $80,000	Depends on distance and number of minutes

There are alternatives that may make sense when connecting sites. For instance, fractional T-1 enables you to add and delete 56 Kpbs channels as needed (T-1 allows up to 28 56 Kpbs channels). Frame relay is a good alternative that lets you send packets of data over a public or private data network, paying only for the data you send rather than for the available bandwidth. Of course, you can often achieve your goals for low-bandwidth connections by using matched high-speed modems over dial-up lines.

 Tip   If you have an existing network link between two sites, consider first trying to use it before adding capacity. Depending on your configuration, you may be able to send Exchange Server data easily over an existing link without adversely impacting other WAN traffic needs. Keep in mind that Exchange Server includes an Internet Mail Connector that enables you to route mail between sites by using existing Internet connections. If you choose this model, however, carefully examine the Exchange Server security capabilities described in Chapter 13, "Administering the Core Components."

When planning your network links, pay careful attention to how much data you expect to send. Consider both peak and average needs. Using simple arithmetic, you should be able to estimate your bandwidth requirements. For instance, if you know that your current e-mail load between sites is as high as 100 MB per hour during peak times, you know that an ISDN connection that handles only about 58 MB per hour (128,000 bits per second equals 57.6 MB per hour) will not be sufficient.

Planning the Client Computers

The fastest server hardware in the world won't help your users if their client computers aren't capable of fast performance as Microsoft Exchange clients. Use table 4.3 to confirm that your client computers have at least the minimum configurations for Exchange and optimally have the recommended configuration.

When evaluating your client needs, remember to look at the average user's needs exclusive of running as an Exchange client. For instance, if most of your users run programs such as Word and Excel concurrently with Exchange Client, 8 MB of RAM is not enough for a Windows 3.*x* or Windows 95 system. Instead, 12 or 16 MB would be more appropriate for such a user.

 Note A Microsoft Exchange client running under Windows 95 uses between 8 MB and 11 MB of virtual memory when running.

TABLE 4.3
Client Computer Requirements for Microsoft Exchange Client

Operating System	Hard Disk Space	RAM (Min/Recommended)
Windows 3.1*x*	20–32 MB	4–8 MB
Windows NT 3.5*x*	20–32 MB	16–24 MB
Windows 95	20–32 MB	8–16 MB
MS-DOS	2–3 MB	1 MB

Getting It Right the First Time

Any implementation as complex as Exchange Server will have problems; it's a simple fact. You need to do your homework as completely as possible to minimize potential problems and ensure a smooth transition to Exchange Server. Spending time on making sure that you've put in place the best underlying hardware and architectures to support Exchange Server will pay off in smoothing the implementation process. You'll also help prevent the need to go back to your budgeting authorities to request additional resources to complete your implementation. As carpenters are fond of saying: "Measure twice and cut once."

CHAPTER 5

Planning for E-Mail Migration

Migration is the process of moving from your existing e-mail system onto Exchange Server. Because e-mail is a crucial business tool for many people in your organization, the migration process needs to be thought out and implemented carefully.

Implementing Microsoft Exchange Server from scratch, although an involved process, is child's play compared to migrating from an existing system. There are many factors to consider when migrating from another e-mail system (even from MS Mail), many different ways to accomplish the migration, and many things that can go wrong. The fact that, in most organizations, e-mail is used almost constantly by virtually everyone in the company makes doing the job right even more important.

The best way to help ensure that migration goes smoothly is to plan your migration carefully. You need to understand all your choices fully and decide how to carry out the migration. Many factors have an impact on these decisions. In this chapter, you learn about all the facets involved in planning your migration: the key issues, decisions, and outcomes for which you need to prepare.

Understanding Levels and Types of Migration

There are three broad types of automated or semiautomated migration: you can choose to let Exchange Server coexist with your existing system during the cut-over; you can choose to migrate your mailboxes, but without their contents; and you can choose to migrate your entire existing e-mail system, including mailbox contents.

Coexistence

Microsoft Exchange Server offers two methods for coexistence if you need to run your old e-mail system alongside Exchange Server for a period of time, using special client software or running gateways.

Using Mail Applications Programming Interface (MAPI) 1.0 connectivity, you can install the Microsoft Exchange Client onto all the computers. They can then access both your new Microsoft Exchange Server, as well as your existing system, by using a MAPI transport provider installed into Exchange Client. In this way, your clients can access both systems during the migration. This is the most graceful way to handle coexistence, provided that a MAPI transport provider that will work with the Exchange Client is available for your existing system. A coexistence strategy using a MAPI transport provider for Exchange Client might follow these steps:

1. Install Exchange Client onto user computers, setting it up so that it is accessing the existing system by using a MAPI provider. Installation of the Exchange Client component that accesses Exchange Server directly can then proceed over time.

2. After all Exchange Clients are installed and working with your existing e-mail system, set up and test Exchange Server.

3. Set up the Exchange Client profiles to begin accessing the Exchange Server instead of the old system. All clients can often be reconfigured over a short period of time if everything is in place and working well. You need to visit each workstation to make these profile changes.

4. Deactivate the old system.

An alternative involves the use of gateways between your old mail system and Exchange Server. In this model, people can run either the old client software or the Exchange client, and both systems are configured to pass messages through to the other system by using some form of custom addressing. Although this type of coexistence may be necessary in some cases, it's a difficult proposition; you have to maintain both systems in parallel during the migration, and few IS departments have the resources to do so. It also requires that you purchase the necessary gateway software for both Exchange Server and your existing mail system. Assuming the gateway software is available, it's probably expensive. Finally, you have to maintain the gateway during the migration period.

What's the answer? First, determine if you *really* need coexistence for a period of time. If you can avoid it, you'll save yourself significant headaches. If you can't avoid it, you need to answer the following questions:

◆ Does a MAPI transport provider exist for your current system that works under Microsoft Exchange Client? If so, you can roll out the client software over time, letting the client software (with the MAPI transport provider installed) handle access to both systems while you do so. If not, you need to pursue a gateway connection.

◆ Does gateway software exist for your existing system and Exchange Server? If so, you need to purchase the gateway software, install and test it, and then start migrating users as quickly as you can, while maintaining both systems during the implementation.

◆ If a MAPI transport doesn't exist and there are no gateways, do you want to develop your own gateway for the transition? This is possible, but it is an expensive and difficult proposition. Microsoft sells an Exchange Software Development Kit (SDK) if you do need to build this kind of solution.

Mailbox Migration

The easiest migration method is one in which you simply migrate the mailboxes, without contents, from your existing system into Exchange Server. You can use one of the Migration Wizards that comes with Exchange Server to help you create the mailboxes. The Migration Wizards help you create all the needed mailboxes en masse. You can do this by using the Migration Wizards, or simply by using a file that contains all your mailbox names and is properly formatted. Then, you use the Administrator program to import the list and create all the mailboxes at once by using a mailbox template that you create. It's really an automated method that enables you to create all your needed mailboxes quickly and easily. Formatting a text file to be imported into Exchange Server is covered in Chapter 10, "Migrating Mailboxes."

You can create the listing of needed mailbox names from many sources within your company:

◆ An employee list

◆ A list from your current e-mail system exported to a text file or printout (captured to a disk file) listing e-mail accounts

◆ An internal company telephone list

◆ A database of employees that your human resource or payroll departments would have readily available

◆ A listing of users from your network operating system; Exchange Server can even directly access the user lists contained in either a Windows NT server or a Novell NetWare server

 On Novell networks, you can use the CAPTURE command to redirect printed output to a disk file. This can often be helpful in extracting information from a system that doesn't support ASCII exports of its information.

If you are migrating all your users at once, using the mailbox creation method is the fastest way to accomplish the implementation. Then, once you create the mailboxes and install the client software, everyone can immediately begin using the new system. Afterward, if the necessary software exists to migrate the mail messages directly from your old system to your new system (supplied by either Microsoft or a third party), you can consider migrating mailbox contents at a future date.

Another advantage to creating the mailboxes all at once and not worrying about moving mailbox contents is that you can more easily correct historical problems in your existing e-mail system. For instance, if naming conventions are poorly observed (or nonexistent), you can create all the new mailboxes by using a single naming convention. By eliminating the need to move mailbox contents, you make it easier to deal with cleaning up your naming conventions for the new system.

Full Mailbox Migration

Full mailbox migration is exactly what its name implies: you move not only the mailboxes from the old system to the new, but also all the contents of the old mailboxes. If your need for existing messages is strong, you may be forced to attempt this approach.

Performing a full mailbox migration is made simpler by the availability of migration tools for your existing system. Microsoft supplies tools for the following:

◆ Microsoft Mail for PC Networks (version 3.*x*)

◆ Microsoft Mail for AppleTalk Networks (version 3.*x*)

◆ Lotus cc:Mail (database version DB6)

◆ Verimation MEMO MVS (version 3.2.1 or later)

◆ IBM PROFS/OfficeVision (all versions)

◆ DEC ALL-IN-1 (versions 2.3 or later)

To assist you with migrating all the existing mailboxes and contents to Exchange Server, several types of migration tools are included with Exchange Server, depending on the system from which you are migrating:

◆ *Source system extractors* copy your e-mail information from the source system into file types that can be imported into Exchange Server. You can use source extractors to copy mailbox listings, messages, and scheduling information from your existing system.

◆ *Migration wizards* take files created from your source e-mail system and import them into Exchange Server.

◆ The *Administrator program* contains features that enable you to import data into Exchange Server.

If you have the necessary expertise and capabilities, you can develop your own tools to extract information from your existing system, format the files in the proper format for Exchange Server, and import the data.

An important factor to keep in mind is that complete mailbox migration takes much longer to perform than mailbox creation, because there is much more data that needs to be imported into Exchange Server. If you are planning a complete mailbox migration, you should perform a test migration first so that you can get a feeling for how long the migration will take for your site. You should also test for data integrity.

Building an Implementation Team

The key to any complex system implementation is forming an implementation team. Your team members should have the following:

◆ Clearly designated responsibilities

◆ Knowledge about their assigned tasks for the Exchange Server implementation process

◆ A clear understanding of how the entire process works and how their job integrates into the project

Every organization has different team needs. However, there are common job functions that should be performed in almost any installation. Whether you assign multiple functions to relatively few individuals or have a number of individuals assigned to each function depends on the size of your organization and the needs of your migration. When developing your team, consider the implementation functions listed in table 5.1.

TABLE 5.1
Implementation Team Functions

Function	Description
Architect	Responsible for the overall implementation process, and the design and testing of the system
Computer hardware support	Installs and upgrades both client and server computer hardware
Network hardware support	Installs and handles networking hardware support, such as routers, bridges, and hardware-based gateways
Exchange administrator	Administers the servers, performs backups, and works on optimizing server performance
User support	Resolves user problems
Network specialist	Knows the underlying network topology and technology for both the LAN and WAN; helps configure and troubleshoot network connectors and other network-oriented problems
Trainer	Trains help desk staff and end users
Tester	Tests the system
Coexistence specialist	Maintains the link between the old system and the new (if necessary) and understands how the two systems interact
Exchange application developer	Develops Exchange Server solutions to replace custom applications being used on the existing system, and develops new applications

You may not need all these functions for your implementation. For instance, if you are not using Exchange Server over a WAN, a networking specialist is not strictly required, or may be a consultant who is available only if problems arise. If you have no custom applications in your existing system, the need for an application developer will not be important until after you have migrated to Exchange Server. Carefully examine each functional area listed and decide what resources you need for your migration.

Choosing a Migration Scheme

Earlier in this chapter, you learned about the three methods available to migrate to Exchange Server (coexistence, mailbox creation, and mailbox migration). Within each of those three methods, you can choose to perform the migration all at once (*single-phase*) or over time (*multi-phase*). Which of these two methods you choose depends on many factors.

Single-Phase Migration

A single-phase migration (moving everything at once, perhaps over a weekend) is always easier than a multi-phase migration if your situation allows it. Consider using a single-phase approach if all the following are true:

◆ You do not need to move mailbox contents from the existing system, or you have tested the migration and you know that the mailbox content migration can be accomplished within the needed time.

◆ All the resources (hardware and software) needed for Exchange Server and the Exchange clients are in place.

◆ You have the necessary personnel to handle a single-phase migration within the window of time available to you.

◆ You have some form of automated software distribution in place so that you can rapidly install Exchange client onto your client computers.

Multi-Phase Migration

A multi-phase migration is more complex than a single-phase migration, because not only do you have to deal with the issues of the migration itself, but you have to deal with the old system while implementing the new. If you require coexistence during the migration, the process becomes even more complex, which makes planning and implementing more difficult.

Because of the following, large sites often have to pursue a multi-phase migration:

◆ The resources don't exist to migrate all users at once.

◆ Existing systems are too complex to migrate all at once.

◆ Hardware that is being used for parts of the existing system is needed for the new system.

◆ Existing mail-specific applications aren't yet available for Exchange and must be developed.

◆ Exchange Client software does not yet exist for all the client platforms in your organization.

If you decide that you require a multi-phase migration, you then should decide whether you need coexistence between the old and new systems during migration. If so, you need to decide how the two systems will coexist, maintain the coexistence mechanisms during migration, and maintain both the old and new systems during the migration time frame.

You may be able to do without coexistence during a multi-phase migration if you can identify groups of users who need to communicate among themselves, but rarely have a need to communicate with other groups in the company. In such a scenario, you can plan a multi-phase migration in which you migrate these groups at each step. During migration, groups are moved from the old system to the new. If your overall timetable is not too long, users may be able to live with not being able to address people still on the old system for a limited period of time. The key to making this work is communication, both with appropriate management within the company, and to the users themselves. Be sure to set expectations carefully.

Understanding Other Migration Factors

There are some other factors you must take into account as part of your migration. These include migrating remote users, dealing with custom applications in use, developing a naming methodology for Exchange Server, and dealing with resulting external name problems if you change your mailbox naming scheme.

Migrating Resource Accounts

Many sites use e-mail scheduling products to schedule resources, such as conference rooms or shared equipment. You need to migrate those e-mail accounts to Exchange Server. Although many of the migration tools will move these types of accounts from your existing system into Exchange Server, you may also have to do some additional work on the accounts within Exchange Server so that they become proper Schedule+ resources that function properly.

Mail Delivery during Migration

When you're doing a multi-phase migration, you need to deal with mail sent to the migrated user's original accounts on the existing system. There are two issues here: mail sent to the existing system after a user has been moved to Exchange Server; and replies to migrated mail in which the original sender's address is from the old system, but the sender has since been migrated to Exchange Server.

To deal with mail sent to the original system after the user has been migrated, try to configure the existing system to forward mail to the user's new address on Exchange Server. Optimally, it should also be able to reply to the sender with information about the person's new address.

If your existing system doesn't have the capability of automatically forwarding mail in the fashion just described, you have two choices:

◆ The migrated user can periodically use the existing system to deal with mail sent there.

◆ You can periodically migrate the contents of the user's mailbox on the existing server to Exchange Server.

Dealing with the second selection—replies in which the sender's address is from the old system but the sender is now using Exchange Server—can be handled within Exchange Server itself. The Address Book in Exchange Server is intelligent in understanding e-mail addresses for replied-to mail. When a person replies to a message, the Address Book first tries to find the sender's address within the global and personal address books. If it finds a unique name, it automatically uses that address. If it finds multiple names that fit the original sending address, it presents users with a list of possible addresses from which they can choose the correct individual. If it cannot match the original sender's name at all, the user can simply choose the proper recipient from either the global or personal address lists.

| Note | In order for the Address Book to find all the necessary names, it must contain addresses for all users of the existing system, on top of the addresses for current users of Exchange Server. Addresses for the existing system can be created as custom recipient addresses within Exchange Server. |

Handling Distribution Lists

Handling distribution lists during a multi-phase migration needs careful planning, because the recipients within the distribution list are constantly being moved from the existing system to Exchange Server, and the distribution lists must always deliver mail to the correct mailboxes. There are many ways to deal with distribution lists during migration.

Disable Distribution Lists

One way to deal with the problem of maintaining distribution lists during the migration is simply to disable them until the migration is complete. However, if your multi-phase migration is expected to be lengthy, this may not be desirable.

Migrate All Distribution Lists to Exchange Server First

If you migrate all your distribution lists to Exchange Server first, the recipients within each list will be created as custom addresses in Exchange Server. As mailboxes are migrated, the distribution lists are automatically modified by the migration wizard to point to the new Exchange Server mailboxes.

Distribution lists at other sites that point to recipients at your site must be manually changed to point to the correct recipient when that recipient's mailbox is migrated. You can deal with this problem in one of two ways: frequently updating, or temporarily restructuring your distribution lists.

First, you can simply have those other sites frequently modify their distribution lists as users are migrated at your site. Second, you can consider changing how you maintain your distribution lists. If you restructure your distribution lists so that all lists point only to recipients within the same site as the distribution list, the migration wizards automatically take care of modifying the distribution lists correctly. Then, to create a distribution list that contains members from multiple sites, have those "cross-site" distribution lists point to smaller distribution lists at each site.

For example, suppose you have three sites, all of which have two management-level people within them. At each site, you create a management distribution list that contains the two recipients within that site only. Then, to create a distribution list that reaches all the managers at all the sites, the new distribution list simply points to each of the smaller management distribution lists at the three sites. In this way, you don't have to worry about updating the individual distribution lists during migration.

Leave Distribution Lists in Place until End of Migration

Another way to deal with distribution lists during a multi-phase migration involves simply leaving the lists in place on the existing e-mail system. Then, using a message forwarding feature in the existing system, mail sent to the distribution lists automatically finds its way to the correct mailbox, whether it be a user still using the existing system or a forwarded message that gets passed to the migrated recipient on Exchange Server. When you finish migrating all your users, you can re-create the correct distribution lists on Exchange Server before shutting down the existing system.

There is one key drawback to this method, though: message traffic between the existing system and Exchange Server will be increased as messages are passed between the two systems. When more than half of your user base is migrated, mail will often be sent through the gateway to the existing system, only to be sent back to Exchange Server as it's forwarded to the correct migrated recipients. In a large site, this may create message traffic loads that delay the delivery of mail to unacceptable levels.

Convert Distribution Lists to Folders

You can often replace the functionality of mail distribution lists with Exchange Server public folders. Members of the original distribution list are given access to view the public folder. They enjoy one key benefit from this conversion: they can see not only new messages just as they do when they receive them via a distribution list, but they can see all the historical messages within the folder as well. Public folders are almost like discussion areas within bulletin board systems, in which it's easy to follow the entire thread of a sequence of messages.

Consider converting your distribution list messages to public folders within Exchange Server. This removes the problems of maintaining distribution lists during migration, although it also means that users will not be able to access the public folders until they have been migrated to Exchange Server.

Migrating Remote Users

Virtually every organization has remote mail users, and yours is probably no exception. These are individuals or small groups of people in remote offices who dial into your e-mail system to send and receive messages. Make sure you consider the following for the remote users:

◆ Do they have the necessary hardware and software in place? If not, what will they require and how will they obtain it?

◆ How will you migrate the remote users, and how will you train them?

◆ How will you maintain their message routing during the migration?

◆ Will you develop a mobile migration team, or will local resources (including consultants) suffice to handle their migration needs?

Microsoft Exchange Server and clients are available in many different languages. Consult your software dealer or Microsoft for more details if you need foreign language support for your Exchange implementation. Note that timetables for product availability can vary depending on the language version desired.

Migrating Custom Applications

Many organizations have custom mail-based applications or mail-enabled applications that must be supported on Exchange Server in order to implement a complete and successful migration.

Exchange Server supports applications that use MAPI and Common Mail Calls (CMC). If your applications don't support either standard, you have to decide whether you will abandon the current applications, convert them to Exchange folders and forms, or add MAPI or CMC capabilities to them.

Be careful that you identify all applications that depend on e-mail for some of their functionality. For instance, your users may be using the mail-enabled feature of a scheduling program used for project management without your being aware of it. Make sure that you talk to other IS staff in your company to identify all the applications that may interface to your existing mail system, and consider polling your current users for feedback on how they use the system now to help identify potential problem applications.

Developing Naming Conventions

Some organizations have naming conventions that often are not followed or that have been used over time and perhaps evolved to be different from how they were first defined. You also may have inconsistent names in your e-mail system that you want to correct. Doing so during the implementation is a good idea, but you need to consider carefully the ramifications.

The following four sections explore different naming areas for Exchange, along with discussions of what they are for and some suggestions on conventions that you can adopt. Figure 5.1 shows the entry screen that contains these different names, and you can use it as a guide to follow along with the different naming areas.

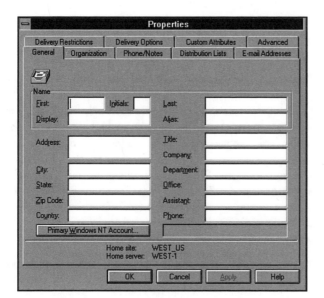

Figure 5.1

*User information
dialog box in
Exchange Server.*

Directory Name

The *directory name* (also known as the *common name*) is used to create the unique name
of a mailbox. You can see a user's directory name on the Advanced tab of the user
properties dialog box. It is visible only in the Administrator program, and by default it
is the same as the alias name. Directory names for a mailbox cannot be changed after
the mailbox is created.

For your directory names, consider staying with the mailbox alias—such as SSmith—
an arbitrary name such as an employee or badge number, or even the user's network
user ID.

Directory names cannot contain spaces.

  Directory names can have up to 64 characters, but remember that some foreign e-
mail systems may be limited to as few as 8 characters.

Display Name

The *display name* is seen in the public address book. You can change it at any time.
Microsoft Exchange Server allows the display name to be the individual's full name, if
you want.

It's important to come up with your standard for display names and to stick to it. You can list people by first and last names (Susan Smith) or by last and first names (Smith, Susan), and choose to include other items, such as middle initials, nicknames, or departments.

 In many Asian countries, people write their names differently from those in the U.S. or Europe, writing out first their family name and then their given name. (For example, "Susan" is a given name and "Smith" is a family name.) If you need to deal with this, consider using given and family name for countries that typically write names in this fashion (Susan Smith), and family name, plus a comma, then given name for your Asian users (Zhou, Qi Ming). The addition of the comma for users in those Asian countries maintains the order of written names usually used in those countries, but also makes it clear to users in other countries how to address them, both in writing and when talking to them on the telephone.

As you see in figure 5.1, Exchange Server is U.S.- and Euro-centric in its user property dialog boxes. Its First Name dialog box should actually be called Given Name and its Last Name dialog box should be called Family Name to allow for other countries' naming systems. The international X.400 standard naming system, however, properly uses given and family names in its fields.

Alias

An *alias* is used for SMTP and Exchange Server e-mail addresses. Aliases are seen by senders when addressing mail, and they can contain spaces if you want. Although it is not required, you should make this name unique for each mailbox to reduce possible confusion.

Aliases can be made from a person's first and last name, first initial plus last name, name plus employee ID, or even network user name.

 You may not want to use a person's network user name as that person's e-mail alias. Because the alias is known to other Exchange users, you will also be letting them know the individual's network, or login, name. From a security standpoint, this may not be desirable for your site, because then only the password, rather than both the person's network user name and password, will allow access the account.

Given Name and Last Name

When you create mailboxes in Exchange Server, you also specify a person's first name and last name. These names are used to create X.400 addresses for the mailbox. Consider how you will deal with double last names, name suffixes (Jr., III, and so on) and hyphenated last names.

Dealing with External Addresses

If your company has an external gateway to a foreign e-mail system, such as X.400, MCI Mail, or the Internet, remember that changing your naming conventions can have wide-ranging impacts. People need to communicate their new e-mail addresses to the "outside world," many people may need new business cards, and so forth. Carefully consider all the impacts of changing your naming conventions during implementation.

Exchange Server does enable you to create multiple e-mail account aliases pointing to the same name for routing incoming mail to the proper recipient. Using this feature, you can implement a new naming convention internally, while still providing the capability of receiving external mail addressed to original addresses. People on the outside can then be informed of the new addresses over time.

Determining the Migration Timetable

Once you determine how you will accomplish the migration, you can then set out a detailed plan with timetables. Make sure you have the following questions answered before laying out your timetable:

◆ How much will be migrated (mailbox or mailbox and contents)?

◆ Will you do a single-phase or multi-phase implementation?

◆ If multi-phase, or if you have other needs, will coexistence be required for a time?

◆ Do you have mail-enabled applications that must be migrated? How will you handle those?

Single-Phase Migration

The simplest migration involves a single-phase migration. Use the checklist in table 5.2 to work through all the steps required for the migration.

TABLE 5.2
Single-Phase Migration Checklist

Area	Task	Complete?
Configuration	Server	
	Connectors	
	Gateways	
	Monitors	
Mailbox Creation	Create Mailboxes	
	Create Windows NT Accounts	
	Create distribution lists	
Testing	End-to-end messages	
	Outbound and inbound messages across gateways	
	Check public folder permissions	
	Perform backup and test restoration	
	Update login scripts	
	Perform test migration	
Training	Train help desk on Exchange Client	
	Train end users on Exchange Client	
	Train administrators	
Roll-out	Revoke access to current system	
	Wait for all outbound messages to send	

Area	Task	Complete?
	Close existing gateways	
	Wait for inbound messages to post to mailboxes	
	Start Exchange Server gateways and connectors	
	Migrate mailboxes and contents	
	Install Exchange Client software	
	Perform full backup of Exchange Server	

Multi-Phase Migration

Multi-phase migrations involve more steps and are more complex than single-phase migration. Table 5.3 contains the steps required, but the exact order will vary from site to site. Use the tasks listed to form your own migration checklist appropriate for your migration.

TABLE 5.3
Multi-Phase Migration Checklist

Area	Task	Complete?
Configuration	Server	
	Monitors	
	Gateway to existing system	
	Public folders	
	Custom recipients	
	Migrate foreign system addresses	
	Migrate distribution lists	

continues

TABLE 5.3, CONTINUED
Multi-Phase Migration Checklist

Area	Task	Complete?
Testing	End-to-end messages	
	Check public folder permissions	
	Back up and perform test restoration	
	Test gateway messages	
	Test directory synchronization between existing system and Exchange Server	
Training	Train help desk on Exchange Client	
	Train end users on Exchange Client	
	Train administrators	
For each phase	Notify group of users about changeover	
	Create mailboxes and Windows NT accounts	
	Update login scripts	
	Migrate mailbox contents	
	Install client software	
	Disable existing system mailboxes	
	Modify address lists accordingly	

Testing Your Migration

After developing your migration plan, perform a pilot migration in which you can test all the migration steps and test the installation with actual data from your site. Perhaps more than any other step you can take, performing a pilot migration gives you a strong understanding of how Exchange Server works, how the migration will be accomplished, how long it will take for your site, and what to expect.

Consider having the migration team start using Exchange Server for its own e-mail needs within the group. This helps familiarize the team with the product, and it also helps you illuminate potential trouble spots before naïve users are exposed to the product.

If your migration team is too small to offer a good test for Exchange Server, look for other groups within the company that are capable of being testers of the system. Groups within the IS department, or groups elsewhere in the company that can handle the challenge of being testers, are good choices.

 While you're running your pilot test, you can take a close look at the performance of Exchange Server in your site. In particular, test how quickly directories synchronize both within and between sites.

As part of your pilot migration, pay careful attention to how quickly the migration tools perform their job on your hardware and with your data. This will help you choose which migration (mailbox-only versus mailbox contents) is best for you and how much time you have to plan for the migration process.

Training the Migration Team

During the pilot period, you have an excellent opportunity for various members of the migration team to work with the software and to play with it in a "safe" environment. Administrators can maintain accounts and distribution lists, folders, and so forth. They should spend a lot of time with the Administrator program, learning all its features. In fact, it's a good idea to let the administrators try to make mistakes within Exchange Server. By being free to try out features in a safe environment, they will more rapidly learn the software and its capabilities and limitations.

Administrators should use the following resources to get up to speed on Exchange Server administration:

◆ *Inside Microsoft Exchange Server* (this book)

◆ The Getting Started public folder in Exchange Server

◆ The Administrator program's online help

◆ Any of a variety of books or training materials to understand Windows NT Server fully

◆ CompuServe, AOL, or USENet discussion groups that cover Exchange

During the pilot test, you have an opportunity to work out the finer details of your migration. Specifically, you can more thoroughly address how you will deal with issues such as coexistence, mail delivery, handling resource accounts, and so forth. Ensure that you fine-tune your migration checklist with the knowledge that you gain during the pilot migration.

Maintenance of Directories

Throughout a multi-phase migration process, your address lists will change as you move users from the existing system to Exchange Server. You need to deal with the synchronization of directories of users in both the existing system and Exchange Server so that mail is always delivered. Careful planning ensures that this happens smoothly.

You first need to determine what directory synchronization will be required during the migration. By looking at your detailed plan, your needs should be clear to you. Then, take a careful look at how you'll accomplish the synchronization.

There are tools that enable you to handle synchronization during the migration process more easily. Specifically, you can use the data extractors, migration wizards, and any available import and export commands from your existing system and the matching commands within Exchange Server. Practice doing these tasks during the pilot test.

 Don't forget to pay attention to addresses of users on foreign systems when you examine directory synchronization issues.

A Word to the Wise

In most companies, migrating from an existing e-mail system to *any* other system is a major project, rife with the potential for problems. An e-mail migration is much more complicated than any other type of end-user application migration, although many issues may not be apparent at first glance.

In this chapter, you learned about a number of issues that you will wrestle with prior to your migration to Exchange Server. It is likely that there will be other issues for your company beyond those discussed here, and the larger and more complex your company, the more chances there will be for trouble spots.

This can't be emphasized enough, and is the most important thing to remember from this chapter: to ensure a smooth migration, plan and test the migration until you are *completely* assured that you have identified all the issues for your company and systems and can deal with all of them. If this means you perform three or four test migrations, or spend two months planning the migration, then do it. Don't try to implement your real migration until you, the other members of the team, and your users are ready.

PART III

Installation

CHAPTER 6

Installing Exchange Server

Installing the Microsoft Exchange Server software is a relatively easy process, although there are a number of steps to go through that aren't immediately obvious. In this chapter, you learn how to install the following:

- ◆ The base Microsoft Exchange Server software

- ◆ The client software to a shared installation source

- ◆ The client software from a shared installation source onto a client computer

- ◆ The Microsoft Exchange Form Designer software

Installing Microsoft Exchange Server Software

Before installing Exchange Server onto a server computer, ensure that you properly installed Windows NT Server (not Workstation) version 3.51 or later onto the computer, and that all necessary Windows NT services have been properly installed. These services include Windows NT administrative tools, as well as all network services (protocols, and so on) needed for your Exchange Server. The networking and NT services may include the following:

◆ IPX/SPX protocol

◆ TCP/IP protocol

◆ NetBEUI protocol

◆ NetBIOS protocol

◆ RAS support

◆ Windows NT Backup (needed for Exchange Server backup)

> **Note** You must be using Windows NT Server version 3.51, build 1057 with Service pack 3 applied, or later.

Test your Windows NT server computer to ensure proper operation of all necessary services before attempting to install the Exchange Server software.

Make sure that the server hardware is properly configured for use with Microsoft Exchange Server. Consult Chapter 4, "Deciding on Hardware," for more information on configuration choices.

Installing Microsoft Exchange Server begins with accessing the CD-ROM containing the Exchange Server software using Windows NT File Manager. In the CD-ROM's directory structure, you will see the directories shown in figure 6.1. Open the SETUP directory, then open the subdirectory corresponding to the type of Windows NT server on which you are installing Exchange Server. Your choices are Alpha for DEC Alpha-based machines, MIPS for any of the MIPS-based machines, or i386 for any Intel-based machines. Within the appropriate machine directory, you will see the SETUP.EXE program. Double-click on it to begin the installation.

After starting the Setup program, you see it initially search for any previously installed components and then see the Copyright screen for the Exchange Server software. Click on OK to proceed. You then see the main installation screen shown in figure 6.2.

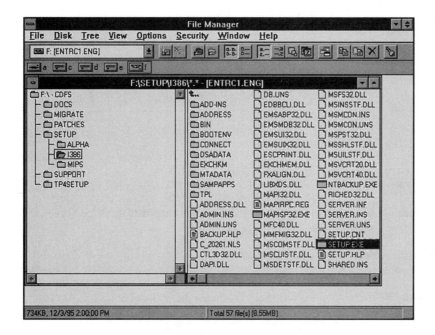

Figure 6.1

Use File Manager to locate and run the appropriate SETUP program.

Figure 6.2

The main installation screen.

A minimal installation installs the core Exchange Server software and the Optimizer. Choosing this installation type means that you will perform all administration of this Exchange Server system across the network by using another Windows NT computer running the Exchange Administrator program remotely.

The Exchange Server Administrator program does not have to run directly on an Exchange Server computer. You can run the Administrator program from any Windows NT workstation or server that has network connectivity with an Exchange Server computer. Because of this, you can easily administer multiple Exchange Servers from one Windows NT workstation or from a single Exchange Server computer.

A typical installation installs the following:

◆ **Core Exchange Server software.** The basic software needed for any Exchange Server

◆ **Optimizer.** A program that optimizes the file locations for Exchange Server based on performance testing that it performs on your disk(s)

◆ **Exchange Server Administrator program.** The program used to administer all aspects of an Exchange Server

◆ **Migration Wizard.** A program that automates the process of migrating data from different existing sources

◆ **Setup Editor.** Software that enables you to customize and automate the installation of Exchange Client software onto client computers

Finally, a Complete/Custom installation enables you to choose exactly which components to install, including three connectors that aren't installed during a minimal or typical installation: MS-Mail Connector, SMTP/Internet Connector, and the X.400 Connector.

Before choosing an installation type, use the Change **D**irectory button to select a new location for the main Exchange Server software, if needed.

The rest of this section assumes that you use the Complete/Custom installation. Clicking on that button on the main installation screen reveals the dialog box shown in figure 6.3, in which you choose which components to install.

In the dialog box shown in figure 6.3, you can choose which components to install by selecting and deselecting the appropriate check boxes next to the listed options. The first option, Microsoft Exchange Server, also has suboptions available. To see those, select the line that says Microsoft Exchange Server and then click on the Chan**g**e Option button. This displays the dialog box in which you can choose which connectors to install, as shown in figure 6.4. After you choose the needed connectors, click on the OK button to return to the previous dialog box.

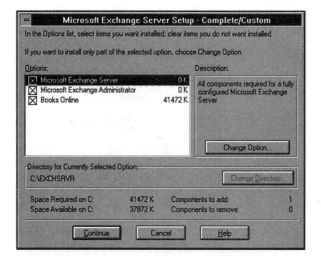

Figure 6.3

*The Complete/
Custom
installation
selection dialog
box.*

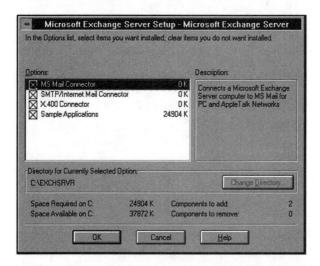

Figure 6.4

*Choosing which
connectors to
install.*

Another feature of the dialog box shown in figure 6.3 is that it enables you to specify where on the Exchange Server computer to install the Exchange Administrator components. (The core Exchange Server software's location was determined with the Change **D**irectory button on the dialog box shown in figure 6.2.) To change the location for the Administrator components, select that line and then click on the Change **D**irectory button. You see the dialog box shown in figure 6.5, in which you can select a new location for the Administrator components.

Figure 6.5

*The Change
Directory
dialog box.*

After setting the installation options, click on the **C**ontinue button to proceed with the installation.

You now see the dialog box shown in figure 6.6. In this dialog box, indicate whether this Exchange Server will be part of an existing Exchange Server site (as an additional server) or if it will be the main server for a new site.

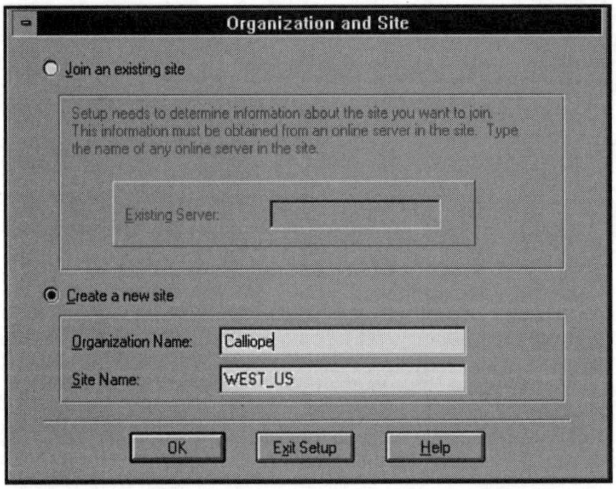

Figure 6.6

*The Organization
and Site dialog
box.*

To make this installation become an additional server for an existing Exchange Server site, click on the **J**oin an existing site button and then fill in the **E**xisting Server field with the name of the main Exchange Server computer. Otherwise, to create a new site, make sure that the **C**reate a new site option button is selected and then type in the **O**rganization Name for your new site. The **S**ite Name should match the Windows NT server name of this computer (this field is automatically filled in for you, so you shouldn't have to change it).

After clicking on the OK button, you see a message asking you to confirm the creation of a new site, as seen in figure 6.7.

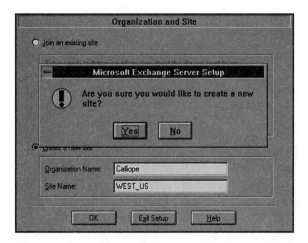

Figure 6.7

The site creation confirmation dialog box.

You now come to the dialog box shown in figure 6.8. Here, you indicate the name of the administrator account on the Windows NT Server onto which you are installing Exchange Server and that account's password. Complete the necessary fields and click on OK to continue.

Figure 6.8

The Site Services Account dialog box.

The Microsoft Exchange Server software is now installed onto your system. At the end of the installation, you are asked if you want to run the Optimizer application to locate the Exchange Server files on the system (see fig. 6.9). Click on the **R**un Optimizer button to do so.

The Optimizer is a program that does performance testing on your server's hard disks and then recommends to you the optimum locations for key Exchange Server files in order to extract the best possible performance from your system. If you choose to accept Optimizer's recommendations, it takes care of relocating the affected files for you. Figure 6.10 shows you the first dialog box you see when you run the Optimizer.

Figure 6.9

Click on Run Optimizer to relocate files after installation.

> **Warning** Clicking on the **N**ext button causes Optimizer to halt all Microsoft Exchange Server services for the duration of the testing.

Figure 6.10

The opening dialog box for the Optimizer.

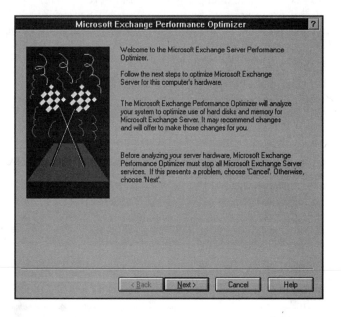

Next you see a dialog box, shown in figure 6.11, that requests information about your intended usage of this Exchange Server. For each field, select the choices that match up with your planned server's configuration.

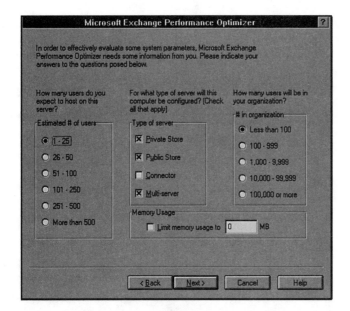

Figure 6.11

Before Optimizer runs, you must enter configuration estimates.

For the Estimated # of users field, enter the number of concurrent users that you expect rather than the total number of user mailboxes. Then, select the check boxes for the Type of server that matches your server configuration:

◆ Select **P**rivate Store if user mailboxes will be stored on this server.

◆ Select Pu**b**lic Store if public folders (or replicas) will be stored on this server.

◆ Select **C**onnector if this server will be acting as a backbone or will be forwarding messages from one system to another.

◆ Select **M**ulti-server if your organization will have more than one Exchange Server; disable this choice only if you expect users to connect to only this Exchange Server.

For the # in organization selection, indicate the total number of mailboxes that your users will have defined in their public address book. Generally, this is the total number of mailboxes within your organization, plus perhaps an additional 10 percent for custom recipients on outside systems.

By default, Exchange Server uses all available RAM installed in your server. However, if you need to limit its RAM usage (perhaps because other services also will be running on your server), you can define this limitation in the **L**imit memory usage field. This value cannot be lower than 16 MB (setting it to 0 enables Exchange Server to use all available RAM).

Clicking on the <u>N</u>ext button begins the performance testing. Testing should not take a very long time, but varies depending on your server configuration. Expect it to complete well within 10 minutes (you will see disk activity while testing continues). At the end of the test, a simple dialog box informs you that testing is complete and that you can click on the <u>N</u>ext button to continue (see fig. 6.12).

Figure 6.12

The test completion dialog box.

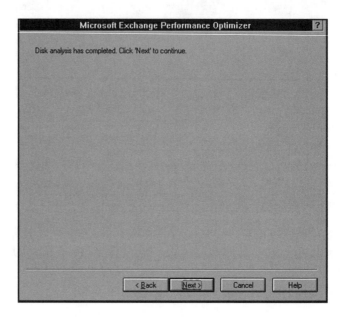

After continuing, you see the dialog box displayed in figure 6.13. In it, Optimizer shows you where it recommends you locate all the different components of Exchange Server. In the example shown, with a small number of expected users, Optimizer has recommended that all files continue to be located on drive C. In your system, multiple drives may be recommended. Keep in mind that there are additional considerations such as disk read/write head contention issues and the type of file system you have formatted the disk to use (FAT or NTFS). You can easily define different paths for the different components in the dialog box shown, and Optimizer takes care of moving the relevant files to their new locations.

After finishing with the Optimizer, you see the final dialog box of the Optimizer Wizard that indicates that Optimizer will automatically restart Exchange Server services that were originally stopped. Clicking on the Finish button restarts the services and completes your installation of Microsoft Exchange Server.

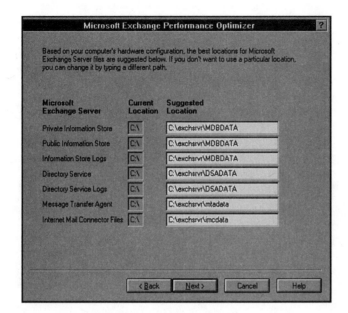

Figure 6.13

The Optimizer recommendation dialog box.

Installing Client Software

Exchange Client software is best installed from a shared network directory so that you can use the Exchange Setup Editor to make default selections for the installations in your organization. From the client computer, you execute the appropriate SETUP program on the network, and Exchange Client is then installed on the local machine.

 "Exchange Client software" includes not only the different flavors of Exchange Client for various operating systems, but also the Exchange Forms Designer, which is also run from client workstations.

Installing Client Software to a Shared Directory

Installing the Exchange Client software to a shared directory is a simple task. Follow these steps:

1. Insert the Exchange Client CD-ROM into your system.

2. Using File Manager, locate the directory on the CD-ROM that contains the correct language version of the client software. Figure 6.14 shows the English language folder open.

3. Copy the entire directory structure to the shared directory on the desired server. You can copy all subdirectories at once, or copy only those for client versions that you will need in your organization. For example, the entire \ENG directory can be copied from the CD-ROM to a directory called \ENG on the file server (or any other directory name that you prefer).

4. Make sure that you grant Read-Only access to the shared directory to all users who will need to install the software (generally, this is everyone).

Figure 6.14

The Exchange Client directory with the English directory open.

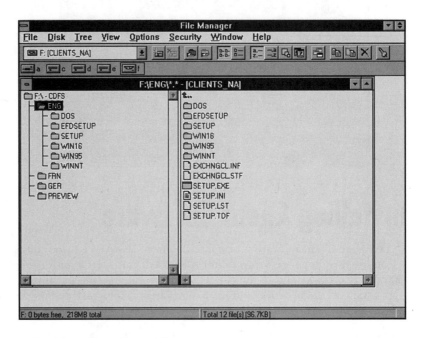

Table 6.1 shows you the contents of the subdirectories within the English directory.

TABLE 6.1
Exchange Client Subdirectories

Directory Name	Contents
\ENG\DOS	MS-DOS Exchange Client
\ENG\EFDSETUP	Exchange Forms Designer
\ENG\SETUP	Shared setup information

Directory Name	Contents
\ENG\WIN16	Windows 3.*x* Exchange Client
\ENG\WIN95	Windows 95 Exchange Client
\ENG\WINNT	Windows NT Exchange Client

Setting Installation Defaults

A tool installed on your Exchange Server enables you to choose default settings for the client installations. This tool is called the Microsoft Exchange Setup Editor, and its icon can be found in the Microsoft Exchange group on the server.

 Note Microsoft Exchange Setup Editor is not installed on the server when you use the minimal installation of the server software.

Double-clicking on the Setup Editor icon starts the program, as shown in figure 6.15.

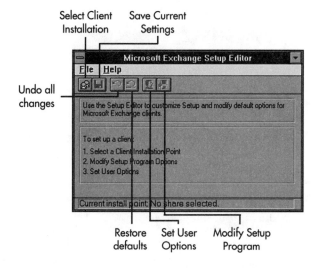

Figure 6.15

The Microsoft Exchange Setup Editor.

You begin to use the Setup Editor by accessing the **F**ile menu and choosing Select **C**lient Installation Point. This brings up the dialog box shown in figure 6.16, in which you select a directory that contains one of the versions of Exchange Client.

Figure 6.16

The Select Client Installation Directory dialog box.

The Setup Editor reads in a file called EXCHNG.STF, located in a directory containing one of the versions of Exchange Client. This file holds all the default choices that are applied when you install Exchange Client onto a workstation. The Setup Editor enables you to change those settings for your organization's particular needs.

Begin customizing the installation defaults by pulling down the **F**ile menu and selecting Set **U**ser Options. This displays the notebook dialog box shown in figure 6.17.

Figure 6.17

Selecting Set User Options.

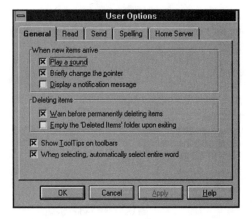

The options in the User Options dialog box are the same seen by users when they use the Options command when running Exchange Client. Changes that you make to this dialog box are then used as the default choices for every installation using that version of Exchange Client. Although the options you can choose in this dialog box are self-explanatory, consider filling in the **H**ome Server field on the Home Server tab if you know that all users will be connecting to a particular Exchange Server. (Leaving this field blank means that the user is prompted to choose a server when installing the client software.) After changing the user options, click on the OK button to return to the Setup Editor.

Next, pull down the <u>F</u>ile menu again and choose Modify Setup Program <u>O</u>ptions. You see the dialog box shown in figure 6.18.

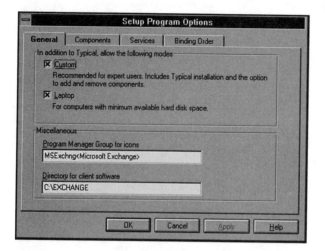

Figure 6.18

The Setup Program Options dialog box.

In the Setup Program Options dialog box, choose how the Exchange Client setup program will behave when it is used.

The General tab enables you to choose whether the user is able to perform C<u>u</u>stom or <u>L</u>aptop installations. If both check boxes are deselected, the user can perform only a Typical installation. In the Miscellaneous section, you define the name of the Program Manager group into which the Exchange Client icon is placed by default, as well as the default directory on the user's computer.

The Components tab enables you to choose what Exchange Client components can be installed by the user (see fig. 6.19). Use the check boxes next to each component to select or deselect them. There are also subcomponents that you can select. To see them, highlight either Exchange or Schedule+ in the dialog box and click on the Chan<u>g</u>e Option button.

The Services tab (see fig. 6.20) enables you to select which messaging services are installed on the client computer. The left window displays the available services, and the right window displays the selected services. Use the A<u>d</u>d and <u>R</u>emove buttons to add or remove services displayed in the right window.

Use the Binding Order tab, shown in figure 6.21, to choose the protocols to be installed onto the client computers, as well as the order in which they are bound. You can change the order with the Move <u>U</u>p and Move Do<u>w</u>n buttons. You also can add protocols by clicking on the <u>A</u>dd button and then indicating the name of a server machine on the network that contains the desired protocol stack in the resulting dialog box.

Figure 6.19

The Components tab.

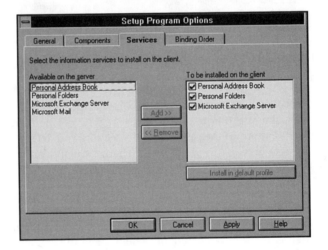

After you finish defining all the Setup Program Options, click on the OK button to return to the Setup Editor main screen. You can then save all your choices with the **S**ave command in the **F**ile menu, or you can reverse your changes with the **U**ndo All Changes command in the **F**ile menu, or you can restore the original defaults with the **R**estore Defaults command, also in the **F**ile menu. When finished, exit the program or choose a new installation directory to make changes for other client versions.

Installing a Windows Exchange Client

After you customize the installation files in the shared directory, users can install the Exchange Client themselves, or your implementation team members can perform the installation on each machine. Installation begins by opening the shared folder that contains the operating system version of the Exchange Client that you wish to install and double-clicking on the appropriate SETUP.EXE program (see fig. 6.22).

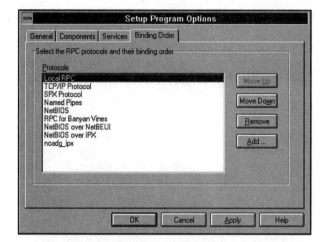

Figure 6.21

The Binding Order tab.

Figure 6.22

Starting Exchange Client installation.

Setup begins with a copyright screen display. Click on Continue after you've read it.

After continuing past the copyright notification, you're asked to enter your name and organization (see fig. 6.23).

If you are installing the Exchange Client onto one of the computers on your network, consider putting your company name in the **N**ame field. Because the **N**ame field must be filled in to continue, doing it this way avoids the annoyance of having incorrect user names appear as computers are moved within your organization, or as people change jobs (and usually computers). You might also use the computer's serial number or property tag number in the **N**ame field.

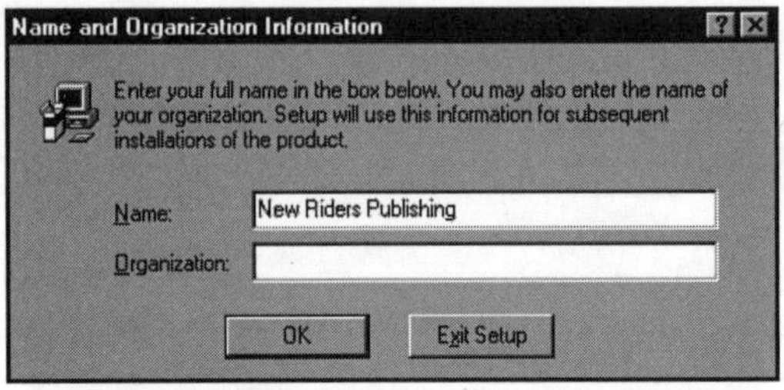

Figure 6.23

The Name and Organization Information dialog box.

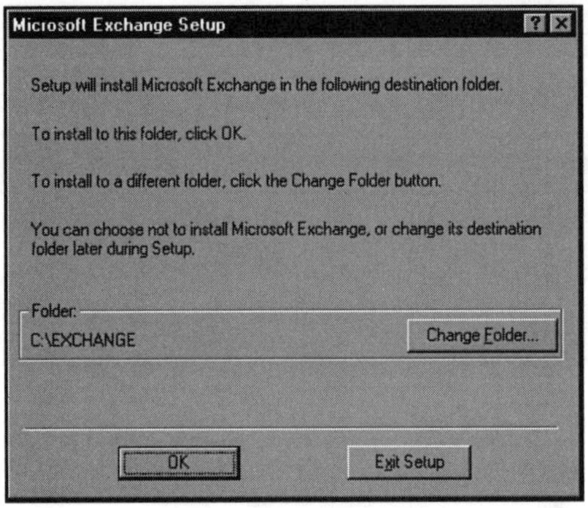

> **Name and Organization Information**
>
> Enter your full name in the box below. You may also enter the name of your organization. Setup will use this information for subsequent installations of the product.
>
> N̲ame: `New Riders Publishing`
>
> O̲rganization: `_____`
>
> [OK]   [E̲xit Setup]

Figure 6.24

Choosing the installation directory.

> **Microsoft Exchange Setup**
>
> Setup will install Microsoft Exchange in the following destination folder.
>
> To install to this folder, click OK.
>
> To install to a different folder, click the Change Folder button.
>
> You can choose not to install Microsoft Exchange, or change its destination folder later during Setup.
>
> Folder:
> C:\EXCHANGE   [Change F̲older...]
>
> [OK]   [E̲xit Setup]

Click on Continue to move forward. You are then asked in a new dialog box to confirm your name and organization entries. Click on OK to continue. Next, you see the dialog box shown in figure 6.24 in which you select the directory where the Exchange Client files will be installed. The directory shown is the default directory you selected when you customized the installation scripts, as described in the Setting the Installation Defaults section. If necessary, change the installation directory with the Change **F**older button. Otherwise, click on OK to continue with the default directory.

You next see the screen shown in figure 6.25, in which you can choose a **T**ypical, C**u**stom, or **L**aptop installation. Table 6.2 shows the components installed for each installation.

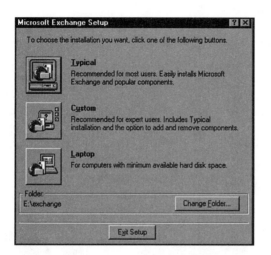

Figure 6.25

The installation type selection dialog box.

TABLE 6.2
Installation Type Components

Component	Installation Types	Size (KB)
Microsoft Exchange Program	All	10649
Personal Address Book	All	2
Personal Folders	All	2
Spelling	Typical/Custom	1217
MS Exchange Help	Typical/Custom	1121
Microsoft Exchange Server	All	677
Microsoft Mail	Custom	433
Microsoft Schedule+ Program Files	All	4306
Print Layouts and Paper Formats	All	705
Help	Typical/Custom	641
Additional Exporters and Importers	Typical/Custom	3361
Seven Habits Tools	Typical/Custom	1473

A Typical installation installs all components and consumes 21.6 MB of hard disk space. A Laptop installation installs a minimum set of components and consumes a bit less than 14 MB of disk space. For most desktop systems, perform a Typical installation to install all components.

After selecting an installation type, all the appropriate files are copied to the local computer's hard disk. At the end of the installation, a message box appears informing you that the installation is complete. After clicking on the OK button, you are returned to the Windows desktop.

Next, you must configure the profile for the Exchange Client. This is easily done by double-clicking on the Inbox icon on the desktop. You see the dialog box shown in figure 6.26.

Figure 6.26

The Inbox Setup Wizard dialog box.

In the Inbox Setup Wizard dialog box, select or deselect the services that will be used on this client computer. Depending on the services you select, you see dialog boxes that ask for necessary information about each service. For Exchange Server connectivity, you must specify the name of the Exchange Server in the appropriate dialog box. Other services require other information. For example, Microsoft Fax requires the user's name and fax number.

Installing Exchange Forms Designer

Installing Exchange Forms Designer proceeds along the same lines as installing the Windows version of Exchange Client, with the following changes:

◆ Run the SETUP.EXE program from \ENG\EFD setup (substitute the correct directory for \ENG if you're using a different language version) or directory name.

◆ There are only two components to choose from for Exchange Forms Designer. You can choose to install the Forms Design software itself (5.7 MB), and you can choose to install the sample applications (2.5 MB). Neither component has suboptions that you need to select or deselect.

Figure 6.27

The DOS Exchange Client installation program.

Installing DOS Exchange Client

Installing the DOS-based Exchange Client is a bit different from installing the Windows-based Exchange Clients. However, consider that the DOS client, although being needed on some older machines that aren't Windows-capable, is also a good choice for laptop computers, on which disk space is very tight but where mail functionality is needed.

 You cannot use the Microsoft Exchange Setup Editor to make installation option preselections for DOS client installations.

Begin the DOS client installation by connecting to the shared Exchange Client directory on the network and executing the SETUP.EXE program found in the DOS subdirectory. You see the installation screen shown in figure 6.27.

Next, you choose what type of DOS Exchange Client installation you want to perform (see fig. 6.28). You can choose between three types of installations:

◆ Local installation copies all DOS Exchange Client files onto the computer's local hard disk.

◆ Workstation installation runs the DOS Exchange Client program from a shared network copy and keeps settings files on the computer's local hard disk (or network directory).

◆ Shared installation enables you to set up an installation of the DOS Exchange Client from which other DOS computers on the network can then perform Workstation installations.

Choosing a Workstation installation displays the screen shown in figure 6.29, in which you define the directory for the Exchange program files. After specifying the correct directory, press Enter to continue.

Figure 6.28

Choosing the installation type for DOS client.

Figure 6.29

Choosing the installation directory.

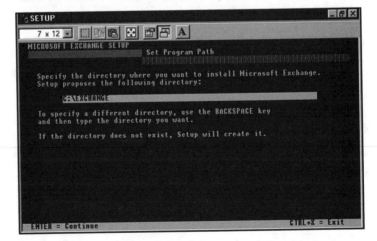

Your next task involves choosing the time zone from which you'll be using the DOS Exchange Client. As shown in figure 6.30, select your time zone and press Enter to continue.

Next, you tell the installation program what language you'll be using (see fig. 6.31). This selection defines how sorting takes place, and also is communicated to Exchange Server so that the appropriate language is used when sending instructions or notifications to the user.

Figure 6.30

Choosing your time zone.

Figure 6.31

Choosing a desired language.

Now, you see the screen shown in figure 6.32. In it, you choose the DOS Exchange Client options you want to install. As you can see, installing all the DOS Exchange Client files takes 2.4 MB on the computer's hard disk (considerably less than the Windows Exchange Client files, although there are fewer features). Press Enter to continue after you choose the options you require.

Figure 6.32

Choosing installed features.

Your final step involves choosing, in the screen shown in figure 6.33, whether you want the installation program to make some minor changes to the computer's AUTOEXEC.BAT file. In almost all cases, you can safely let the installation program make these changes. However, if for some reason you want to move these settings into a batch file that starts the DOS Exchange Client, you can. There are two lines that you should add to the batch file:

```
SET EXCHANGE = C:\EXCHANGE\
SET RPC_BINDING_ORDER = ncalrpc,ncacn_np,ncacn_spx,ncacn_ip_tcp
```

If the computer's environment already contains many settings and cannot store both these SET commands, you may have to increase its size with this command in the computer's CONFIG.SYS file:

```
SHELL=C:\COMMAND.COM /E:1024 /P
```

You can substitute different sizes for the /E parameter if needed. Using /E:1024 dedicates 1 KB of RAM to holding environment variables, which is typically enough even for very large environment needs.

After the installation is complete, you can run the DOS Exchange Client with the command EXCHANGE.EXE from the directory into which you installed the program.

As you have seen in this chapter, installing Exchange Server is a relatively straightforward task (the hard part is in configuring it once you've installed it).

You now know how to install various versions of Exchange Client and how to use network copies of the installation programs to make the job of installing the client software faster and easier. Using these tools can pay big dividends when you need to install hundreds or thousands of clients.

Figure 6.33

The Modify System File installation screen.

CHAPTER 7

Configuring Sites

Many organizations have more than one site in which they do business and use e-mail. In these cases, you need a way to communicate between your Microsoft Exchange Server sites. Exchange Server provides built-in functionality to connect your different sites by using a number of different communication methods, each with a variety of options that enable you to control the connection properties. In this chapter, you learn how to configure and connect between your different Exchange Server sites.

Choosing a Connection Medium

There are three methods that you can use to link Exchange Server sites:

◆ Site Connector using an underlying WAN link

◆ Dynamic Remote Access Service (RAS) for asynchronous modem connections

◆ X.400 Connector that uses an underlying X.400 backbone

There are advantages and disadvantages to each method.

Site Connector

Using the built-in Site Connector is the most efficient way to connect different Microsoft Exchange Server sites. In order to use the Site Connector, you must have an underlying WAN link between the sites that uses a protocol that supports Remote Procedure Calls (RPCs). IPX/SPX (NWLink) and NetBEUI both support RPCs.

The Site Connector is the easiest connector to set up and maintain. When configuring the Site Connector, the remote site's Site Connector can be automatically installed without having to have an administrator at the remote site duplicate the installation.

When using the Site Connector, the two sites are always connected, and you do not have the ability to schedule communications between sites or control message size. If you have many sites on your WAN, there may be times in which many servers attempt to connect to a particular site at once, swamping that site's network connection. Finally, you are limited by the bandwidth of the underlying WAN link, which usually varies from 56 Kbps (leased line) to 1.544 Mbps (T-1) or even 44.184 Mbps (T-3).

Dynamic Remote Access Service

If you have more limited communication needs between sites, or there is no underlying WAN in place, you can connect sites using Remote Access Service (RAS) over an asynchronous link running through modems. This is a simple way to connect sites, and it can be very cost-effective to implement; however, be aware that if you are using dial-up lines excessively, a more traditional WAN link may be more cost-effective overall.

Dynamic RAS connections enable you to schedule connection times and control message size. You can connect by using asynchronous connections, and you can also use Integrated Services Digital Network (ISDN) connections.

Dynamic RAS may not make sense for some sites due to limitations in modem speed. At the time of this writing, asynchronous connections are limited to 28.8 Kbps, and ISDN connections (using both B channels) to approximately 128 Kbps (both uncompressed).

X.400 Connector

If your organization has an existing X.400 messaging backbone, you can configure Exchange Server to use that backbone to send messages between sites.

Using an existing X.400 backbone can have several advantages. First, you can exert control over message-passing parameters, such as scheduling and message size. You can take advantage of several X.400-compliant protocols, such as TCP/IP, TP4, and X.25. If you are connecting to foreign X.400 systems, you can utilize the same backbone for those connections on top of your Exchange Server connections, which may be the most efficient for your organization.

Disadvantages include limitations to the protocols listed; if your bridges or routers don't support TCP/IP, TP4, or X.25, you either have to upgrade them, install new bridges or routers, or choose another connection scheme.

Installing the Site Connector

If you have chosen to use an underlying WAN link to link your sites using the Exchange Server Site Connector, you'll find that setting up and using the Site Connector is an easy process. And because the Site Connector can use RPCs to communicate with the remote Exchange Server, you can configure both sides of the connection at the same time, from your local site.

 Using the Site Connector does not preclude you from installing other connectors using other communication methodologies. Exchange Server supports multiple simultaneous connectors.

Laying the Groundwork

In order to show you how to set up and configure a Site Connector, let's use the example company, Calliope, Inc. Table 7.1 shows you the vital statistics for the example connector.

TABLE 7.1
Calliope, Inc. Organization Information

Parameter	Setting
Organization Name	CALLIOPE
Domain Name	WEST_US
Local Exchange Server Site Name	WEST_US
Remote Exchange Server Site Name	NORTHWEST_US
Local Server Name	WEST-1
Remote Site Server Name	WEST-2
Underlying Connection Protocols	IPX/SPX (NWLink) and NetBEUI

In this example, each Exchange Server site has several recipients and desires full messaging between the two sites.

Installing and Configuring the Connector

To install the Site Connector, first select the Connections container in the Configuration tree using the Administrator program, as shown in figure 7.1.

Next, choose the **F**ile menu, then **N**ew Other, and finally Site **C**onnector. You see the dialog box shown in figure 7.2.

For this example, you enter WEST-2 in the dialog box before clicking on the OK button. Exchange Server then tries to connect to the remote server using your WAN connection. You then see the General page of the Site Connector Properties notebook shown in figure 7.3.

The following fields of the General page are available to you:

◆ **D**isplay name contains the name that appears in the Exchange Server Administrator program window. You are allowed up to 255 characters, and they are not case-sensitive.

◆ Directory **n**ame holds a descriptive name for the connector, up to 64 characters, that is used for diagnostic log messages. This name is permanent and cannot be changed once the connector is installed.

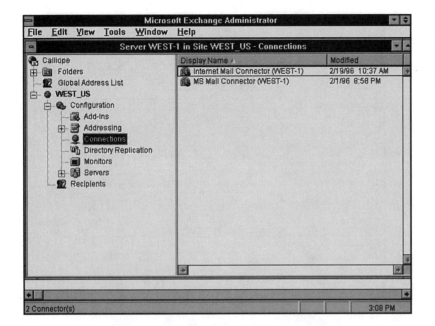

Figure 7.1

Choosing the Connections container.

Figure 7.2

Selecting the remote site.

◆ Target site contains the name of the target Exchange Server site. You cannot change this field.

◆ Cost is used by Exchange Server to determine the best way to route messages. If there are multiple connectors available that all connect to the remote site, the one with the lowest cost is always chosen. If the lowest cost connection is not functioning, the next highest cost connection is then used. Using the Cost field and multiple connectors gives you fine control over how Exchange Server routes messages to the remote site, while enabling you to implement a fault-tolerant messaging system.

◆ You use the Messaging Bridgehead in the local site box to choose which server handles messaging between the sites. In a busy messaging environment, this enables you to control the load balancing among your Exchange Servers.

Figure 7.3

The General tab of the Site Connector Properties notebook.

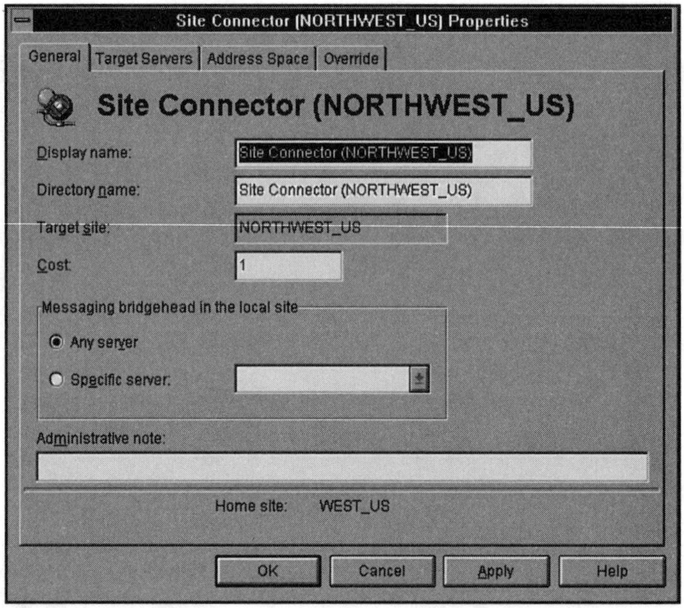

Site Connector [NORTHWEST_US] Properties

General | Target Servers | Address Space | Override

Site Connector (NORTHWEST_US)

Display name: Site Connector (NORTHWEST_US)

Directory name: Site Connector (NORTHWEST_US)

Target site: NORTHWEST_US

Cost: 1

Messaging bridgehead in the local site

⦿ Any server

○ Specific server:

Administrative note:

Home site: WEST_US

OK   Cancel   Apply   Help

◆ Use the Administrative note field to type any notes relating to this Site Connector. For instance, you could enter the time and date the connector was installed and the name of the installer.

The Target Servers property page, shown in figure 7.4, enables you to control which servers in the remote site are used to process messages from your local site.

By default, all servers in the target site are listed in the Target Servers window. You can add or remove servers from the list, and you can also vary the Target server cost for each server (select the server, change the cost, and then click on Set Value). Server costs are used for load balancing among the target servers. If all listed servers have the same cost, the messaging load is roughly balanced between them. Servers with a cost of 1 are used first; servers with a cost of 100 are used only when all other servers are unavailable.

The Address Space notebook property page (see fig. 7.5) enables you to control how messages are routed to different sites.

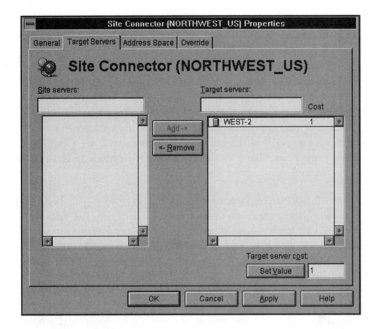

Figure 7.4

The Target Servers notebook property page.

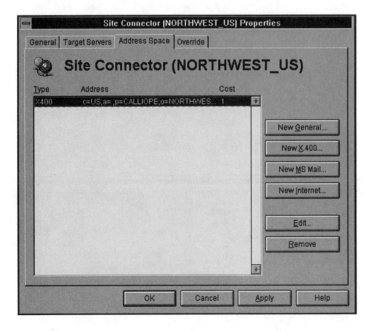

Figure 7.5

The Address Space notebook property page.

Using the Address Space page, you can direct that certain messages from your local site are routed to the remote site, even if that remote site is not the final destination. This is the purpose of the address space settings. For instance, consider the scenario in which the NORTHWEST_US site has a gateway connection to the Internet, but WEST_US does not. You could provide Internet (SMTP) mail services to the people in the WEST_US site by routing messages containing an SMTP address to NORTHWEST_US, which then forwards the messages to the Internet. This is controlled with the Address Space property page. You add a new Internet address space in which you enter an asterisk for the Internet address used. See Chapter 8, "Configuring MS Mail Connectors," for more information on establishing Internet connections.

The final Site Connector Properties notebook page, Override (see fig. 7.6) is used if your current server does not have an existing trust relationship with the remote server. In these cases, you can provide the Windows NT **u**sername, **P**assword, and Windows NT **d**omain name in order to allow the Exchange Server Administrator program to carry out the necessary setup tasks on the remote server when establishing the Site Connector.

 You need to use the account on the remote server that is the Microsoft Exchange Server service account. Often, this is the main administrator account on the Microsoft Exchange server.

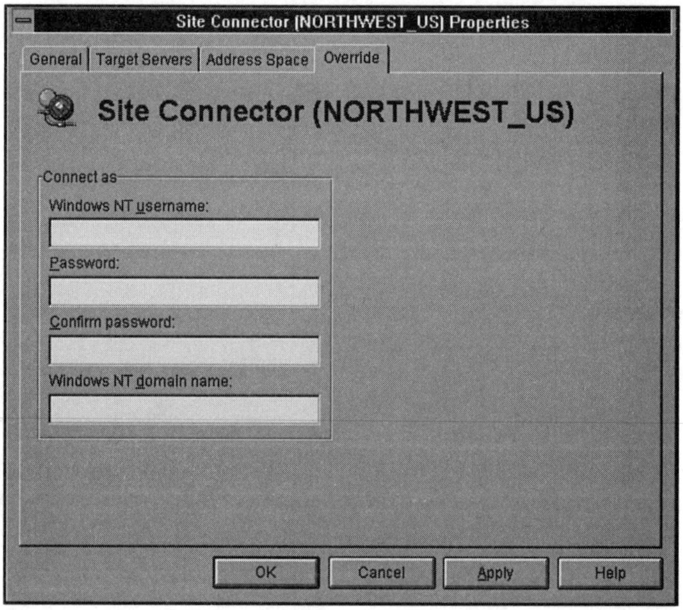

Figure 7.6

The Override notebook property page.

Site Connector [NORTHWEST_US] Properties

General | Target Servers | Address Space | Override |

Site Connector (NORTHWEST_US)

Connect as

Windows NT username:

Password:

Confirm password:

Windows NT domain name:

OK | Cancel | Apply | Help

Completing Site Connector Installation

After installing the Site Connector, you still must install and configure directory replication so that each server lists the recipients and can properly direct messages to the remote site. You learn how to do this in Chapter 9, "Managing Replication and Synchronization."

Installing Dynamic RAS

You can use Dynamic RAS to connect sites using modems (or ISDN connections) and matching asynchronous or ISDN telephone lines. This type of connector requires the least capital investment to get started, but may cost more to run over time than a higher-bandwidth WAN link. One approach you can take is to link sites initially with unknown mail needs by using Dynamic RAS, then upgrade to a higher-bandwidth WAN link by using the Site Connector only when you can justify the upgrade cost.

In order to use Dynamic RAS, you must first have RAS services installed on the Windows NT Server computer at each site. See your Windows NT documentation for details on installing RAS services.

Laying the Groundwork

In order to show you how to set up and configure the Dynamic RAS Connector, let's use the example company, Calliope, Inc. Refer to Table 7.1 for the vital statistics for the example connector.

Before attempting to configure the Dynamic RAS Connector, first ensure that you can establish a normal RAS connection to the remote site. In addition to this, you need to know the remote system's administrator account name and password. Finally, you need the administrator of the remote system available to duplicate your setup in the remote site.

Preparing the RAS MTA Transport Stack

Before installing the Dynamic RAS Connector, you first must install the RAS Message Transfer Agent (MTA) Transport Stack. To do this, follow these steps:

1. In the Exchange Server Administrator program, choose Servers and then select your server from the list.

2. Access the **F**ile menu, choose **N**ew Other, and then select the **M**TA Transport Stack command. You see the dialog box shown in figure 7.7.

Figure 7.7

The New MTA Transport Stack dialog box.

3. Choose RAS MTA Transport Stack from the **T**ype window and click on the OK button to continue. You see the notebook shown in figure 7.8.

Figure 7.8

The Transport Stack notebook.

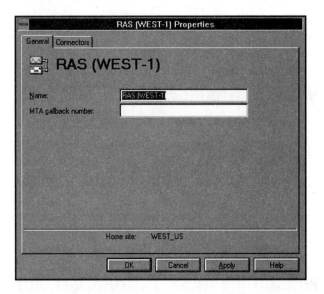

4. If you want, change the name in the **N**ame field; this name is used for the transport stack's display name. If you intend to use callback security, enter the number of the server you are working with in the MTA **c**allback number field.

5. Click on OK to finish creating the RAS MTA Transport Stack. The Server window updates to display the transport stack, as shown in figure 7.9.

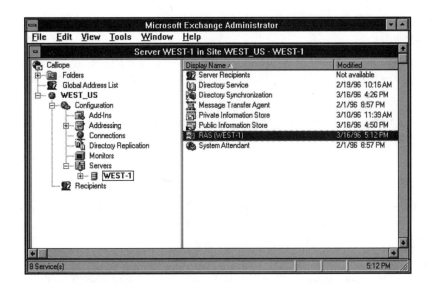

Figure 7.9

*RAS MTA
Transport Stack
displayed in the
Server window.*

Installing the Dynamic RAS Connector

After successfully adding the transport stack, you can then add the Dynamic RAS
Connector. In the Administrator program, select the Connections container. Then
pull down the File menu, choose New Other, and select Dynamic RAS Connector.
You see the notebook shown in figure 7.10.

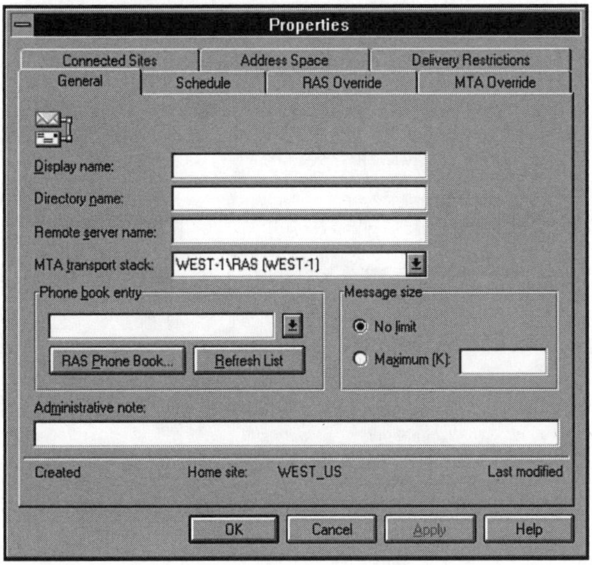

Figure 7.10

*The Dynamic
RAS Connector
notebook.*

On the General page of the Dynamic RAS Connector's properties notebook, complete the following fields:

◆ **D**isplay name should contain the name you want to view in the Exchange Server Administrator program to identify this connector. You are allowed up to 255 characters, and they are not case-sensitive.

◆ Directory **n**ame is used to identify this connector uniquely in the logs. Directory names can be up to 64 characters long.

◆ Enter the name of the remote server to which you are connecting in the Remote **s**erver name field.

◆ The MTA **t**ransport stack field should already contain the name of the transport stack you added in the previous section. If not, use the drop-down list box to select it.

◆ When you configure a RAS connection, you create an entry in the RAS phone book. In the Phone **b**ook entry field, select the appropriate RAS phone book entry that Exchange Server will use. If you've just added a new RAS phone book entry, the Refresh button will cause it to display.

◆ If necessary, you can set a maximum message size in the Message size box.

When you're finished, your screen should look something like figure 7.11.

Figure 7.11

The completed General page.

Next, you must supply the necessary information for Exchange Server to log in to the remote system over the RAS link. You do this on the RAS Override page, shown in figure 7.12.

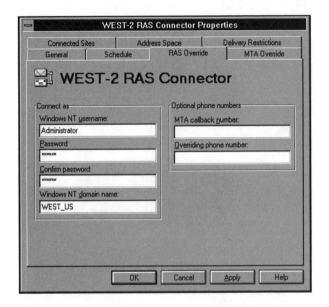

Figure 7.12

The RAS Override page.

In the RAS Override page, enter the remote system's administrator account name (or the account set up for Exchange Server services) and the domain name of the remote system.

Your final required step is to add the remote site to the Connected Sites page, shown in figure 7.13.

In the Connected Sites page, click on the **N**ew button to define a new site. You see the properties notebook for the new site shown in figure 7.14.

Complete the **O**rganization and **S**ite fields. If necessary to add routing, you can use the Routing Address page to do so.

After completing these pages, click on the Dynamic RAS Connector's OK button to save the new connector. You see the warning dialog box shown in figure 7.15 as you do so.

Figure 7.13

The Connected Sites page.

Figure 7.14

Connected Sites new site properties.

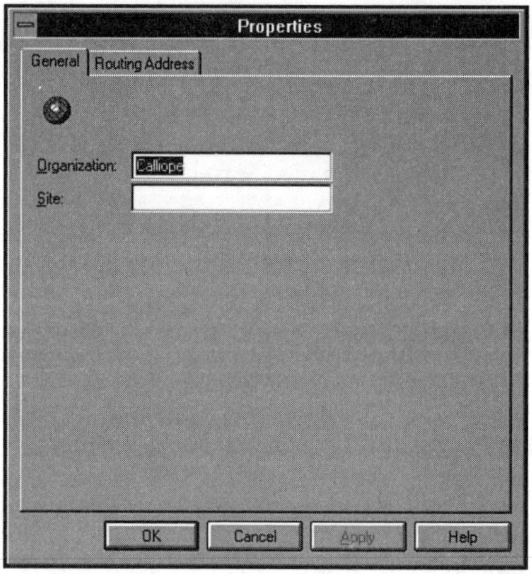

Figure 7.15

The Dynamic RAS Connector new site warning dialog box.

Once you complete the steps shown previously, have the remote administrator complete the same series of steps. After that, you can either define a custom recipient for the remote RAS site and exchange messages with the other site, or you can move on to establish directory synchronization over the Dynamic RAS connection.

 When you first set up the Dynamic RAS Connector, set the connection schedule to Always on the Schedule page of the connector. After you are satisfied that communications are working correctly, you can use the Schedule page to set an appropriate schedule for your connection needs.

Using Exchange Server with multiple sites adds a new level of complexity to your e-mail system. However, as you've seen here, actually connecting two sites using the two most likely methods is not really very difficult.

Connecting the sites is only half of the battle, however. Next, you need to configure and set up replication between the sites so that directories of users and folders are properly shared between the sites. You learn how to do this in Chapter 9.

CHAPTER 8

Configuring MS Mail Connectors

I f your organization will maintain some sites or LANs on MS Mail
or AppleTalk for a while, you need a connector to integrate those
services with Microsoft Exchange Server. Perhaps you are migrating your organization to Microsoft Exchange and there are some
unmigrated sites, or you have customized your mail systems and have
not yet converted those customizations to Exchange Server.

Connecting to MS Mail

You should install the MS Mail Connector to transfer messages between Exchange Server sites and Microsoft Mail for PC Networks. Every server in the organization can run one instance of the Microsoft Mail Connector, which can service one or more connections to MS Mail post offices and gateways.

Although the MS Mail Connector is configured by using the Microsoft Exchange Server Administrator program, you can administer it on any Windows NT Workstation or server on your network.

Setting Up the Connector

Exchange Server uses three components of the Microsoft Mail Connector to communicate with MS Mail (PC) systems:

◆ Microsoft Mail Connector interchange, which routes and transfers messages between Microsoft Exchange Server and the Microsoft Mail Connector post office

◆ Microsoft Mail Connector post office, which temporarily holds messages that are in transit

◆ Connector Message Transfer Agent (MTA), which performs the transfer of messages between the Connector post office and the MS Mail post office

A message from Microsoft Exchange to MS Mail is picked up by the interchange, converted to MS Mail format, and held in a temporary information store of the connector post office. The MTA then delivers the message to the MS Mail post office.

Understanding Connectors

Configuring the interchange and the general properties is the same, whether the connection is a LAN, an asynchronous transport, or an X.25 connection.

The third configuration, the connector, is the one that varies. Setting up the connection and configuring an MTA instance is unique for each of those connection types because messaging services between an MS Mail (PC) post office and Exchange Server need RPCs, so they have to be performed over a LAN connection.

Asynchronous or X.25 connections require an instance of the MS Mail External (or Multitasking MTA) at the remote post office. Of course, if you are using a LAN connection, there is no necessity for the MS Mail External program.

Configure the Interchange

You must configure the Interchange tab before you establish settings for any other option:

1. From the Administrator's window, choose Configuration, then choose Connections.

2. Find the MS Mail Connector in the right pane and double-click on it. The Properties dialog box displays with the Interchange tab in the foreground (see fig. 8.1).

Figure 8.1

Use the Interchange tab to configure the way messages are handled between Exchange Server and the MS Mail post office.

3. By default, the administrator's mailbox for this connection is the current administrator. Choose **C**hange to select a different mailbox from the address list. This mailbox is used for receiving administrative messages from the connector.

 Create a special mailbox for this administrative mailbox and name it so that it is obvious what the mailbox is for (you have to do that before getting to this step). You might want to create several administrative mailboxes and then have a distribution list. Hide the mailbox in the address list so that it doesn't accidentally receive mail from other users.

4. In the **P**rimary Language box, choose the language for Exchange Server clients that will use this connector.

5. Select Ma**x**imize MS Mail 3.x Compatibility if you have to support versions of OLE previous to 2.0 in messages moved from Exchange Server to MS Mail 3.*x.*

Note | If you don't care about OLE compatibility, deselect this option. The maximization process means that two versions of every OLE object are created and sent, which adds substantial size to messages. However, if Exchange Server clients send embedded objects in messages, MS Mail 3.x users won't be able to view (or save) them without this selection.

6. Select **E**nable message tracking if you want to add the messages sent through this connector to your message tracking log.

The Interchange tab also has the capability of configuring an MS Mail AppleTalk MTA if you have added that connector to your Exchange Server system.

Configure General Properties

Move to the General tab to establish fundamental elements for the connect (see fig. 8.2):

◆ Select **M**aximum to place limits on the size of individual messages for this connector, then specify the maximum size (up to 9,999,999 kilobytes).

◆ Enter any Administrative **n**ote about the connector you want to use.

This tab also displays the creation date and last modification date for the connector.

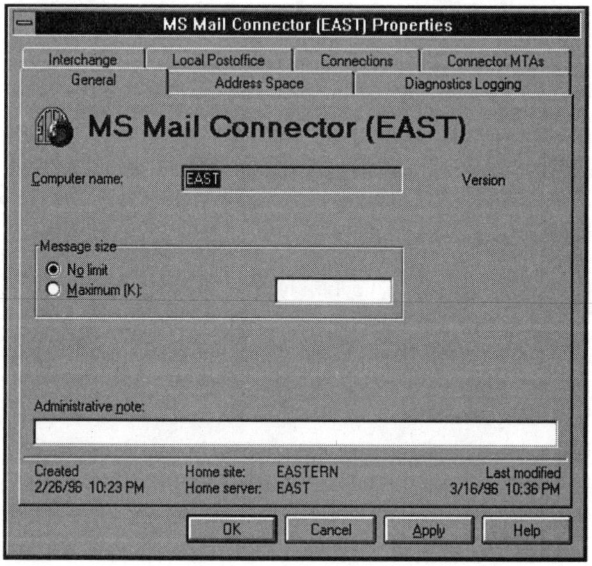

Figure 8.2

The basic configuration options for the connector are set on the General property page.

Configuring LAN Connections

For a LAN connection, the connector can extract the network and post office names from the external post office, so you do not have to enter any information (although you do need to know the network path to the directory for the external post office).

Configure the Connection

Move to the Connections tab and choose **C**reate to begin the configuration of the connection (see fig. 8.3).

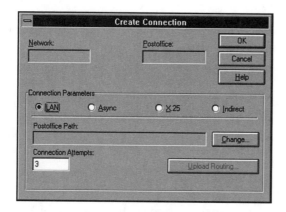

Figure 8.3

The Create Connection dialog box—options are accessible or greyed out depending upon the parameter you select.

Under Connection Parameters, select LAN (which is the default).

To enter the Postoffice Path, choose **C**hange to display the Postoffice Path dialog box (see fig. 8.4):

◆ For **P**ath, enter full path to the server using the Uniform Naming Convention (UNC) format.

◆ For Connect **A**s box, type the logon identifier.

◆ For Pass**w**ord, enter the account password if there is one.

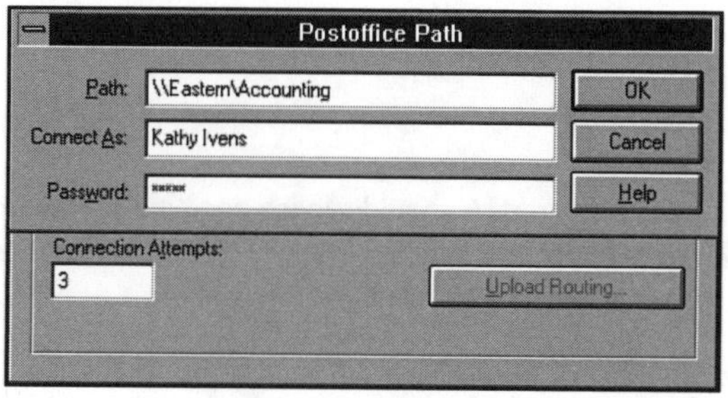

Figure 8.4

A LAN connection needs only the information about the Postoffice Path.

If you are configuring a connection to a NetWare server, your Windows NT Server must be running Gateway Service for NetWare. When setting a network path to a NetWare server, use the uniform naming convention (UNC) format (*servername*\ *sharename**path* for a Windows NT Server or *servername**volumename**path* for a NetWare server).

Choose OK when you finish to return to the Create Connection dialog box.

In the Connection A̲ttempts box, type a value (up to 99) to specify the number of attempts at sending mail before returning the message to the sender with a non-delivery report (NDR). The default is 3.

Choose U̲pload Routing to see a list of any indirect post offices connected to the MS Mail post office. Any of these can be included on the routing list.

Choose OK to return to the Connections property tab.

Once you create a connection, you can M̲odify or D̲elete it. At the bottom of the page is an option to Co̲nfirm before Connection changes are applied. Select or deselect this option depending upon whether or not a confirming dialog box should display whenever any changes are made to this property page.

Configure the Connector MTAs

Move to the Connector MTAs tab to define and configure Microsoft Mail Connector MTAs for transferring the messages between the connector and one or more MS Mail post offices.

Each Connector MTA you define is a separate Windows NT service, which you can start or stop by using the Windows NT Server Manager or Control Panel. You can run as many instances of the Connector MTA as you need.

Connector MTAs can service MS Mail post offices for three connection configurations:

- ◆ LAN-only

- ◆ Asynchronous/LAN

- ◆ X.25/LAN

 Each instance of the Connector MTA should service one type of connection, and you should create a separate instance of the Connector MTA to service those post offices that have the same connection.

To begin configuration, choose <u>N</u>ew to display the New MS Mail Connector (PC) MTA Service dialog box (see fig. 8.5).

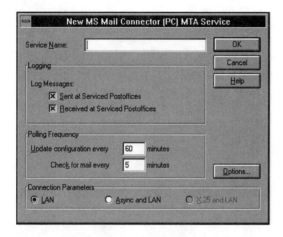

Figure 8.5

Set up a new connector instance—you can configure as many instances as you need.

Configure the options, following these steps:

1. Enter a Service <u>N</u>ame, which is used to register a new instance as a Windows NT service. Up to 30 characters can be used, including lowercase and uppercase letters and spaces character. This name cannot be modified.

2. Enter the Log Messages options you want (logs are stored at the Connector post office in the \LOG directory):

   ◆ Select <u>S</u>ent at Serviced Postoffices to log messages delivered to MS Mail post offices.

   ◆ Select <u>R</u>eceived at Serviced Postoffices to log messages received from MS Mail post offices.

3. Specify the frequencies for polling:

   ◆ <u>U</u>pdate configuration specifies how often the Connector post office and the MS Mail post office are checked for updated user and network information. Valid entries are 1–999 minutes.

   ◆ Chec<u>k</u> for mail specifies how frequently the Connector MTA checks the Connector post office and the MS Mail post office for mail. The default is 5 minutes. Valid entries are 1–999 minutes. Entering 0 minutes means there will be continuous polling.

Once the basic configuration for each instance of MTA connectors is complete, you can select an instance and choose **O**ptions to complete the configuration (see fig. 8.6).

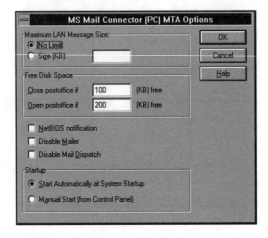

Figure 8.6

Use MTA Options to establish the way the connector handles specific situations that occur during message transfers.

Configure the options, using these parameters:

1. Set options for message size, choosing either No **L**imit or specifying a Si**z**e in Kilobytes.

2. Set Free Disk Space specifications:

   ◆ **C**lose the post office if free disk space falls below your specification. The post office is marked as unavailable and no messaging takes place.

   ◆ **O**pen the post office if free disk space exceeds your specification. If the post office has been closed, it is made available again and messaging resumes.

3. Select **Ne**tBIOS notification if you want to use NetBIOS to notify MS Mail users when new mail arrives.

4. Select Disable **M**ailer to disable this instance of the connector.

5. Select Disable Mail **D**ispatch to stop this instance of the connector from processing directory synchronization messages.

6. Choose a Startup option for this instance of the connector: **S**tart Automatically at System Startup, or M**a**nual Start, which means you start it through the Control Panel.

Choose OK when you finish configuring the options for this connector instance.

Specify the Post Offices for the Connector

You also use the Connector MTAs property page to specify which MS Mail post offices each Connector services. Follow these steps to accomplish this task:

1. In the MS Mail Connector MTA Services box, select a connector, then choose List to display the available post offices on the LAN.

2. Select a post office and choose Add to place the post office in the Postoffices Serviced box.

3. When you finish adding post offices, choose OK.

Other Configuration Options

Choose Edit to modify the parameters for a selected instance:

◆ You can assign a specific network user account for each occurrence of an MTA service. For instance, if the connector logs on to a NetWare server, you can assign an account name and a password, and enter the appropriate user rights for the post office directory.

◆ You can specify that you want to send, but not receive, messages from this post office.

Configure the Local Post Office

When you finish setting up the connector, you can configure each MS Mail post office you listed for the connector. However, it is usually not necessary to make any changes. If you have multiple post offices at the same site, you may want to group them by using a single network name.

Move to the Local Postoffice tab (see fig. 8.7) if you need to make changes to the Post office configuration:

◆ You can change the Network name and/or Postoffice name. These names identify your server for routing services between it and MS Mail post offices. The default names that display are derived from your Microsoft Exchange Server organization and site names.

◆ You can change the existing Sign-on Password for this post office.

Figure 8.7

*You can modify
the information
about a post office
if you want,
although it's
rarely necessary to
do so.*

If you make any changes, choose **R**egenerate to regenerate all the MS e-mail addresses for this post office throughout your system. If messages are in transit, they will
be returned. You should also stop and restart all MS Mail gateways, MS Mail external
programs, and all other connections at the same site, because the Connector interchange and all instances of the Connector MTA read the network and post office
name at startup.

Configuring Asynchronous and X.25 Connections

The procedures for setting up asynchronous and X.25 connections are very similar.

For configuring either connection, the following data is needed:

◆ The network name

◆ The post office name

◆ The sign-on ID number

◆ The password (if one is required)

The differences between these connectors are in the communication settings:

◆ Asynchronous connections need a phone number to dial.

◆ X.25 connections need the X.121 addresses for both the Microsoft Exchange
Server computer and the external post office.

To establish asynchronous and X.121 connections, move to the Connections tab of the MS Mail Connector Properties dialog box and follow these steps:

1. Choose **C**reate to get to the Create Connection dialog box.

2. Choose **A**sync or **X**.25, which makes the appropriate options accessible (see fig. 8.8).

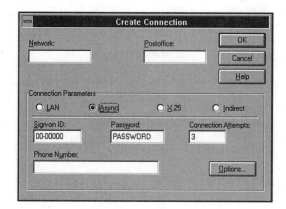

Figure 8.8

The configuration options vary depending upon the connection you're configuring—if this were an X.25 connection, the Phone Number box would be called X.121 Address.

3. Enter the data as follows:

   ◆ **N**etwork is the network name for the post office (you can use up to 10 characters).

   ◆ **P**ostoffice is the post office name (up to 10 characters).

   ◆ **S**ign-on ID is the serial number identifier for the post office, in an *XX-XXXX* format.

   ◆ Pass**w**ord is the password needed to log on to the post office.

   ◆ Connection A**t**tempts is the number of times you want to attempt to send mail before returning it to the sender with a nondelivery report (the choices are 1–99, the default is 3).

   ◆ X.121 Address (if you are configuring an X.25 connection) is the X.121 address of the external post office (use up to 16 numeric characters).

   Phone N**u**mber (if you are configuring an Asynchronous address) is the number that must be dialed to reach the external post office.

Set Additional Options

There are additional options for these connectors, which can be configured by choosing **O**ptions in the Create Connection dialog box (see fig. 8.9):

◆ The Message Size options are the same as those for LAN connectors.

◆ Failed connection retry for **U**rgent Mail is an interval range (1–999 minutes) for connection attempts for mail marked urgent.

◆ Failed connection retry for **N**ormal Mail is an interval range (1–999 minutes) for connection attempts for mail marked Normal.

◆ **D**ial Every is an interval range (1–999 minutes) for the modem to dial.

◆ **A**llow mail reception after sending means you can send, and then receive, messages from an MS Mail post office during the same connection session. If this option is not selected, the connector receives mail only during connections initiated by the external post office.

◆ **R**eturn registered mail confirmation indicates you want to issue a confirmation receipt automatically when users send registered mail to and from this MS Mail post office.

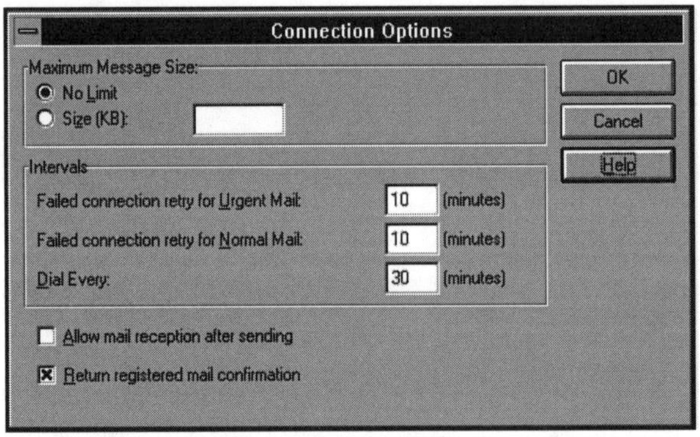

Figure 8.9

Message transfer options specific to Async and X.25 connections are configurable from the Connection Options dialog box.

Choose OK when you finish configuring the options for the connector(s).

Configure the Connector MTAs Properties

The configuration for the Connector MTAs properties are established exactly the same way as discussed previously in the configuration for a LAN connection. However, each instance of the Connector MTA should really service only one type of connection—LAN, asynchronous, or X.25—to ensure the optimum performance.

Therefore, you should create a separate instance of the Connector MTA for each connection type you're using.

When you configure the Connector MTA properties for asynchronous or X.25 connections, you will find some additional configuration entry boxes.

For asynchronous connectors, enter the following:

◆ Communications Port

◆ Modem Scripts

◆ Modem Timeout

For X.25 connectors, enter the following:

◆ The X.25 adapter port number

◆ The listen user data information (up to 218 hex characters, specified by your X.25 service provider)

◆ The listen user facilities information (up to 218 hex characters, specified by your X.25 service provider)

Taking Care of the Finishing Details

Once all the configuration options are completed on your Microsoft Exchange Server computer, you need to make sure each of the MS Mail post offices you integrated in this system is aware of the Microsoft Exchange Server computer.

Then, go to a computer running Exchange Server Client software and test your connections.

CHAPTER 9

Managing Replication and Synchronization

Directory replication updates each of your Exchange Server sites with directory entries (mailbox names) from all the other sites. Once set up, this process becomes automatic and ensures that each site will always have up-to-date listings for the other sites, with no intervention required on your part.

You don't need to worry about directory replication between servers within a single site. Servers in a site automatically replicate their directories to each other, with no intervention on your part required.

Between Exchange Server sites, directory replication is easy to establish. However, it is more complex when you need to synchronize directories between an Exchange Server site and a foreign mail system, such as MS Mail for PC Networks or for AppleTalk Networks. Software for performing directory synchronization with these systems is included with Exchange Server and is called *dirsync requestors.*

 Updating directory data between Exchange Server sites is called *directory replication,* whereas updating Exchange Server directory information with foreign mail systems is called *directory synchronization.*

Public folder replication is the process of updating each site with replicas (copies) of data in public folders in other sites. You select which folders are replicated between sites and how often they are updated. In this way, each site has its own copy of needed data in public folders, as well as new changes, on an ongoing basis.

In this chapter, you learn how to establish directory replication between Exchange Server sites (or within a single site with multiple servers), how to use dirsync requestors to synchronize directory entries with foreign systems, and how to establish replication for public folders.

Understanding Directory Replication

Exchange Server stores information about all the e-mail recipients in the system as well as other resource information within the mail system. Being able to exchange this information automatically between all your sites is crucial. By keeping recipient and resource information current between all sites, you guarantee that the system users will always be able to address mail within the organization accurately, no matter where a recipient is located.

Within a particular site, directory replication between Exchange Servers is automatic. However, when you have Exchange Servers in different sites, you must set up directory replication manually (the first time). Setting up directory replication follows connecting the sites using one of the connection methods outlined in Chapter 7, "Configuring Sites."

Before you install and configure directory replication, first ensure that each Exchange Server is installed and running correctly, and that the two sites are connected (see Chapter 7). Then, you use the Administrator program to install directory replication.

Setting Up Directory Replication

Once you connect two Exchange Server sites, you need to set up directory replication between them. Depending on the connection method that you used to connect the sites, you can often set up both your local site and the remote site without having to take any action at the remote site. This happens with Remote Procedure Calls (RPCs) and requires that your link to the remote site supports RPCs. Most LAN and WAN connections will support RPCs, whereas an Internet connection between sites will not.

Replicating Directories within a Site

Directory replication within a single site is automatic and begins within five minutes of making a change to one of the server's directories.

The process uses RPCs and follows these steps:

1. The directory in which a change is made notifies the other directories that a change has been made.

2. The notified directories request, as appropriate, updated information from the changed directory.

3. The changed directory sends the updated data to the other directories.

Replicating Directories between Different Sites

To establish directory replication between different Exchange Server sites, you must install a directory replication connector. The connector contains the settings needed to maintain the replication between the sites. In each of the sites, you designate one server that will handle the directory replication duties between the sites, and that server will then automatically update any other servers within the site. These designated servers are called *bridgehead servers*. In a site with multiple servers, you can designate the server that will act as the bridgehead server so that the load of the site's messaging system will be balanced appropriately.

The process of directory replication works like this: at set times, the bridgehead server requests an updated directory from the remote site. The remote site then prepares and sends a message containing any changes since the last update. This message is processed by the requesting site automatically and updates the site directory with the changes. Then, any other servers in the same site as the bridgehead server receive the updated directory entries. Once configured, this all happens automatically, without intervention on your part.

Before installing a directory replication connector, ensure that the messaging connector is installed and working properly. For sites linked by a LAN or WAN, this is the Exchange Server site connector. You also need to know the name of the bridge-head server at the remote site and need Administrator-level privileges on the remote server.

Begin the process of setting up the directory replication connector by selecting Directory Replication in the Administrator program, as shown in figure 9.1.

Next, access the File menu and choose New Other. Then choose Directory Replication Connector (see fig. 9.2).

Figure 9.1

Selecting Directory Replication in the Administrator program.

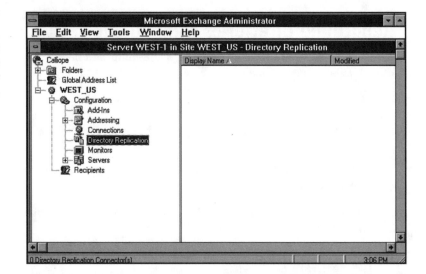

Figure 9.2

Choosing Directory Replication Connector.

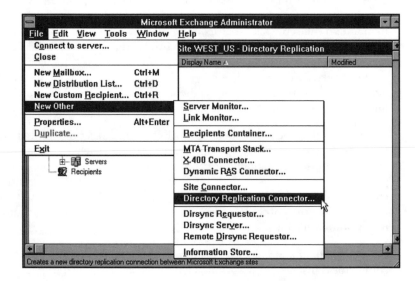

You now see the New Directory Replication Connector dialog box shown in figure 9.3.

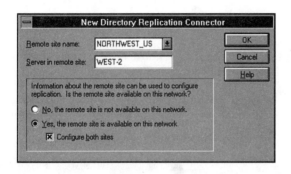

Figure 9.3

The New Directory Replication Connector dialog box.

In the displayed dialog box, complete the following information:

◆ **R**emote site name contains the name of the other Exchange Server site for which you are installing the connector. Using the drop box, you can see all the sites that have an installed messaging connector.

◆ In the **S**erver in remote site field, type the name of the server that will act as the remote bridgehead server. You need to know the name of this server.

◆ If the remote site is not available on the network, as is the case if it is connecting using either the Internet connector or an X.400 connector, you select **N**o, the remote site is not available on this network. Otherwise, select **Y**es, the remote site is available on this network.

◆ If you want to configure the remote site at the same time as the local site, and the remote site is on the same network (LAN or WAN link), you can check the Configure **b**oth sites check box. This causes your configuration to be duplicated at the remote site automatically, with no need for an administrator of the remote site to do anything to complete the installation.

Click on OK to continue after completing the needed fields shown in figure 9.3.

You now see the Properties notebook for the Directory Replication Connector, shown in figure 9.4.

To complete a basic installation of the directory replication connector, complete the following fields on the General page of the Properties notebook shown in figure 9.4:

◆ **D**isplay name is a 256-character alphanumeric field that defines the name shown in the Administrator program window for this connector.

◆ Directory **n**ame is a 64-character field in which you define a unique name for this connector.

◆ **S**ite name cannot be changed by you, but displays the name of the remote site for which you are installing the connector.

◆ **L**ocal bridgehead server is where you choose which of the local site's Exchange Servers will perform directory replication with the remote site.

◆ **R**emote bridgehead server is where you choose which of the remote site's Exchange Servers will perform directory replication with your local site.

◆ If you wish, you can enter an Administrative n**o**te. Your organization may have standards developed for what you enter in this field, which may simply consist of the creation date and your name.

Figure 9.4

The Directory Replication Connector Properties notebook.

After completing the preceding fields, click on the OK button to finish creating the connector.

The first directory replication may take a while to complete, depending on the amount of data to be exchanged, the speed of the link between the sites, and how busy the bridgehead servers are with other tasks. When the first replication completes, you will see the remote site shown in the main Administrator tree, as shown in figure 9.5.

Granting Directory Replication Permissions

Going back into the Directory Replication Connector dialog box (see fig. 9.4), you can designate which users or groups can modify or maintain the directory replication connector with the Permissions property page shown in figure 9.6.

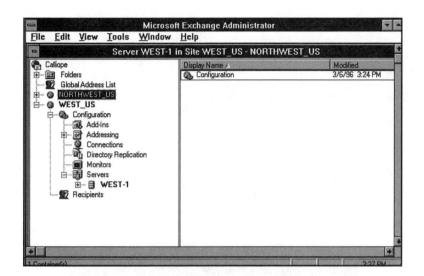

Figure 9.5

Directory replication completed; NORTHWEST_US is now visible in the Administrator object tree.

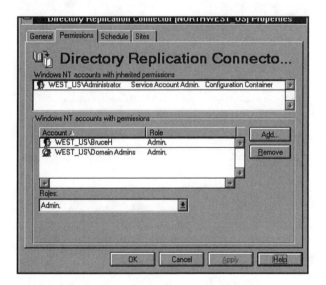

Figure 9.6

The Permissions property page.

In the Permissions property page, you designate accounts, in addition to the Administrator account, that can maintain the replication connector. Click on the A**d**d button to select either a group or account to give privileges (see fig. 9.7). For each account selected and added to the Windows NT accounts with **p**ermissions box, you can further select a role with the Ro**l**es drop box.

Roles are sets of rights that you can grant. For the replication connector, you can choose from Admin, Permissions Admin, Service Account Admin, View Only Admin, and User roles. You can also create custom roles that have only the specific rights that you want to grant. The following are the available rights:

◆ Add Child enables creation of objects within the selected object.

◆ Delete enables deletion of the selected object.

◆ Modify Admin Attributes enables changing the administrator attributes for the selected object.

◆ Modify Permissions enables changing the permissions for the selected object.

◆ Modify User Attributes enables changing the user attributes for the selected object.

Figure 9.7

Selecting groups or accounts to which to add permissions.

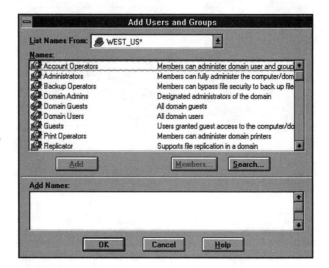

Scheduling Replication

Use the Schedule page of the Directory Replication Connector Properties to control how often new directory information is replicated to other sites. Figure 9.8 shows this page in the notebook.

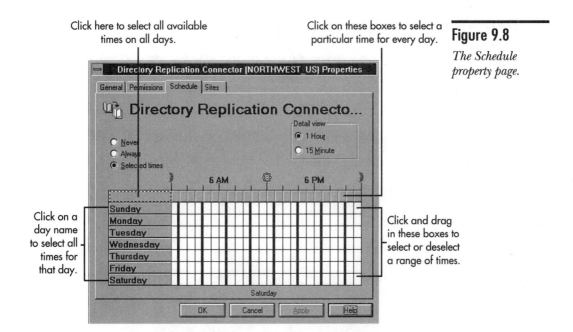

Figure 9.8

The Schedule property page.

The Schedule property page has the following settings:

◆ **N**ever disables all directory replication, except for forced updates performed on the Sites page of the Properties notebook.

◆ A**l**ways is equivalent to choosing every possible 15-minute interval.

◆ **S**elected times uses the time boxes so that you can pick and choose the times to perform directory replication.

◆ Choosing 1 Hou**r** sets the selected times to 1-hour increments.

◆ Choosing 15 **M**inute allows 15-minute time selections.

When selecting a schedule for directory replication, make sure that you consider any underlying schedule for the actual connectivity between the sites. For instance, you may have a scheduled Internet connection that occurs once a day, but if your replication schedule is after the connection schedule, replication messages will wait in the queue until the next available connection. Try to coordinate replication schedules with connection schedules, when necessary.

Using the Sites Properties Page

The Sites page of the Directory Replication Connector's Properties notebook displays inbound and outbound sites for directory replication. *Inbound sites* are those that send directory information to your current sites, and *outbound sites* are those to which your sites send updates. Figure 9.9 shows this page.

Figure 9.9

The Sites property page.

You can select sites in the **I**nbound sites window and then click on the **R**equest Now button to force an immediate update of directory information. When you do this, you see the Directory Update Type dialog box shown in figure 9.10, in which you choose either to update only new and changed items or to request an entire copy of the remote site's directory.

Replicating Directories without Network Connectivity

As you've seen in the preceding sections, setting up a directory replication connector between sites that are on the same LAN or WAN is a relatively easy and straightforward process. However, you may have connected your Exchange Server sites using a method that does not rely on LAN or WAN connectivity, as when you link Exchange Server sites using the Internet connector or an X.400 connector. In these cases, you still must enable directory replication between sites, but you must perform the installation a little differently.

Figure 9.10

The Directory Update Type dialog box.

The first step involves ensuring that the remote site has been added to the Connected Sites property page. For instance, for an Internet mail connection, you open the Properties notebook for the Internet Mail Connector, as shown in figure 9.11.

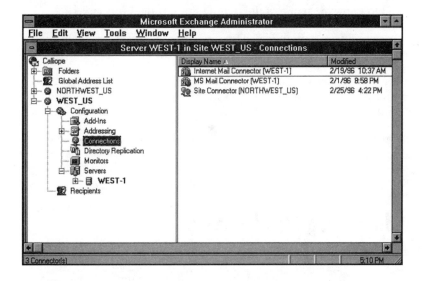

Figure 9.11

Finding the Internet Mail Connector.

Then, open the Internet Mail Connector object and activate the Connected Sites page shown in figure 9.12.

Figure 9.12

The Connected Sites property page.

If necessary, add the remote site's mail address to the Connected Sites page.

You will then need to know the name of the remote site's bridgehead server.

After fulfilling those requirements, follow these steps to install directory replication between the sites without network connectivity:

1. Create a directory replication connector as shown earlier in this chapter. You need to do this at both sites manually. You specify, **N**o, the remote site is not available on this network as you perform this.

2. Specify the remote system's bridgehead server name in each site's replication connector manually.

3. Set the schedule for directory replication in both sites.

Understanding Bridgehead Servers

When working with bridgehead servers, there are some things to keep in mind:

◆ If you have a site with multiple servers that replicates to many remote sites, you can specify different bridgehead servers for each site. This enables you to balance the load among servers in a site.

◆ If you change the bridgehead server for a site, the directory information in the site is completely rewritten.

◆ When you change a bridgehead server, make sure that you not only change the configuration in the site with the different bridgehead server, but that you also change the setting in the remote site so that it connects to the new bridgehead server. You can do this with the General page of the appropriate directory replication connector's properties if you have network connectivity (the changes are made in the other site through the network). Otherwise, an administrator of the remote system has to change the configuration at that site simultaneously.

Setting Up Foreign Directory Synchronization

Microsoft Exchange Server can automatically exchange directory information with any foreign system that supports the MS Mail directory synchronization protocol. In this scheme, you establish both directory synchronization servers and requestors. There will be one server and possibly many requestors. Exchange Server can function as either a directory synchronization server or requestor.

 Exchange Server calls its components for directory synchronization *dirsync servers* and *Dirsync requestors*.

When you configure Exchange Server with a dirsync requestor, it queries the Exchange Server recipient database for new entries or changes. When recipients are added or changed, it sends the update to the MS Mail directory synchronization server post office, based on scheduled updates. During the update, it also requests any changed information from the MS Mail directory synchronization server.

When Exchange Server is set up with a dirsync server, on the other hand, it responds to requests from the MS Mail directory synchronization requestors. New or changed addresses from the MS Mail requestor post offices are added to Exchange Server as custom recipients.

You can have only one directory synchronization server for a single site. Exchange Server cannot be both a requestor and a server; it has to fulfill one role only. Generally, your directory synchronization server should be the system to which all other messaging systems connect. In a site in which many MS Mail post offices exist and you are installing a single Exchange Server system, one of the MS Mail servers will be a dirsync server. In a site in which Exchange Server will be implemented as the "main" system, you will likely configure the system being phased out as a dirsync requestor.

In order to set up the directory synchronization process with a MS Mail post office, you need to have the MS Mail DISPATCH.EXE program accessible on the LAN. It can be located in any directory to which the Exchange Server system has access. This program coordinates the tasks necessary for MS Mail to carry out directory synchronization over the network.

Understanding Dirsync Prerequisites

Before you can set up the directory synchronization process on your LAN or WAN, you must first ensure that Exchange Server is installed and running properly, and that messages can be passed between it and the MS Mail post offices with which you'll be working.

You must also install and test the Microsoft Mail Connector onto the Exchange Server computer. See Chapter 8, "Configuring MS Mail Connectors," for more information on connectors.

Setting Up a Dirsync Requestor

You can configure Microsoft Exchange Server to function as a requestor to a single MS Mail directory synchronization server. Communications between the dirsync requestor and the server flow like this:

1. The dirsync requestor sends a list of new or changed recipients to the server.

2. The server compiles the changes, creates the global address list (that may include updates from other requestors), and sends the complete list to the Exchange Server dirsync requestor.

3. The Exchange Server with the dirsync requestor adds the new or changed addresses to its global address list.

4. The updated global address list is replicated to other Exchange Server servers that are linked to the dirsync requestor server.

To set up the dirsync requestor, follow these steps:

1. Using the Microsoft Exchange Administrator program, select the Connections container (see fig. 9.13).

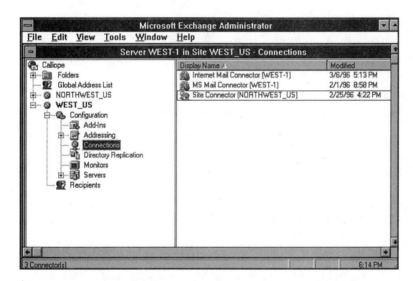

Figure 9.13

Selecting the Connections container.

2. In the **F**ile menu, select **N**ew Other and then choose Dirsync **R**equestor. If you see a dialog box prompting you for the correct MS Mail post office, select it and click on OK. You then see the Properties dialog box shown in figure 9.14.

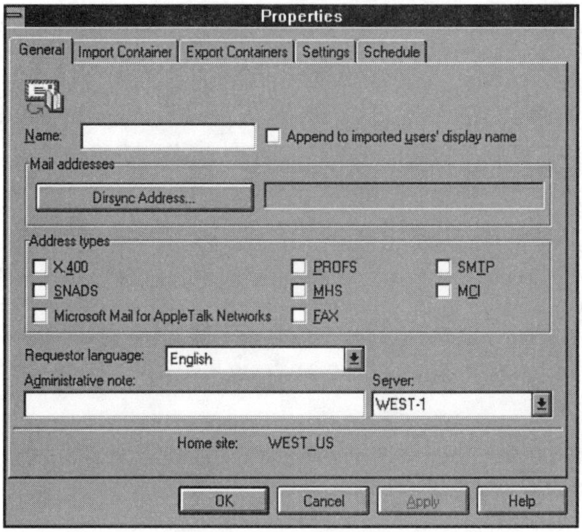

Figure 9.14

Dirsync Requestor properties.

The General property page enables you to set the basic configuration for the Exchange Server dirsync requestor. The first step is to fill in the <u>N</u>ame field with a 64-character display name for the requestor. Then, choose Append to imported <u>u</u>sers' display name. This enables users of the system to see where the addressee is located.

Next, you can choose which foreign address types the requestor will request from the synchronization server. Because the synchronization server may be handling many different address types, you need to select which ones will be requested and updated.

 MS Mail addresses are requested and serviced by default. Each Address Type selected will be in addition to the MS Mail address type.

The Dirsync Address field contains a hidden mailbox on the directory synchronization server by default, which is named $SYSTEM. As a rule, do not change this name to another mailbox.

If you require, you can also change the language for the requestor in the Requestor language field, and, of course, you can enter an administrative note in the field provided if your organization does so.

Your next step is to move to the Import Container page shown in figure 9.15. In this page, you need to select in which recipient container the imported addresses will be stored. Click on the <u>C</u>ontainer button to do so. You can make address information from multiple directory synchronization servers available to your Exchange Server recipients, but if you want to keep them in separate address books, you can do so by first creating a new recipient container to hold the imported addresses.

 When your users browse e-mail addresses, they normally see the main address list for their sites and have the option of viewing other address lists. Each recipient container appears as a separate address list to your users. It can be helpful to segregate different types of addresses into different containers to ease administration and keep your address lists better organized.

You can also assign a trust level for the directory objects being imported. These trust levels are used to control directory synchronization with other mail systems. User accounts with a trust level that is higher than the value assigned to the synchronization connector are not synchronized; those with a lower trust level are synchronized. Trust levels are arbitrary numbers that you can set from 0 to 100.

 Once you select a directory import container, you cannot change it without deleting the existing requestor and reinstalling.

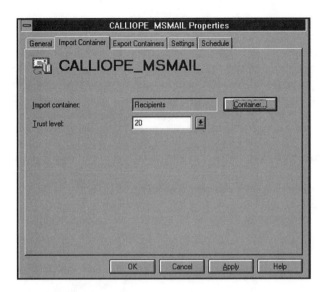

Figure 9.15

The Import Container page.

The next page to work with is the Export Containers page, shown in figure 9.16. With this page, you select which of your recipient containers will be exported to the directory synchronization server. Select the appropriate containers from those displayed in the left window, and click on the A**d**d button to list them in the right window. You can also select which recipients are selected with the **T**rust level field. All recipients with a trust level equal to or lower than that shown will be exported. Finally, choose whether custom recipients (those in foreign e-mail systems whose addresses are in the address book) will be exported with the Export **c**ustom recipients check box.

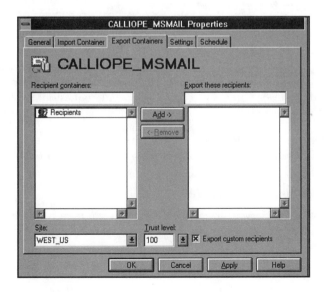

Figure 9.16

The Export Containers page.

Next, move to the Settings page, displayed in figure 9.17. Using the Settings page, you can choose whether updates to the address list can be sent or received. You can also choose whether to send or receive template information. Finally, if you select either **I**mport on next cycle or **E**xport on next cycle, you can force a complete address update during the next scheduled communication with the directory synchronization server. Selecting either **I**mport on next cycle or **E**xport on next cycle applies only to the next cycle; the check boxes are deselected once the update completes.

 Note   If you select to send or receive template information, you must map the template details to the equivalent MS Mail template strings. This is handled in the Directory Synchronization object and is described later in this chapter.

Figure 9.17

The Settings page.

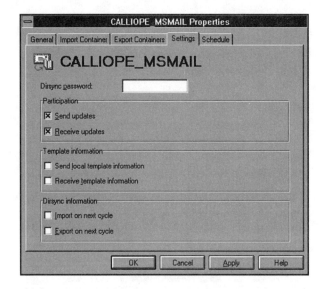

You use the Schedule page, shown in figure 9.18, to set the schedule used for directory synchronization. The dirsync requestor drives the process; the server merely responds to requests at whatever time they occur. The dirsync requestor lets you choose the synchronization schedule in one-hour increments only.

Once you finish configuring the various pages in the dirsync requestor properties notebook, click on OK to store them and return to the Administrator program.

Setting Up the MS Mail Dirsync Server

After setting up the Exchange Server dirsync requestor, you can then configure the MS Mail directory synchronization server. You need to configure it so that it can recognize your Exchange Server as a valid requestor. This is done with the MS Mail ADMIN program.

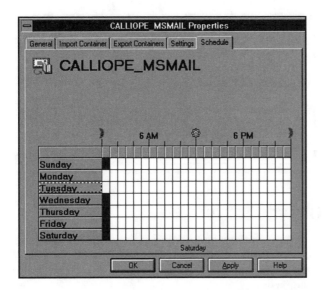

Figure 9.18

The Schedule page.

When setting up the MS Mail directory synchronization server, you need to tell it with which MS Mail post office it will be synchronizing. The MS Mail Connector in Exchange Server simulates an MS Mail post office to the MS Mail server. Use the MS Mail Connector properties page to set the MS Mail names that Exchange Server uses and that need to be entered into the real MS Mail directory synchronization server.

 Microsoft Exchange Server often abbreviates Directory Synchronization with the letters *DXA* in both the online help files and in the printed documentation.

Once you have configured both the requestor and the MS Mail server, you then need to start the directory synchronization services on the dirsync requestor server. Follow these steps:

1. Open the Windows NT Control Panel, then double-click on the Services icon. You see the dialog box shown in figure 9.19.

2. Locate the entry called Microsoft Exchange Directory Synchronization.

3. To manually start the service, click on the **S**tart button.

4. To set the service to start automatically when the server starts, click on the Sta**r**tup button and then choose Automatic.

Figure 9.19

The Control Panel Services dialog box.

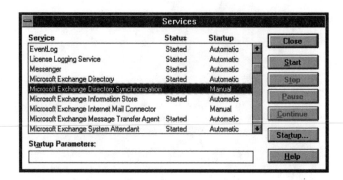

Setting Up a Dirsync Server

There are three main steps to configuring Exchange Server as a dirsync server. First, you install and configure the dirsync server from within the Exchange Administrator program. Second, you define each valid requestor that will use the server. Third, you set up the actual requestor systems.

Adding a Dirsync Server

To create a dirsync server in Exchange Server, start by selecting the Connections container in the Administrator program. Then, pull down the File menu and choose New Other. In the New Other menu, choose Dirsync Server. You see the Properties notebook shown in figure 9.20.

 You will not be allowed to create a dirsync server if your system already has a dirsync requestor defined.

Use the Name field to enter a 64-character display name for the dirsync server. Then, click on the Dirsync Administrator button and choose the recipient that will receive directory synchronization messages.

For debugging purposes, you can select either the Copy administrator on outgoing messages or Forward incoming dirsync messages to administrator check boxes.

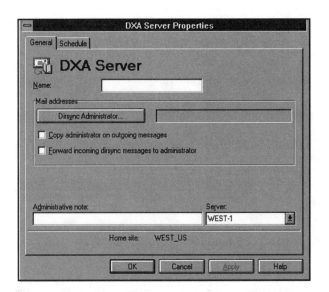

Figure 9.20

The DXA Server Properties notebook.

You can then use the Schedule page to determine when the Exchange Server dirsync server sends its own updated lists to the requestors (in one-hour increments). The Schedule page is shown in figure 9.21.

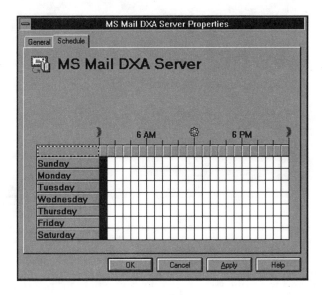

Figure 9.21

The Dirsync Server Schedule page.

By default, the Schedule page is set to send updates at midnight every day. If you want more frequent updates, select the appropriate time boxes. Updates are sent at the beginning of each hour selected.

Click on the OK button to finish creating the dirsync server and save your selections.

Configuring Remote Dirsync Requestors

Once you finish installing the Dirsync (DXA) Server, you must then define each valid requestor that will be working with the DXA Server. For each remote requestor, you define an object for that requestor and then configure the properties for the requestor so that you select which directory containers are used for exporting and importing address information.

To create a remote dirsync requestor, pull down the **F**ile menu in the Administrator program, choose **N**ew Other, and then select Remote **D**irsync Requestor from the menu. You see the Properties notebook shown in figure 9.22.

Figure 9.22

Remote Dirsync Requestor properties.

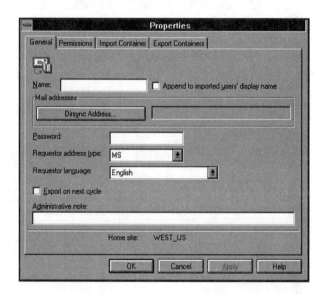

As you have previously seen, you first enter a 64-character display name for the remote DXA requestor in the **N**ame field.

You can then choose to select the check box labeled Append to imported **u**sers' display name. This causes the name you used in the **N**ame field to appear after the custom recipient names that are imported from the remote DXA requestor. It's recommended that you select this check box.

By default, the Dirsync Address is set to a hidden mailbox on the MS Mail post office called $SYSTEM. You should not change this name.

If you have defined a password in the remote MS Mail requestor, you must enter this password in the **P**assword field. By default, passwords are not used for this function.

The Requestor address **t**ype field offers two choices: MS or MSA. MS is used for remote dirsync requestors that are compatible with MS Mail for PC Networks, and MSA is for connecting to MS Mail for AppleTalk Networks.

If desired, you can select a language for the requestor in the Requestor lan**g**uage field. By default, this is set to English. You can also choose the check box marked **E**xport on next cycle, which forces a complete update during the next directory synchronization cycle and then resets the check box to the deselected state.

Use the Permissions page to define who can modify the Remote Dirsync Requestor object with the Exchange Server Administrator program. As with the other Permissions pages, you can grant access to specific accounts, and you can assign each account a different role or set of rights.

Next, move to the Import Container page, which is shown for you in figure 9.23. In the **I**mport Container field, choose which recipient container is used to store the custom recipients that are created when addresses are imported from the remote DXA requestor. You can also choose a default trust level for the created custom recipients with the **T**rust level field. The default is trust level 20, which you can override on an individual basis if you wish.

If you update all recipients from a remote requestor, the default trust level that you select will overwrite any previously chosen trust levels for specific recipients.

Once you choose an import container, you cannot change it without removing and reinstalling the Remote Dirsync Requestor object.

The Export Containers page enables you to specify which of your Exchange Server recipients containers are exported to the remote dirsync requestor (see fig. 9.24). Copy the relevant recipient containers from the left window into the right window by selecting them and clicking on the A**d**d button. You can, of course, also remove export containers by selecting them in the right window and clicking on the **R**emove button.

You can use the S**i**te drop-down list to choose different servers, which lets you then choose recipient containers located on the selected server.

Figure 9.23

The Import Container page.

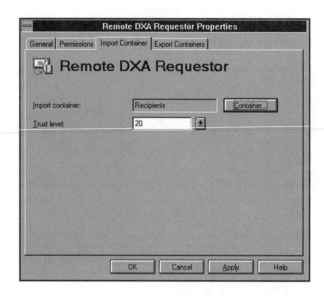

The <u>T</u>rust level field is used to select which recipients will be exported. All recipients with a trust level equal to or less than that chosen in the <u>T</u>rust level field will be exported to the remote system.

Selecting the Export C<u>u</u>stom Recipients check box causes custom recipients that you've created to be exported.

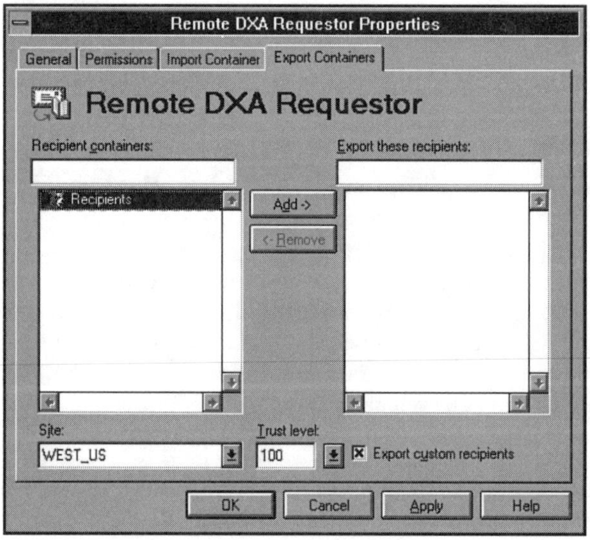

Figure 9.24

The Export Containers page.

After defining all the properties for the Remote Dirsync Requestor, click on the OK button to save your selections and close the dialog box.

Configuring Remote Systems

Your final step in setting up a dirsync server and the dirsync requestors is to set up the remote MS Mail system. Note that, as far as the MS Mail system is concerned, you follow the same steps to have the MS Mail system connect to an Exchange Server Dirsync server as you do to connect it to another MS Mail directory synchronization server. The Exchange Server Dirsync server emulates an MS Mail post office for this purpose. You configure the MS Mail system using its ADMIN.EXE program.

Before setting up the MS Mail system, ensure that the following tasks are complete:

◆ Your Exchange Server is installed and running correctly.

◆ You have installed and configured both the MS Mail Connector and the Dirsync server on the Exchange Server, and both are working.

◆ You can send and receive messages between Exchange Server and the MS Mail post office.

◆ You have installed the MS Mail EXTERNAL.EXE program (or multitasking MTA program), and it's available on the network on which the MS Mail post office is running.

◆ The MS Mail DISPATCH.EXE program is available on the network on which the MS Mail post office is running.

After verifying that these facts are all true, use your MS Mail for PC Networks manual for assistance in configuring a directory synchronization requestor.

Configuring Directory Synchronization

Once you set up directory synchronization as described in the preceding sections of this chapter, you're probably done with the whole thing. However, there are some additional procedures that you may need to perform, depending on your needs. These include the following:

◆ Changing directory synchronization e-mail addresses

◆ Mapping MS Mail templates to Exchange Server recipient fields

◆ Setting restrictions on delivery or reception of messages

In this section, you will learn how to perform these tasks.

Changing Directory Synchronization Addresses

You can control the addresses used for sending and receiving directory synchronization messages by accessing the appropriate properties page of the Directory Synchronization object. To get to this properties notebook, select the appropriate server in
the Administrative window, and then double-click on the container marked Directory
Synchronization (see fig. 9.25).

Figure 9.25

*Accessing the
Directory
Synchronization
object.*

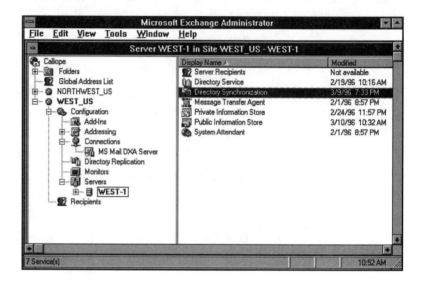

Once you open the Directory Synchronization object's Properties notebook, you see
the screen shown in figure 9.26.

To control the e-mail addresses used for directory synchronization, select the E-mail
Addresses page, shown in figure 9.27.

You can select any of the automatically generated addresses shown and click on the
Edit button to change them. You can also add a new address with the **N**ew button.

 Changing directory synchronization addresses may have unforeseen impacts and
may cause directory synchronization to fail. Other Exchange Server services rely on
these addresses.

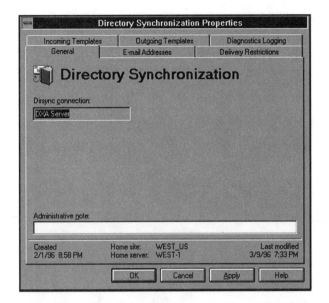

Figure 9.26

*The Directory
Synchronization
Properties
notebook.*

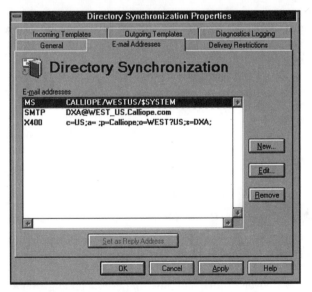

Figure 9.27

*The E-mail
Addresses page.*

Setting Delivery Restrictions

As an administrator, you may need to reject messages from the other system or accept
messages only from certain valid recipients. This can be controlled with the Delivery
Restrictions page of the Directory Synchronization Properties notebook, which you
can see in figure 9.28.

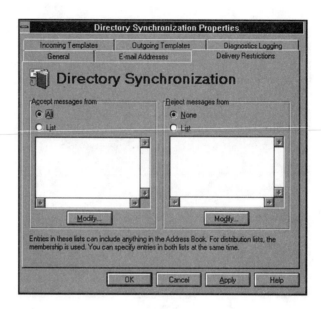

Figure 9.28

The Delivery Restrictions page.

By default, all messages are accepted. You can choose either to accept all messages except certain ones with the **R**eject messages from window, or you can choose to accept only messages from valid recipients by defining them all in the A**c**cept messages from window. To enable either feature, select the List option button in the appropriate window and then use that window's Modify button to maintain the list of rejected or accepted messages.

 An external e-mail system may be sending messages to an account on your system that you no longer wish to see. Use the Delivery Restrictions page to refuse mail under these circumstances.

Maintaining Dirsync Templates

MS Mail uses templates to define additional information about recipients. These templates are very flexible and enable the MS Mail administrators to define any information they like. They might, for instance, define template entries for telephone extension, department, employee number, or anything else. Exchange Server uses a defined database of entries in place of the older MS Mail scheme. In order to exchange template information between Exchange Server and a connected MS Mail system, you need to map the Exchange Server fields to the MS Mail template entries. This mapping has to occur for both directions: you need to map Exchange Server fields to MS Mail template entries and also map MS Mail template entries to Exchange Server fields.

Note In order to send or receive template information between an MS Mail post office and the connected Exchange Server, you must turn on incoming or outgoing templates. Refer to figure 9.17 for the properties page that enables you do to this.

To modify incoming template information, move to the Incoming Templates page of the Directory Synchronization Properties notebook, shown in figure 9.29.

Figure 9.29

The Incoming Templates page.

On this page, you define which string in the MS Mail template should map to which descriptive attribute for each recipient. To add a new entry, click on the New button, which displays the dialog box shown in figure 9.30.

In the Map the string field, enter the MS Mail template string with which you want to work. Then, in the To the attribute field, select the Exchange Server recipient attribute in which you want to store the incoming information.

 Note MS Mail enables you to define completely arbitrary fields for its templates. Exchange Server needs to know which character string (sequence of letters) in the template labels the information you're after for mapping.

Outgoing Templates functions in the same way, but in the Outgoing Templates page you select an Exchange Server attribute and then type the text that should be sent to the MS Mail post office for use.

Figure 9.30

*The Incoming
Template
Mapping dialog
box.*

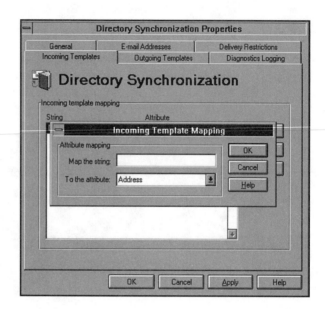

 Changing template mappings results in a complete update of directory information during the next communication between the Exchange Server and the MS Mail post office.

Understanding Public Folder Replication

One of the most exciting features of Microsoft Exchange Server is that it enables the creation of public folders. Recall that a public folder is a folder that can contain diverse information to which many people have access. It can contain customer information, organizational information, a history of messages about a particular topic analogous to a bulletin board system, or just about anything you want.

Note Public folders are created by users of Exchange Server; they are not created in the Administrator program. However, the Administrator program is used to set up and maintain replication for the folders once they exist.

When public folders are created by users on their home Exchange Server sites, the public folder entry in the public folder hierarchy is automatically replicated to all other connected Exchange Server sites. However, the contents are not; you must set up replication for that folder or folder tree in order to update other sites with the folder contents. After you've done this, the folder contents are automatically updated among your different Exchange Server sites. This is the meaning of *public folder replication*. When you set up replication, all replicas throughout an organization are equal; there is no master replica.

Another key concept is *public folder affinity*. When users of a site try to open a public folder, any replicas in their own sites are first tried, one by one. If none of the replicas in their sites are available, either because they don't exist or because the servers that hold the replicas are down, other sites are then tried *if* affinities to those sites are set up. You can configure public folder affinities under the following circumstances:

◆ You do not want to replicate a particular public folder to another site. Perhaps the other site does not have enough capacity to hold the replicated data, or the communications link between the sites is not fast enough to support replication of the data the folder contains, but it is fast enough to enable occasional access to users through the WAN link.

◆ You want to provide backup public folder access to users in a site. In case their main Exchange Server goes down, you still want them to have access to the data in the public folder, even if it's over the LAN/WAN link and will be slower than accessing a replica in their main site.

You need to balance the need for public folder affinities against the available bandwidth between sites. Accessing a large public folder over a slow link may exhaust your available bandwidth, hurting other network services.

 Note In order for a user to access a public folder at another site through an affinity, they must have LAN or WAN access to the other site.

Creating and Managing Public Folder Replicas

To create a public folder replica, access the server in the Administrator program and then access the Public Folder's Properties notebook. The selection in the Administrator program is shown in figure 9.31; the notebook is shown in figure 9.32.

Figure 9.31

Accessing Public Folder properties.

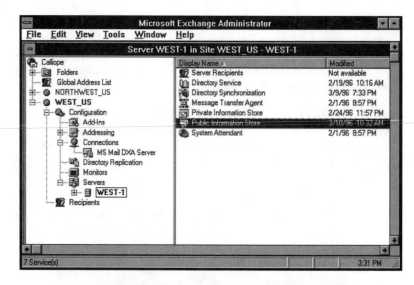

Figure 9.32

The Public Folder Properties notebook.

You maintain public folder replicas with the Instances page in the notebook, shown in figure 9.33.

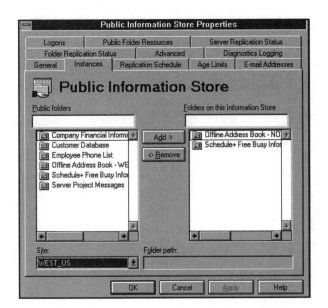

Figure 9.33

The Instances page.

The left window (**P**ublic folders) shows available public folders in the site selected in the S**i**te drop box. To replicate the remote public folder to the site you're administering, select the folder you're interested in and click on the A**d**d button. This causes the folder (and any of its children) to replicate. You can also remove the replication by selecting a folder in the **F**olders on this Information Store and then clicking on the **R**emove button.

Checking Replication Status

You can see how current your replicas are by moving to the Folder Replication Status page in the Public Information Store Properties notebook. This page is shown in figure 9.34.

In the Folder Replication Status page, you can see the last update for any of the replicas on the server for which you are administering. If you require, you can update the display by clicking on the **R**efresh button. You can also change the information displayed and the order of the columns with the **C**olumns button shown.

Figure 9.34

The Folder Replication Status page.

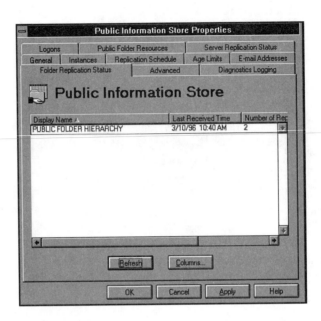

Managing Folder Replication Schedules

You can control the schedule for replication of all public folders, as well as individual folders. For a specific folder, select Public Folders in the Administrator program tree and then access the properties for the specific public folder you want to control. To set the overall schedule for all public folders, select the server in the Administrator program tree and then access the properties for the Public Information Store. In both cases, you then select the Replication Schedule page. The Replication Schedule page for a specific folder is shown in figure 9.35.

As you can see in figure 9.35, folders default to the setting **U**se Information Store Schedule. However, you can override this for specific folders merely by selecting one of the options. If you select **S**elected times, you can define which hours on which days replication is performed.

The Advanced page in the Public Information Store's properties also enables you to choose the interval that is meant by the **A**lways check box in the Replication Schedule page (see fig. 9.36). By default, selecting **A**lways causes replication to occur every 15 minutes, and replication messages are rejected if they are over 100 KB. You can change either of these settings.

Employee Movie Reviews Properties
Distribution Lists
E-mail Addresses
Custom Attributes
Advanced
General
Replicas
Folder Replication Status
Replication Schedule
Employee Movie Reviews
Use Information Store Schedule
Never
Always
Selected times
Detail view
1 Hour
15 Minute
6 AM
6 PM
Sunday
Monday
Tuesday
Wednesday
Thursday
Friday
Saturday
OK
Cancel
Apply
Help

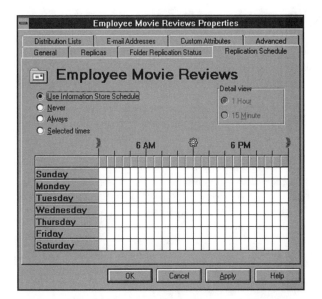

Figure 9.35

The Replication Schedule page.

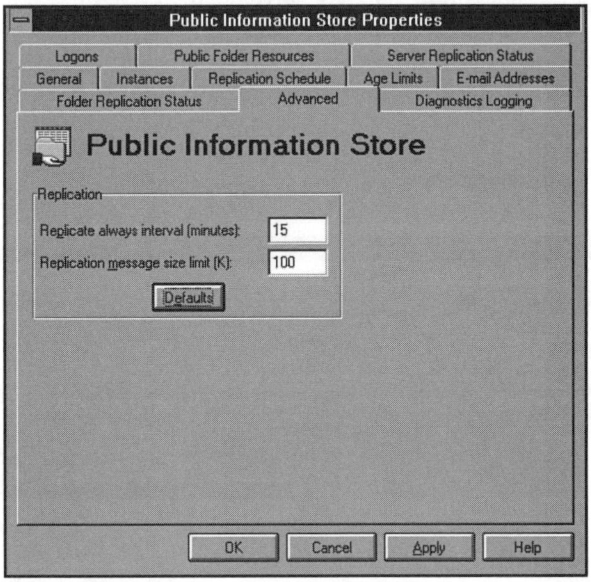

Public Information Store Properties
Logons
Public Folder Resources
Server Replication Status
General
Instances
Replication Schedule
Age Limits
E-mail Addresses
Folder Replication Status
Advanced
Diagnostics Logging
Public Information Store
Replication
Replicate always interval (minutes):
15
Replication message size limit (K):
100
Defaults
OK
Cancel
Apply
Help

Figure 9.36

The Advanced properties page.

Managing Public Folder Affinities

To manage affinities between public folders, access the properties page for the Information Store Site Configuration, found in the Configuration object in the Administrator program. Figure 9.37 shows you how to access this notebook.

Then, move to the Public Folder Affinity page shown in figure 9.38. You can select which sites have affinity with the site being administered and can assign a cost to each site.

In this example, public folder affinity has been defined with site NORTHWEST_US. You can also set a routing cost for each site, which controls the preference that will be used in connecting to a remote site; lower cost sites (those with more bandwidth to the current site) will be chosen preferentially to sites with a higher routing cost. Use the Set Value button to change the routing cost for a selected site.

Connecting an Exchange Server to another Exchange Server, or to another system, is only half the battle. Once your connection is established, you need to carry out a couple of additional steps to complete the job.

When connecting to a foreign (non-Exchange Server) e-mail system, you need to find a way to keep address lists on both systems synchronized. Dirsync requestors and servers are the best tools to use, provided the foreign system can use the MS Mail protocol to communicate changes.

Connecting two Exchange Server sites also requires that you establish replication for both directories and for public folders.

Figure 9.37

Accessing Information Store Site Configuration.

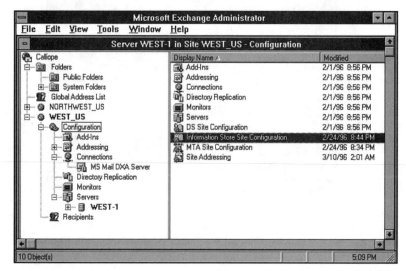

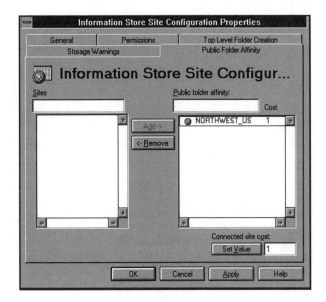

Figure 9.38

The Public Folders Affinity page.

CHAPTER **10**

Migrating Mailboxes

When creating new recipients for your new Exchange Server site as part of a migration, you can greatly speed the process by using the Import features available for creating new accounts. Using this method, you can edit or create a text file that contains all the recipients for your site and then import them all at once.

Creating Mailboxes

You can prepare a text file in a Comma Separated Value (CSV) format that contains all the needed information for each of your Exchange Server users. Then, by importing this file, you can rapidly create all the accounts you need. If you are setting up a new site with hundreds or thousands of users, this method will save you enormous amounts of time.

As a starting point for creating the import text file, consider these possible sources in your company:

◆ A file may be exported from your existing e-mail system. Remember, also, that most systems enable you to find a way to capture printer output to a file and then edit it, if necessary. On Novell systems, for example, the CAPTURE command can be used to redirect printer output to a file.

◆ A database or program in the payroll or human resource departments may be able to export a listing of all active employees in the company.

◆ If you maintain a company phone book listing all extensions in the company, consider using that file.

◆ Your telecommunications department may have an up-to-date listing of all employees.

◆ The network administrator may be able to create a listing of all system users that you can then modify.

Once you have a file that lists all mailboxes you want to create, your next step is to modify it so that Exchange Server can recognize its contents and use the file as a basis for creating new mailboxes.

Creating the Import File

Exchange Server can import an ASCII text file and create mailboxes based on entries in that file. Specific fields in the file are separated by commas. Quotation marks are not needed around any of the fields.

Use a comprehensive text editor, such as a programmer's text editor, to modify the source file into one that Exchange Server will recognize. Using the text editor's macro programming or recording features may also help speed the process.

Each line in the file is a record. Each piece of data between commas is a field in the file. The fields, in order of their appearance from left to right, are listed in table 10.1.

Table 10.1
Mailbox Import File Layout

Field Name	Contents
Obj-Class	The name of the object class that is being created. `Mailbox` is used for new mailboxes. `Remote` is used for custom addresses (addresses that are for external recipients) that you want to create in Exchange Server.
First Name	The user's first, or given, name.
Last Name	The user's last, or family, name.
Display Name	The user's name as it appears in the address book.
Alias Name	An alias for the user, which is usually used as the mailbox name. For instance, John Smith may have an alias of `JohnS`.
Directory Name	Typically, identical to the Alias Name.
Primary Windows NT Account	The account name for Windows NT in the form of `domain\account_name`. An example is `WEST_US\JohnS`.
Home-Server	The home Exchange Server for this user.
E-mail Address	Leave this field blank by adding a comma with no data between it and the preceding comma.
E-mail Addresses	In this field, enumerate the different addresses for the user. See following sections for more information on this field.
Members	A list of all the distribution lists to which this recipient belongs. See following sections for more information on this field.
Obj-Container	The container that holds this record. For mailboxes, this is `Recipients`.
Hide from AB	Short for Hide from Address Book, this entry is either blank if the recipient should not be hidden, or contains the number 1 if it should be hidden.

E-Mail Addresses Field

The E-mail Addresses field contains a listing that enumerates all the e-mail addresses for each recipient. Each address starts with its address type, such as `MS:`, `SMTP:`, or `X400:`. Note that each address type ends with a colon. The address information then follows the address type. A percent sign terminates each address entry on that line. You do not use a comma until you have completed the entire E-mail Addresses field (with all its entries) and are continuing on to the next field.

For example, consider the user John Smith. John has addresses defined in Exchange Server for MS Mail, Internet Mail, and an X.400 address. Here are the addresses for John:

◆ John Smith's MS-Mail address is

```
MS:CALLIOPE/WESTUS/JOHNS
```

◆ John Smith's SMTP address is

```
SMTP:JohnS@WEST_US.Calliope.com
```

◆ John Smith's X.400 address is

```
X400:c=US;p=Calliope;o=WEST?US;s=Smith;g=John;
```

John Smith's complete entry in the E-mail Addresses field would therefore be the following:

```
MS:CALLIOPE/WESTUS/
JOHNS%SMTP:JohnS@WEST_US.Calliope.com%X400:c=US;p=Calliope;o=WEST?US;s=Smith;g=John;
```

Members Field

The members field contains a list of all of the distribution lists to which the recipient belongs. Here is its format:

```
Recipients/cn=distribution_list1%Recipients/cn=distribution_list2
```

Note that each distribution list entry ends with a percent sign, except for the final entry that terminates with the comma for the field. Using this format, if John Smith belongs to the groups Everyone, WEST_OFFICE, and Engineers, his Members field would look like this:

```
Recipients/cn=Everyone%Recipients/cn=WEST_OFFICE%Recipients/cn=Engineers,
```

Note You cannot include new mailboxes in distribution lists that do not yet exist in Exchange Server. You must either first create the distribution lists in Exchange Server before importing the mailbox file, or you can include distribution list information at the top of the import file. See the section Creating Distribution Lists later in this chapter for information on including distribution list information in the import file.

Complete Example

The following file listings demonstrate how a complete import file might appear. Use this as a guide to building your own file.

```
Obj-Class,First Name,Last name,Display Name,Alias Name,Directory Name,[cr]

Primary Windows NT Account,Home-Server,E-mail address,E-mail Addresses,[cr]

Members,Obj-Container,Hide from AB[nl]

Mailbox,Bruce,Hallberg,Bruce Hallberg,BruceH,BruceH,WEST_US\BruceH,WEST-1,,[cr]

MS:CALLIOPE/WESTUS/BRUCEH%SMTP:BruceH@WEST_US.Calliope.com%X400:c=US;[cr]

a= ;p=Calliope;o=WEST?US;s=Hallberg;g=Bruce;i=A;,Recipients/cn=WEST_OFFICE%[cr]

Recipients/cn=Everyone,Recipients,0[nl]

Mailbox,David,Chernicoff,David Chernicoff,DavidC,DavidC,WEST_US\DavidC,WEST-
➡1,,[cr]

MS:CALLIOPE/WESTUS/DAVIDC%SMTP:DavidC@WEST_US.Calliope.com%X400:c=US;a= ;[cr]

p=Calliope;o=WEST?US;s=Chernicoff;g=David;,Recipients/cn=Everyone%[cr]

Recipients/cn=WEST_OFFICE,Recipients,[nl]

Mailbox,Kathy,Ivens,Kathy Ivens,KathyI,KathyI,WEST_US\KathyI,WEST-1,,[cr]

MS:CALLIOPE/WESTUS/KATHYI%SMTP:KathyI@WEST_US.Calliope.com%X400:c=US;a= ;[cr]

p=Calliope;o=WEST?US;s=Ivens;g=Kathy;,Recipients/cn=Everyone%[cr]

Recipients/cn=WEST_OFFICE,Recipients,[nl]

Mailbox,Emmett,Dulaney,Emmett Dulaney,EmmettD,EmmettD,BUILTIN\Guests,WEST-
➡1,,[cr]

MS:CALLIOPE/WESTUS/EMMETTD%SMTP:EmmettD@WEST_US.Calliope.com%X400:c=US;a= ;[cr]
```

```
p=Calliope;o=WEST?US;s=Dulaney;g=Emmett;,Recipients/cn=Everyone%[cr]

Recipients/cn=WEST_OFFICE,Recipients,[nl]

Mailbox,Becky,Campbell,Becky Campbell,BeckyC,BeckyC,BUILTIN\Guests,WEST-1,,[cr]

MS:CALLIOPE/WESTUS/BECKYC%SMTP:BeckyC@WEST_US.Calliope.com%X400:c=US;a= ;[cr]

p=Calliope;o=WEST?US;s=Campbell;g=Becky;i=J;,Recipients/cn=Everyone%[cr]

Recipients/cn=WEST_OFFICE,Recipients, [nl]

Remote,Administrative,,Administrative,Administrative,Administrative,,,[cr]

MS:CALLIOPE/MAIL-1/
Admin,SMTP:Administrative@WEST_US.Calliope.com%X400:c=US;[cr]

a= ;p=Calliope;o=WEST?US;s=Administrative;%MS:CALLIOPE/MAIL-1/Admin,,[cr]

Recipients,[nl]

Remote,Fred,Flintstone,Fred Flintstone,FredF,FredF,,,MS:CALLIOPE/WESTUS/
FREDF,[cr]

SMTP:FredF@WEST_US.Calliope.com%X400:c=US;a= ;p=Calliope;o=WEST?US;[cr]

s=Flintstone;g=Fred;%MS:CALLIOPE/WESTUS/FREDF,,Recipients,[nl]
```

Creating Distribution Lists

Just as you can import lists of mailboxes, you can also import distribution lists and have them created automatically. Use the fields listed in table 10.2 to create the fields for your distribution lists.

Table 10.2
Distribution List Import File Layout

Field Name	Contents
Obj-Class	The name of the object class that is being created. dl is used for new distribution lists.
First Name	Leave this field blank for distribution lists.
Last Name	Leave this field blank for distribution lists.

Field Name	Contents
Display Name	The display name for the distribution list.
Alias Name	The alias name for the distribution list, which is typically the same as the display name.
Directory Name	The directory name for the distribution list, which is typically the same as the display name.
Primary Windows NT Account	Leave this field blank for distribution lists.
Home-Server	Leave this field blank for distribution lists.
E-mail Address	Leave this field blank for distribution lists.
E-mail Addresses	In this field, you enumerate the different addresses for the distribution list. See following sections for more information on this field.
Members	A list of all the members that belong to this distribution list. See following sections for more information on this field.
Obj-Container	The container that holds this record. For distribution lists, this is `Recipients`.
Hide from AB	Short for Hide from Address Book, this entry is either blank if the distribution list should not be hidden, or contains the number1 if it should be hidden.

A distribution list called WEST_OFFICE would contain the following standard addresses:

◆ MS-Mail Address

```
MS:CALLIOPE/WESTUS/WESTOFFICE
```

◆ SMTP Address

```
SMTP:WEST_OFFICE@WEST_US.Calliope.com
```

◆ X.400 Address

```
X400:c=US;a=;p=Calliope;o=WEST?US;s=WEST?OFFICE;
```

Notice that MS-Mail addresses strip out nonalphanumeric characters, and X.400 addresses replace them with question marks.

Members Field

The Members field for distribution list entries lists all members of the distribution list and their mailbox containers. Each entry terminates with a percent sign, except the last one. Here is an example of a listing that references each member of the distribution list:

```
Recipients/cn=BruceH%Recipients/cn=DavidC%Recipients/cn=KathyI%Recipients/
cn=EmmettD%Recipients/cn=BeckyC
```

Complete Example

The following is a complete example of a distribution list import file:

```
Obj-Class,First Name,Last name,Display Name,Alias Name,Directory Name,[cr]

Primary Windows NT Account,Home-Server,E-mail address,E-mail Addresses,[cr]

Members,Obj-Container,Hide from AB[nl]

dl,,,WEST_COAST,WEST_COAST,Everyone,,,,MS:CALLIOPE/WESTUS/EVERYONE%[cr]

SMTP:Everyone@WEST_US.Calliope.com%X400:c=US;a= ;p=Calliope;o=WEST?US;[cr]

s=Everyone;,Recipients/cn=BruceH%Recipients/cn=DavidC%Recipients[cr]

/cn=KathyI%Recipients/cn=EmmettD%Recipients/cn=BeckyC,Recipients,[nl]

dl,,,WEST_OFFICE,WEST_OFFICE,WEST_OFFICE,,,,MS:CALLIOPE/WESTUS/WESTOFFICE%[cr]

SMTP:WEST_OFFICE@WEST_US.Calliope.com%X400:c=US;a= ;p=Calliope;o=WEST?US;[cr]

s=WEST?OFFICE;,Recipients/cn=BruceH%Recipients/cn=DavidC%Recipients[cr]

/cn=KathyI%Recipients/cn=EmmettD%Recipients/cn=BeckyC,Recipients,[nl]
```

Combining Import Files

You can combine the import files for both distribution lists and mailboxes into a single file. To do this, your file should be organized like this:

◆ In the first line, list all the fields, just as was shown in the preceding Complete Examples.

◆ The second set of lines should include the distribution lists.

◆ The third set of lines should include the recipient mailboxes.

Notice that you can define distribution group membership in two places. First, each recipient mailbox has a field that lists all the groups to which they belong. Second, each distribution list lists all the recipients that are members. You do not need to duplicate these fields. For instance, you can leave out the member lists from the distribution group records, and then simply include membership information in the mailbox records. The key thing to avoid is adding mailboxes that reference distribution lists that don't yet exist.

Importing the Data

Once you finish creating your import file and have saved it to a directory accessible to Exchange Server (with whatever file name you like), you perform the import using the Tools menu in the Exchange Server Administrator program. Choose Directory Import from the menu. This displays the Directory Import dialog box shown in figure 10.1.

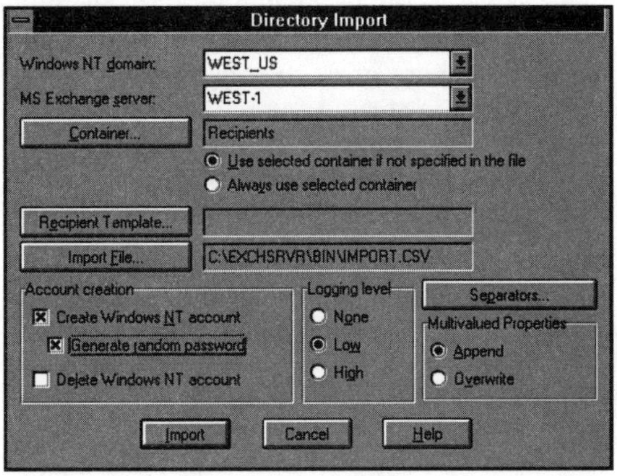

Figure 10.1

The Directory Import dialog box.

Choose the appropriate Windows NT domain and MS Exchange server in the top two fields of the dialog box. Using the Container button, select the Exchange Server container into which to add the imported mailboxes. Note that you can use the Use selected container if not specified in the file to choose a default container; the container specified in the file will override the container specified with the Container button.

If there is a template that should be used to create the new mailboxes, select it with the R<u>e</u>cipient Template button.

 Note Templates define what information recipient objects hold. You can have many different templates, if you like. The standard templates are found within the Addressing container in the Exchange Administrator program.

Choose the import file you created with the Import **F**ile button, which then displays a standard File Open dialog box from which to select the file.

Account Creation contains checkbox fields that enable you to choose to create appropriate Windows NT accounts automatically for each recipient so that they can log into the Exchange Server computer. If you choose to create random passwords, they will be stored in a file called *filename*.PSW where *filename* matches your import filename. You are told what this filename is when the import completes. Figure 10.2 shows you an example of the random passwords generated in a file called IMPORT.PSW. You can view this file with NOTEPAD and can then communicate the generated passwords to the new recipients. If you do not choose to create random passwords, the user's username is used for the password.

The Logging Level of the Directory Import dialog box controls the log entries created by the import process. Log entries are viewed in the Windows NT Event Viewer. A level of N<u>o</u>ne causes no logging. A level of Lo<u>w</u> causes only the beginning and ending of the import process to be logged, plus any error messages. A level of Hi<u>g</u>h causes a log entry to be entered for each recipient created.

Figure 10.2

The IMPORT.PSW file.

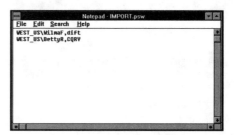

Multivalued Properties refers to both the E-mail Addresses and Members fields of the import file. If you choose **A**ppend, the entries in those two fields will be added to an existing recipient. Choosing O**v**erwrite causes those two fields to replace any existing information.

Finally, if your file uses separators different from commas, you can select those separators with the dialog box displayed by clicking on the Se**p**arators button.

PART IV

Administering Exchange Server

CHAPTER **11**

Backing Up and Restoring

Hard drives die. Machines crash. Files and directories get corrupted or are accidentally deleted. You can't prevent these things, but you can recover from them. Design a backup scheme and use it.

Backing up Microsoft Exchange Server is a bit different from doing your usual backup of software and data files, but the principles you put into place for your backup strategy are the same.

As you plan your backups, remember that it's not important that the backup be quick, simple, fast, or easy. It's important that you have a backup system that makes *restoring your servers easy* so you can get everybody back to work in the shortest amount of time in the event of a catastrophe.

The easiest way to restore data after a hard drive has gone to hard drive heaven, or a computer has exploded, or some other devastating misadventure has taken place, is to put a tape into a drive, load software, and click on a button titled Restore. If everything that was on the original drive is on the tape, it won't take very long to be back in business.

Using Windows NT Backup Software

The best way to back up your Microsoft Exchange system is to use the Windows NT Backup application. When you installed Microsoft Exchange Server, additional features for the Windows NT Tape Backup software were also installed. This addition to the NT Backup application contains a component that is specifically designed for backing up Microsoft Exchange Server components. In fact, regular third-party backup software cannot handle the needs required to back up your Microsoft Exchange Server system. (As of this writing, several backup software companies are planning to release new software with the necessary features for backing up Microsoft Exchange Server.)

Warning If you get a patch or update, or have to reinstall your Windows NT system, be sure to check whether the original NT Backup software was reinstalled. If so, you have to reinstall Microsoft Exchange Server in order to put the Exchange Server-aware features back into the NT Backup software.

When you launch Windows NT Backup, you see a new window in addition to the original NT Backup window. This is the Microsoft Exchange Organization window, and it displays the organization, sites, and servers on your system (see fig. 11.1).

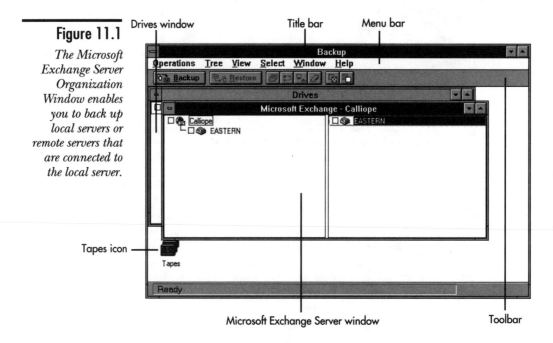

Figure 11.1

The Microsoft Exchange Server Organization Window enables you to back up local servers or remote servers that are connected to the local server.

Drives window   Title bar   Menu bar

Tapes icon

Microsoft Exchange Server window   Toolbar

If the Microsoft Exchange Organization window is not displayed in the Backup window, its icon (bearing the organization name) should be. Double-click on it to display the window.

Understanding the Rules

Before you start using the Windows NT Backup software, there are a few things you should know about the software and its relationship to your system:

◆ You must be logged in with an account that has backup permissions for every server you are backing up.

◆ The directory of a server is specific to that server and cannot be restored to another server that is part of a replication group.

◆ You cannot split the private and public information stores, but must back them up as a single entity. You can, however, restore them separately.

◆ During the backup procedure, users can continue to work on the server being backed up.

◆ If there is a problem with backing up any component on any server, an error message will display, then the backup will continue. To see more detailed explanations of any backup problems, you look at the Applications Event Log in the Windows NT Event Viewer.

Understanding Backup Types

There are four types of backups you can perform when backing up your Microsoft Exchange server. This is slightly different from the "normal" Windows NT Backup software, which provides five backup types. The missing type is the type named Daily. With the Daily backup option in NT, you back up only files that have been modified that day, and there is no attribute applied to indicate that the file has been backed up. With Windows NT, this is useful for users who want to back up the files they worked on during the day so that they can take them home to continue their work. Because a backup of a Microsoft Exchange server is centered around components rather than files, this option isn't viable.

Normal Backup

A Normal backup is a full backup. All the Microsoft Exchange components are backed up, and the disk is marked to indicate that the full backup was made (useful for future incremental backups). This is not just a matter of copying some files, however. It's far more complicated and ingenious.

The Microsoft Exchange backup feature understands the transaction logs and database functions of the Microsoft Exchange components. (Detailed information about these components are found in Chapter 13, "Administering the Core Components.") One of the procedures performed during a Normal backup is cleaning up the transaction logs by erasing log files that contain data that has been committed to the database. The deletion is made, of course, after all the transaction logs and database file have been copied to tape.

If users continue to perform transactions during the backup procedure, Microsoft Exchange uses a temporary patch file as the transaction log, and the backup program looks for it at the end of the backup procedure and backs it up.

 It's important to invoke a Normal backup occasionally (if your standard backup type is not Normal) in order to delete the transaction logs. It is not advisable to delete these logs manually.

Copy Backup

A Copy backup is a backup of all Microsoft Exchange components. The disk is not marked, however, so any subsequent incremental or differential backups are not affected.

Incremental Backup

An Incremental backup is a backup of Microsoft Exchange components that have been modified since the last backup. The backup is indicated on the disk, and log files with transactions that have been sent to the database are deleted.

Differential Backup

A Differential backup is the same as an Incremental backup, except the disk is not marked. The transaction log files are not deleted, regardless of whether their data has been committed to the database.

| Note | Neither Incremental Backup nor Differential Backup are available if you enabled circular logging. More information about circular logging can be found in Chapter 13, but it's probably beneficial to discuss it briefly here so you can understand its relationship to your backup strategies. |

Circular logging means that transaction logs are overwritten as their data is committed to the database. This prevents a large buildup of transaction log files on the disk.

The downside is that if there is a disk disaster you can restore only back to the last Normal (full) backup.

You will have lost the ability to restore transaction logs. That can mean a significant loss of data, because during the recovery process the database uses the log files to re-create itself.

If you are worried about disk storage space, the ideal solution is to enable circular logging and do Normal backups regularly.

Understanding What Is Backed Up

When you back up your Microsoft Exchange system, you won't see filenames scrolling across the backup software window, the way you do when you normally back up your software and data files. Although files are being backed up, they are separated into the various Microsoft Exchange Server components, and it is, technically, the components that are backed up.

In this section, you take a brief look at the components that are backed up.

Transaction Logs

The Windows NT Backup software, as modified by Microsoft Exchange Server, understands the way transaction logs work and backs them up. If you perform a Normal backup, all the transaction logs that have transferred their data to the database are deleted after they are backed up.

When message transactions occur, they are written to a transaction log and then later copied to the Microsoft Exchange Server database. This enables uninterrupted use of the system, because the database is in use only when the system determines there is an opportunity to write to it, using a typical cache-write system.

There is an ordered sequence to the transaction logs, which grow to 5 MB each—when that size is reached, a new log file is automatically created:

◆ The current log file is named EDB.LOG, and it contains the most recent transactions in your Microsoft Exchange Server system.

◆ The previous log files are named consecutively EDB*XXXXX*.LOG (where *X* is a hex number between 0 and f).

◆ There are two files, named RES1.LOG and RES2.LOG, that are placed on the disk to reserve space. If the hard drive containing the database or log files fills up, the chances of having your data corrupted when there is an "out of space" error during a transaction is minimized.

In case you're curious about the procedures, the data in the transaction log file is written to the database on a continuous basis, which means the data in the historical logs is probably no longer needed.

In fact, in a busy system, with lots of transactions and substantial durations of time between the writes to the database, there are probably occasions when messages have been read, responded to, and forgotten before they are sent from the transaction log to the database.

Understanding the Databases

There are three databases on each Microsoft Exchange Server:

◆ SYSTEM.EDB, which is the primary database for the server's information stores

◆ PRIV.EDB, the private information store database, which is a subdatabase of SYSTEM.EDB

◆ PUB.EDB, the public information store database, which is also a subdatabase of SYSTEM.EDB

Microsoft Exchange Server sees PRIV.EDB and PUB.EDB as one unit.

The directory has two databases:

◆ SYSTEM.EDB (a different database from the one described previously in the section on the databases), which stores the objects in the directory

◆ DIR.EDB, which is the database that stores all the details about the objects in your Microsoft Exchange Server system

During backup of the information store (\EXCHSRVR\MDBDATA) and directory (EXCHSRVR\DSADATA), the files that are backed up differ, depending upon the type of backup you are performing.

For a Normal or Copy backup type, the database files, which have the extension EDB, are backed up. Restoring the backup restores the database.

For an Incremental or Differential backup type, the logs, which have the extension LOG, are backed up. Restoring the backup restores the log files, from which the database can be re-created.

 The database is re-created from an Incremental or Differential backup in an interesting way. When you restore the log files, they actually run the transactions in order to force a write to the database. Eventually, when every transaction is run, the database reflects the events in the log.

Backing Up

Making a backup involves the following steps:

1. From the NT Backup window, select the organization, site, or server(s) you wish to back up by clicking on the check box to the left of the appropriate object or by highlighting the object and choosing **C**heck from the **S**elect menu.

2. Click on the Backup icon on the Toolbar or choose **B**ackup from the **O**perations menu.

You can use these normal Windows NT Tape Backup software features for your Microsoft Exchange Server backup functions:

◆ Compress files

◆ Set tape options to Append or Replace

◆ Name tapes

◆ Choose to verify the backup against the original files

◆ Back up the local registry

◆ Restrict access to the tape

◆ Establish logging

Choosing the Exchange Servers to Back Up

You can back up based on a selection of an organization, a specific site in the organization, or a specific server.

Regardless of the hierarchical level you select, it is the directory and information
stores of the Exchange servers that are backed up. Because these are the objects
needed to use Microsoft Exchange Server, they are the only objects of interest to the
backup software application.

 If your Microsoft Exchange servers contain other important data (for instance,
application files) you should use either the "normal" Windows NT Tape Backup
software or a third-party application to perform a backup of those files. Do such
backups in addition to the Microsoft Exchange Server backup, however, so that you
have specific tapes for restoring the Microsoft Exchange Server system.

The choices about what to back up depend on your organization's configuration:

◆ If you select an organization, all the attached servers in the organization will be
backed up.

 You can back up only those servers that share direct network connectivity.

◆ If you select a site and there are multiple servers on that site, the directory and
information stores for each server will be backed up discretely.

◆ If you select a specific server, that is the only set of directory and information
stores that will be backed up, even though it might have direct connections to
other servers.

Connecting to a Server

If the computer on which you are running NT Backup is not a Microsoft Exchange
server, you have to connect to the server you want to back up. When you do that, you
can back up all the servers in your organization to which your Microsoft Exchange
server directly connects.

 Of course, without a Microsoft Exchange Server installation, the NT Backup
software won't have the appropriate features for backing up the databases. You
have to install the additional backup software onto the NT server from which you
perform the backup.

Here are the steps:

1. Choose **M**icrosoft Exchange from the **O**perations menu to bring up the Microsoft Exchange dialog box (see fig. 11.2).

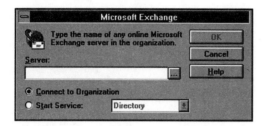

Figure 11.2

Connect to any Microsoft Exchange server in your organization to perform a backup of the Microsoft Exchange databases and transaction logs.

2. Enter the name of the server to which you want to connect. If you don't remember the exact name, click on the button to the right of the **S**erver box to see a list of all the accessible servers in your organization.

3. Choose OK to complete the connection.

Using a Batch File

If you want to save some time and mouse-clicks, you can write a batch file. You can attach it to an icon for even faster access.

Here is the syntax for a simple batch file that works for a Microsoft Exchange Server backup:

```
ntbackup operation component \\server /a/v/r/d ["text"]/hc:on/off/t/[option]/
l["filename"]/e
```

On my system, the batch file reads as follows:

```
ntbackup backup DS \\east /hc:on
ntbackup backup IS \\east /hc:on /a
```

The following summarize an analysis of the syntax:

◆ *operation* is backup.

◆ *component* is DS (for directory) or IS (for information store).

◆ *server* is the name of the server you want to back up and must be preceded by two backslash characters.

◆ /a appends the backup to the last backup set on the tape.

◆ /v specifies a verification process after the backup is completed.

◆ /r restricts access to the tape.

◆ /d ["text"] uses the specified text as a description for the backup set (you must use the quotation marks).

◆ /hc:on or /hc:off specifies hardware compression or the lack of it.

◆ /t[option] specifies a backup type.

◆ /l[filename] specifies a filename for a backup log.

◆ /e instructs the program to list only exceptions (files that failed to be backed up) in the backup log.

> **Note** When you use Windows NT Backup, there are two backup sets—one for the information store (IS) and one for the directory (DS). Write a batch file that calls for the backup of one component followed by the backup of the next. Make sure the second component is backed up with the /a option so that it is appended to the end of the first (otherwise, it will overwrite it).

Restoring

There are three basic scenarios that may require a restore operation:

◆ File corruption and other problems on a server require a restore of the Microsoft Exchange Server data.

◆ A major disaster occurs, requiring a new computer installation followed by a restore of the Microsoft Exchange Server data.

◆ Specific messages have become corrupted or have disappeared (or been erased) and have to be restored.

For the first two scenarios, the restore process differs, depending upon the backup types available:

◆ If your last backup was a Normal backup or a Copy backup, that backup tape is all you need to restore your system.

◆ If your last backup was an Incremental or Differential backup, you have to go back to the last Normal backup and restore that first. Then you have to restore each incremental backup made after the Normal backup. The tapes have to be restored in the same order in which they were made.

◆ If a directory for a server needs to be restored, any changes that occurred since the directory was backed up will be replicated from the other servers online (unless there is only one server, in which case the tape is all you have).

 Restoring a directory is a server-specific function. You cannot restore the directory that was backed up from one server onto a different server.

Restoring to the Original Server

There are a few tasks to take care of before you restore a tape backup set.

First, you have to fix the computer problem that caused the situation.

Then, if you are going to restore a directory or information store, each service currently being run on the server must be stopped before you can begin the restore process.

Now you can begin the restore, following these steps:

1. Open the Windows NT Administrative Tools program group, then open Windows NT Backup.

2. In the Tape window, select the tape(s) you want to restore. (If the Tape window is not open, double-click on the Tapes icon.)

3. Choose **R**estore from the **O**perations menu, or click on the **R**estore button on the toolbar.

4. Restore the data.

5. Run the DS/IS consistency adjustment tool (see Understanding the DS/IS Tool, later in this chapter).

There are several options for restoring tapes to a server:

◆ Erase All Existing Data deletes any data on the drive that is related to the information contained on the tape. This is most useful if the data is being restored to a different server, but you can choose this option if you want to delete database information currently on the hard drive.

◆ Private and Public are options available when you are restoring the information store. You can choose both the private and public information store databases, or just one of them. Remember that when you back up, you cannot separate them—you can restore them separately (in case only one is corrupted and needs restoring).

◆ Start Service After Restore automatically starts the information store or directory service after the restore is completed; otherwise, you have to start the service manually.

◆ Verify After Restore verifies the contents of the disk against the tape and logs any exceptions in a file named BACKUP.LOG.

Restoring to a New Server

If you had a complete and utter disaster on a server and have to replace the hard drive or the entire computer, follow these steps to restore your Microsoft Exchange Server data:

1. Install Windows NT on the new or repaired server. (You may have to delete the Windows NT account and re-create it—in fact it's a good idea to do that automatically rather than waiting for an error.)

2. Install Microsoft Exchange Server on the new or repaired server. During configuration, do not let it participate in the replication process until you have finished all the restore tasks. Run setup\R.

3. Give the server its original organization and site name.

4. Restore the directory from the last backup tape(s).

5. Restore the private/public information store from the last backup tape(s).

6. Run the DS/IS consistency adjustment tool (see Understanding the DS/IS Tool, later in this chapter).

Restoring Specific Messages

Restoring a backup replaces the existing components, so if you're just trying to restore specific data from the information store you have to take some special steps.

You have to restore the information store to a separate computer, one with the hardware required to run a Microsoft Exchange Server. Do not use an existing, working server. To restore to a different computer, follow these steps:

1. Install Microsoft Exchange Server on this computer. Make sure the organization and site names are the same as the server whose backup you are going to restore. To avoid confusion, however, give it a unique computer name.

2. Restore the information store to the new server.

3. Give yourself all the appropriate permissions for the mailbox you want to restore if you are restoring a private folder. You can use any mailbox if you are restoring a public folder.

4. Log on to the server from a Microsoft Exchange Client, and then place the items to be restored into a PST file (use a new *filename*.pst). This PST file must be accessible by the original server.

5. Go to the original server and move the messages from the PST file onto the online server.

Remember, this does not work for backups of the Microsoft Exchange Server directories, which are computer-specific and cannot be restored to another computer.

Understanding the DS/IS Tool

A server's directory (DS) stores the properties for mailboxes and public folders. A server's information stores (IS) hold the mailboxes and public folders and the contents of both. These entities are linked and they have to be consistent.

If there is a mailbox entry or a public folder in the directory that does not exist in the information store (or the other way around), that inconsistency has to be resolved.

Inconsistencies usually occur after a restore process, and Microsoft Exchange Server system provides the DS/IS Consistency Adjustment tool to resolve them.

Understanding DS/IS Actions

For every inconsistency found, the DS/IS tool takes one of three actions, depending upon the type of inconsistency encountered:

◆ Deletes an entry

◆ Creates an entry

◆ Issues a report so you can make an adjustment

If there is a public folder or mailbox in the information store with no entry in the directory, a directory entry is created.

If there is a public folder in the directory with no entry in the information store, the directory entry is deleted. However, if there is a mailbox entry in the directory with no entry in the information store, no action is taken (mailboxes are never removed during a DS/IS adjustment).

If there are invalid users (users who no longer exist) attached to public folder permissions, those users are removed.

If there are public folders that have no owners, a report is issued indicating that fact.

Running the DS/IS Tool

To run the DS/IS Consistency Adjustment tool, follow these steps:

1. From the Microsoft Exchange Server Administrator window, highlight the server that needs to be checked.

2. Choose **P**roperties from the **F**ile menu.

3. Move to the Advanced property page (see fig. 11.3).

Figure 11.3

Use the DS/IS selection to make the entries in the directory and the information store consistent.

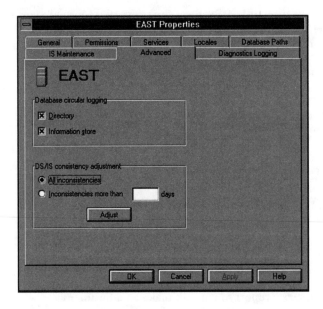

4. Choose a method for adjusting any inconsistencies:

   ◆ Choose A**l**l inconsistencies to adjust all the consistencies found.

   ◆ Choose **I**nconsistencies more than (days) and specify a number of days to adjust only inconsistencies that are older than the specified number.

You must use the A**l**l inconsistencies choice if you have not used the DS/IS tool before. The timestamps that are used are those left behind by the last DS/IS adjustment. If this is the first time you ran the tool, those timestamps do not exist.

If you have run the DS/IS tool before, you may not specify a number of days that is smaller than the number of days that has elapsed since your last use of the tool. The number of days you specify must be at least as many days since the last inconsistencies check so that the timestamp does not fall within the time frame window you are specifying.

Choosing a specific number of days is useful if you believe that some of the recent inconsistencies don't need adjustment because they will be corrected during the next replication event. Recently created entries that are inconsistent won't be deleted and will probably be resolved during replication. If not, they will be taken care of during the next DS/IS adjustment you perform.

5. Click on the Adjust button to begin.

When the process has completed, check the Windows NT Event Viewer, selecting the **A**pplication log from the **L**og menu. Inconsistencies that are not resolved by the DS/IS program will be displayed, and you can decide if and what you want to do about them.

Some of the reported inconsistencies won't necessarily require any action but others might:

◆ Reporting that no user has ever sent messages to a specific mailbox may be caused by the fact that the user no longer exists (corporately speaking, of course). If so, you can delete the mailbox.

◆ A reported missing owner for a public folder can be remedied by adding an owner. Remember that public folders are created at client workstations and owners can be entered only there. (There are other permissions and configuration options you can adjust on a public folder from the server.)

CHAPTER 12

Mailbox Administration

The mailbox is probably the most used, most important, and most basic element in your Microsoft Exchange system. It receives messages and attachments to messages for the owner (or owners, because you can have more than one user assigned to an individual mailbox).

Mailboxes are part of the private information store, and you can create folders within a mailbox if users want to sort and organize the messages and files they receive.

Creating Mailboxes

There are two ways to create a Microsoft Exchange Server mailbox:

◆ By using the Windows NT User Manager, if the mailbox is being assigned to a user new to your NT system

◆ By using the Microsoft Exchange Server Administrator program, if you are creating a mailbox for an existing Windows NT user

Whichever way you begin, the process is the same. Once the mailbox is created, you also have to establish properties for it. That configuration step is discussed in the section of this chapter entitled Setting General Mailbox Properties.

Creating a Mailbox for a New User

If you want to create mailboxes for new users automatically, you first have to make sure your system is configured to perform all the necessary steps:

1. From the Windows NT Program Manager, open the Administrative Tools program group, then open User Manager to see the User Manager dialog box for your domain (see fig. 12.1).

Figure 12.1

The User Manager dialog box lets you administer domains, groups, and user accounts.

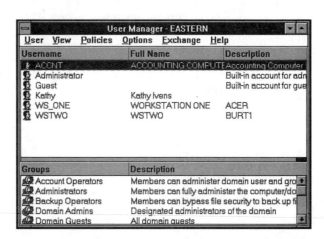

2. Choose **O**ptions from the **E**xchange menu to establish the protocols you need to create an automatic relationship between your new Windows NT users and your Microsoft Exchange Server system mailboxes (see fig. 12.2):

◆ Enable Always **c**reate an Exchange mailbox to have any new users receive a Microsoft Exchange Server mailbox as soon as they are established in your NT system.

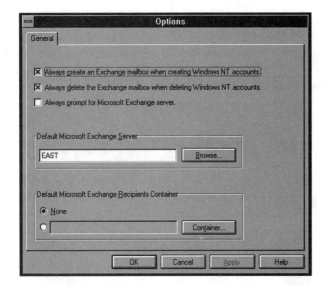

Figure 12.2

*You can configure
your Windows
NT system to
create and remove
mailboxes as your
users are added or
deleted.*

◆ Enable Always **d**elete the Exchange mailbox if you want to delete the
   mailbox when the user is deleted from your system (this also removes any
   messages in the mailbox).

◆ Enable Always **p**rompt if you want to be asked which server you want to
   connect to for this user's mailbox. If all your users will have their mailbox
   objects placed on the current server, you can deselect this option.

◆ In the Default Microsoft Exchange **S**erver box, enter the name of the
   server that will hold the new mailbox.

◆ If you want to create a new/different Default Microsoft Exchange **R**ecipi-
   ents Container (instead of the system default, which is in the Recipients
   object), enter a Con**t**ainer name.

Now, whenever you add a user, you also automatically create a mailbox in your
Microsoft Exchange system. A Properties dialog box for the new mailbox is displayed
when the new user is created so that you can configure the mailbox.

Creating a Mailbox for an Existing User

If you're creating mailboxes as part of your configuration for your new Microsoft
Exchange Server system, or if you chose not to create mailboxes for new NT users
automatically, you use Microsoft Exchange administrative tools to create mailboxes:

1. Open the Microsoft Exchange program group, then open Microsoft Exchange
   Administrator.

2. Choose New **M**ailbox from the **F**ile menu to begin to configure the mailbox.

If the Server window displayed in your Microsoft Exchange Administrator window has an object highlighted, that object is the current parent container. To create a mailbox, you must be working in the Recipients container of the current site. If you're not there, Microsoft Exchange Server displays a dialog box asking whether you want to switch to the appropriate container.

Setting General Mailbox Properties

Regardless of whether you're creating a mailbox for a new user or an existing one, you have to configure the mailbox for the user. Once you follow either of these protocols to create a mailbox, the General tab of the Mailbox Properties dialog box is displayed (see fig. 12.3).

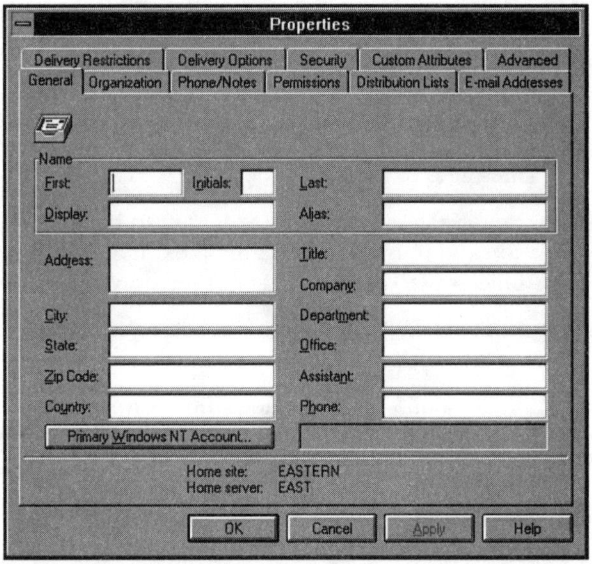

Figure 12.3

Use the General property page to establish the mailbox name and any optional information about the user you feel you need to track.

Only a few of the fields are required, but you might want to make a company policy decision about which of the optional fields you'd like to use in order to have the information. Let's go over the fields on the General page.

The Name Section

The Name section at the top of the General properties page is for information about the user connected to this mailbox:

◆ **F**irst Name is an optional field that can have up to 32 characters.

◆ **In**itials is an optional field that can have up to 2 characters.

◆ **L**ast Name is an optional field that can have up to 64 characters.

◆ **D**isplay is required and is the name that appears in the system's Address Book and in the list displayed when you open the Microsoft Exchange Server Administrator program. It can have up to 256 characters.

◆ **Al**ias name is required and is used in e-mail addresses that are outside the Microsoft Exchange Server system. It can have up to 64 characters. Remember, some external e-mail systems restrict this field to 8 characters, no spaces.

The Address Section

The entire address section is optional, and each organization makes its own rules about which of the fields, if any, should be filled in. If there are occasions when certain portions of the address section are useful, be sure to enter data in those fields.

Primary Windows NT Account

The Primary **W**indows NT Account is the primary user account connected to this mailbox and is a required entry. This is the person who will be the main user of the mailbox (remember, you can assign multiple users to a mailbox). The primary user automatically has full mailbox owner permissions for sending and receiving messages.

Click on the selection button to see the Primary Windows NT Account dialog box (see fig. 12.4).

If the mailbox is for an existing user, choose **S**elect an existing Windows NT account, then choose OK. A list of users is displayed so that you can pick the one you need.

If you have to create a new NT account as you're creating this mailbox, choose the **C**reate option to display the Create Windows NT Account dialog box (see fig. 12.5).

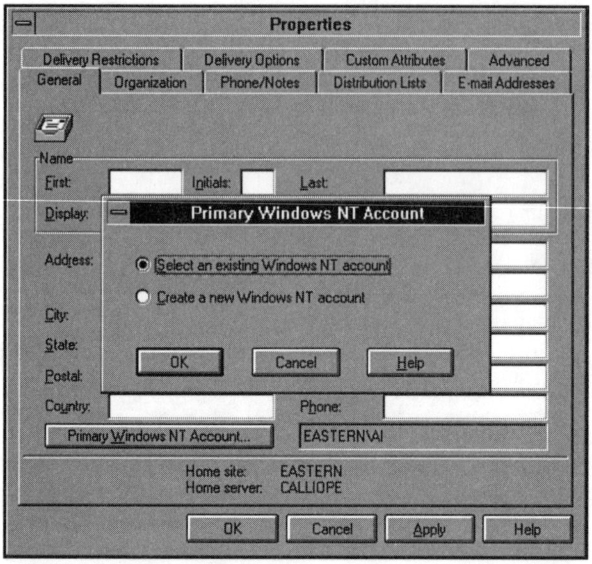

Figure 12.4

Attach a new mailbox to an existing user or create a user to assign to the mailbox.

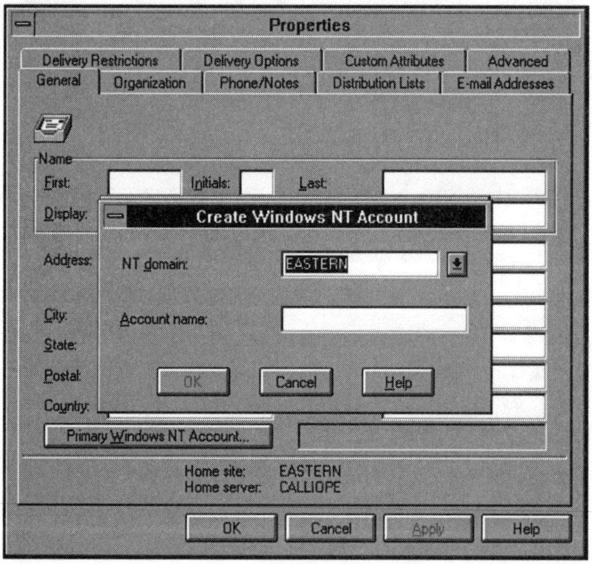

Figure 12.5

You can add a new user to your NT system as you're creating mailboxes.

Adding Users to Existing Mailboxes

Multiple users can be given access to a mailbox, which is useful if you find it productive to create mailboxes for departments or resources (such as libraries or conference rooms).

 On my system, I have a mailbox for certain workstations that are shared by several users. For example, one workstation has a local printer that holds company checks, and the room is kept locked with only authorized personnel holding keys. This is a good way to secure checks, and we found it a better solution than keeping the checks locked up until needed. The staff found it annoying to go through the trouble of getting the checks and loading them into the printer when there was an unexpected need to write one (for instance, when a COD delivery arrived). We made everything more productive by locking up the checks at night, loading them in the morning, and keeping the room locked during the day.

Company protocols require that users check the workstation's mailbox in case there are any messages regarding the tasks performed at that workstation. Frequently, there are notes regarding payments, such as instructions to make only a partial payment to a vendor or to put a vendor's invoice on hold. Sometimes there's an expense report from an employee that requests a check for reimbursement (of course, the paperwork has to be handed in before the check is delivered).

To give additional users access to an existing mailbox:

1. Open the Microsoft Exchange program group, then open Microsoft Exchange Administrator.

2. Click on the appropriate Domain object, then select the Recipients object to display the domain recipients in the right panel.

3. Choose **M**ailboxes from the **V**iew menu to change the display in the right panel to a view of the existing mailboxes (see fig. 12.6).

4. Highlight the mailbox you want to reconfigure, then choose **P**roperties from the **F**ile menu (or double-click on the mailbox listing) to display the mailbox Properties dialog box.

5. Click on the Permissions tab to see the dialog box shown in figure 12.7. (If you don't see a Permissions tab, please read the Note on that subject in this section.)

Figure 12.6

You can display the list of existing mailboxes, then select one and change its configuration.

Figure 12.7

Use the Permissions property page to add users to an existing mailbox.

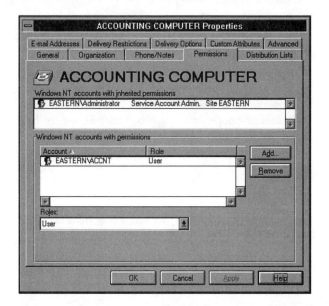

Note   When you install Microsoft Exchange Server, the Permissions tab of the Mailbox Properties is hidden by default. To see it and access it, use the Options choice on the **T**ools menu of the Exchange Administrator window. Move to the Permissions tab and select **S**how Permissions page for all objects.

Be sure to select Display **r**ights for roles on the Permissions page, because you'll want to be able to see that information if you want to configure rights for users (discussed later in this section).

6. Choose A**d**d to display a list of domain users in the Add Users and Groups dialog box (see fig. 12.8).

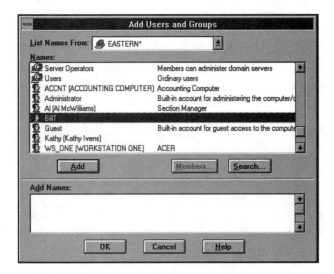

Figure 12.8

All the users and groups in the current domain are displayed so that you can choose additional users for the mailbox you're configuring.

7. Select the user or group you want to give access to this mailbox and choose **A**dd. You can repeat this to add additional users from the list. Choose OK when you finish.

 If you're adding multiple users to a mailbox, after you select the first one, you can continue to highlight users or groups without choosing **A**dd each time by holding down the control key as you click on each name.

If there is a group of contiguous names, you can drag your mouse.

When you complete your selection of additional users, the A**d**d Names section of the dialog box displays your list, and you can remove anyone you added in error (or changed your mind about).

Choose OK when you are satisfied with your list of additional mailbox users.

Configuring Permissions

You can use the Permissions tab to change the rights or permissions for a user (this chapter uses the words "rights" and "permissions" interchangeably). The permissions for the mailbox are designated by assigning roles.

Understanding Roles

Roles are pretty much what you'd expect—in Microsoft Exchange Server the word role is used to define the role a user plays in the administration and use of a mailbox. Each role contains within its definition one or more specific rights to the mailbox. Therefore, you give certain permissions to users by assigning them a role that has those permissions built in.

There are predefined roles, and you can also customize a role for any user, assigning whatever specific rights and permissions that user might need.

The predefined roles and inherent permissions are shown in Table 12.1.

TABLE 12.1
Permissions for Predefined Roles

Role	Permissions
Admin	Modify User Attributes; Modify Admin Attributes
Permissions Admin	Modify User Attributes; Modify Admin Attributes; Modify Permissions
Send As	Send As
User	Modify User Attributes; Send As; Mailbox Owner

Modify User Attributes means you can change any of the user attributes associated with the mailbox object.

Modify Admin Attributes means you can modify the administrator attributes that are associated with the mailbox object.

Send As means you can send messages as the owner (or another authorized recipient) of this mailbox. When you do send a message from this mailbox, a recipient can't tell that the message has been sent by someone other than the user whose name is attached to the mailbox.

 Note   Send As is not the same as Send On Behalf Of (discussed later in the Send On Behalf Of section), which permits one user to send messages for another user, but the sending user's name appears on the message.

Mailbox Owner means you have message sending and receiving rights to this mailbox object.

Modify Permissions means you can access the settings in the Permissions tab of the properties dialog box and make any changes you wish.

Changing a User's Role

You can change the role of any user attached to a mailbox:

1. Highlight the mailbox and choose **P**roperties from the **F**ile menu (or double-click on the mailbox listing).

2. Move to the Permissions tab and select (highlight) the user you want to change.

3. Click on the arrow to the right of the Ro**l**es box and select a role for this user (see fig. 12.9).

Figure 12.9

You can change a user's role for this mailbox by simply selecting the user, then selecting the new role.

Creating a Custom Role

If you have a user for whom you want to give permissions that don't match any of the permutations and combinations available in the defined Roles, you can create a Custom Role for this user:

1. Highlight the mailbox and choose **P**roperties from the **F**ile menu (or double-click on the mailbox listing).

2. Move to the Permissions tab and select (highlight) the user you want to change. The current role for this user is displayed in the Ro**l**es box, and the Ri**g**hts box shows the permissions that are inherent in this role.

If the Ri**g**hts box isn't visible, change the options for displaying the Permissions tab as described in a Note in the Adding Users to Existing Mailboxes section earlier in this chapter.

3. Select or deselect permissions as you wish. The role listed next to the account name in the Windows NT accounts with **p**ermissions box changes to Custom.

There are a couple of things you should be aware of about custom roles. First, each custom role is unique to the user, and you can have several users with custom role designations and different rights for each of them. Second, if you select and deselect rights and end up matching the permissions for an existing role, the user will still be designated as having a custom role. That's because the moment you begin messing around with the permissions in the Ri**g**hts box, Microsoft Exchange Server changes the role to custom.

It's better to start with a plan for assigning roles, permissions, and rights and stick to it than to create custom roles on the fly. Invariably, there's a missing right for someone who expected to be able to perform a certain task or a right given someone who abuses it. If you have a set of standards for various levels of administration, you won't run into trouble.

Keeping Company Information About Users

The Properties dialog box for mailboxes affords a great deal of opportunity to keep an organization structure for yourself as an administrator. The fields on most of these tabs are optional but you should take a careful look at all of them because it may be useful to use some of them to track users, groups, and the structure of various departments.

To help make the decision, let's take a brief look at some of these information tabs.

Organization Property Page

The Organization property page (see fig. 12.10) is the place to enter information about where the mailbox owner fits in the hierarchy of the organization:

Figure 12.10

Use the Organization page to keep track of the personnel to whom the mailbox owner is responsible.

1. Click on **M**odify in the Manager section to see the Global Address List (a list of mailboxes), from which you can select the manager of the mailbox owner's department.

2. Use the **S**how Names section to change the list that's displayed. You also can look at any level of the structure of your organization, choosing a different domain or server.

3. Choose **F**ind to locate any object in the currently displayed list, avoiding the need to scroll through a long list. The Find dialog box offers a variety of fields to search on (see fig. 12.11).

Figure 12.11

The Find dialog box presents most of the fields from a mailbox General property page so that you can enter data to find the user that matches your criteria.

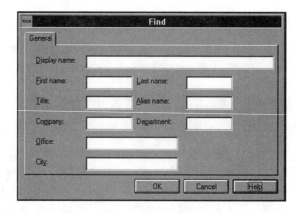

 When you use Find, fill in as much information as you know in order to narrow the scope of the search. Of course, if you're looking for a last name of Scyklskioskmn, the odds are pretty good that you won't have to fill in more than the **L**ast name field. For most situations, however, the more you give Find, the faster it works.

4. Click on Mo**d**ify in the Direct reports section of the Organization page to build an organization chart that shows all the users and departments to which this mailbox owner reports. Highlight any entry in the list, then choose **A**dd to move it to the Direct **r**eports section of the dialog box (see fig. 12.12).

Figure 12.12

All the recipient objects are available, so you can choose the people or groups to whom this mailbox owner reports.

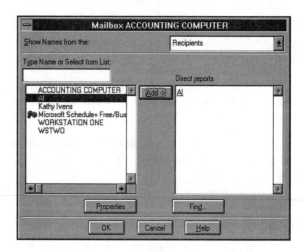

When you enter information about direct reporting, the list that is displayed is the Recipients list, not the mailbox list.

Phone/Notes Property Page

The Phone/Notes tab is the place to keep information that will probably come in handy at some point. You can enter all the telephone numbers connected to this mailbox owner, information about other people in the owner's office, and any notes you think might be useful (see fig. 12.13).

Figure 12.13

The more information you have about mailbox owners, the easier it is to track them down.

Delivery Restrictions

By default, a mailbox accepts mail from anybody. There are occasions, however, when this isn't efficient. For example, the weekly memo on the menu available in the company cafeteria is probably of little interest to the outside sales force, so why clutter their mailboxes with it?

Once a restriction is placed on a sender, rejected messages from that sender will be returned.

There are two ways to restrict delivery:

◆ Keep a list of all those from whom the mailbox will accept messages, so that messages from any sender not on the list will be rejected.

◆ Keep a list of those from whom the mailbox will reject messages, so that messages from any sender not on the list will be accepted.

The choice should be made in view of the length of the list—if you plan to reject only a few senders, use a Reject list. If you have a very limited list of senders you're willing to accept mail from, create an Accept list.

To restrict delivery in a mailbox:

1. Open the mailbox and move to the Delivery Restrictions tab of the Properties dialog box (see fig. 12.14).

Figure 12.14

Use the Delivery Restrictions tab to pick and choose the people from whom you want to accept messages.

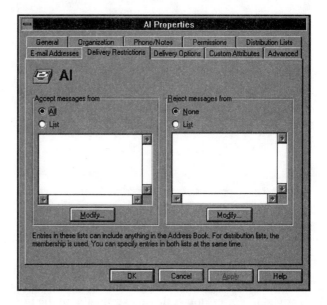

2. Choose **M**odify in the A**c**cept panel or Mo**d**ify in the **R**eject panel, depending on the approach you've chosen. The default address book displays.

3. If the senders you want to reject or accept are not listed in the default address book, use the **S**how Names text box to select a different address book or listing.

4. Select all the names you need, then choose OK.

Delivery Options

You can configure special circumstances for the messages that arrive in a mailbox with the Delivery Options property page (see fig. 12.15).

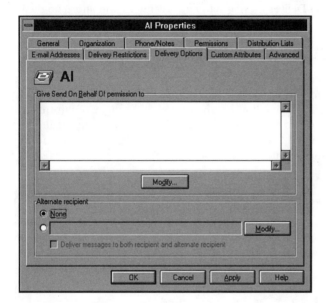

Figure 12.15

You can give permission to another user to send and receive messages with the Delivery Options property page.

Send On Behalf Of

You can establish another user or multiple users to send mail on behalf of the mailbox owner. If a message is sent by the other user on behalf of the owner, there is an indication of that fact on the message. This differs from the Send As feature that is discussed earlier in this chapter in the Understanding Permissions section, in which the actual sender is not noted on the message:

1. Choose Modify in the Give Send On **B**ehalf Of box to display a list of users.

2. Choose the user or multiple users to whom permission to perform this service should be given. Then choose OK.

Alternate Recipient

You can name an alternate recipient for incoming messages to this mailbox. You can also opt to have messages sent to both the alternate recipient and the mailbox owner. (By default, the choice in the Alternate recipient section is **N**one.)

1. Choose **M**odify to name an alternate recipient. The user list displays so that you can choose the recipient you want to perform this task.

2. Choose OK.

3. If you wish, select De**l**iver messages to both recipient and alternate recipient.

Custom Attributes

The Custom Attributes property page is a place to configure specific information that you want placed in each user mailbox. This information may be a payroll number, some other identification, eye color, height, or any other piece of information about the mailbox owner that you need to know. By default, the Custom Attributes property page contains 10 unnamed fields, but you can create whatever field names you want in order to gain additional information about the mailbox owner (see fig. 12.16).

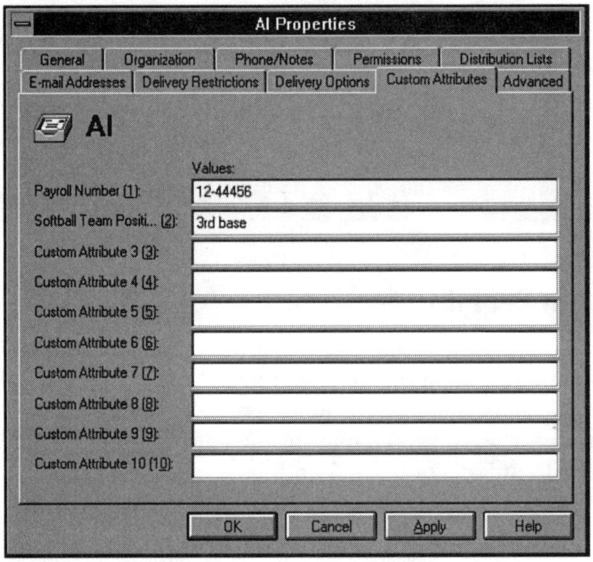

Figure 12.16

Our company finds it important to track the payroll numbers and the position the user plays on the company softball team.

In order to name the fields so that every mailbox displays your configuration, you have to establish the definitions. Use the following steps:

1. In the Microsoft Exchange Server Administrator window, select the Site object in the left panel. This displays the Configuration and Recipients objects in the right panel (or, click on the plus sign to the left of the site object to display the lower objects beneath it in the left panel).

2. Select the Configuration object, which causes the objects under Configuration to display in the right panel.

3. Select the object named DS Site Configuration (see fig. 12.17).

Figure 12.17

Move through the object structure to get to the DS Site Configuration object so that you can create custom attributes for all the mailboxes.

4. Choose **P**roperties from the **F**ile menu (or just double-click on the DS Site Configuration object) to open the Properties dialog box.

5. Move to the Custom Attributes property page.

6. Enter the text for as many custom attribute fields as you need. When you finish, choose OK.

Once you complete these steps, all existing and future mailboxes will display your custom fields on the Custom Attributes property page.

Advanced Mailbox Properties

A great deal of power and a host of configuration options are provided in the Advanced property page (see fig. 12.18).

Simple Display Name

Use Sim**p**le display name to enter a name for the mailbox to be used by outside systems that can't interpret all the characters in the regular mailbox display name.

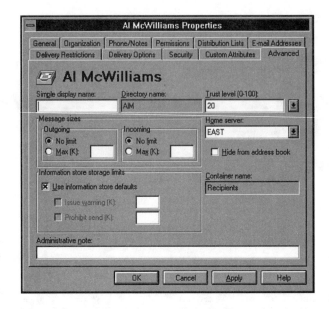

Directory

The **D**irectory name (which is automatically filled in) designates the name that is used when routing mail through the system.

Trust Level

The **T**rust level is used to determine whether information about this mailbox owner is replicated when directories are replicated throughout the organization. If you designate a trust level for a mailbox that is higher than the trust level that was established for the recipient container, data about this mailbox will not be synchronized during the directory exchange procedures. (Information about configuring trust levels for synchronized exchanges is found throughout the installation and maintenance chapters of this book.)

Message Size

You can configure Message sizes for both the outgoing and incoming messages that are sent and received by a mailbox:

◆ For Outgoing messages, choose No **l**imit if you don't care how large a message is sent by this mailbox. Select **M**ax and specify a value (in kilobytes) if you want to limit the size of outgoing messages.

◆ For Incoming messages, choose No limit, or select Ma**x** and specify a value that represents the largest message permitted.

Home Server

H**o**me server specifies the Microsoft Exchange Server computer on which the mailbox resides. Besides representing the server on which the mailbox was placed when it was created, this home server also represents the server that the mailbox owners must log in to when they want to access mailboxes. However, mailboxes can be moved after they're created by choosing **M**ove Mailbox from the **T**ools menu of the Administrator window. If the mailbox moves, you need to change its Home Server.

Information Store Storage Limits

Information store storage limits is a way to change the size of the data kept in the private information store (all mailboxes are kept in the private information store). When you first set up your system, you specify the storage limits for the private information store (on its General property page), and you can override that specification for a mailbox.

Once you deselect **U**se information store defaults, two other choices become accessible:

◆ Issue **w**arning, which instructs the system to issue a disk space warning when the space occupied by the mailbox data reaches a limit you specify.

◆ Prohi**b**it send, which is a specified level (which you enter), after which the mailbox owner will not be permitted to send messages. Messages can still be received.

 If you use the storage limit features (and users aren't careful about their own housekeeping chores), you either have to clean out mailboxes periodically to make disk space available, or give the appropriate rights and permissions to others to accomplish that task.

Hide from Address Book

Hide from address book means that the mailbox listing does not appear in the system address book. Many top-level executives request this property for their mailboxes. It's also useful for making sure nobody sends mail to a mailbox that was created for the purpose of making mailbox templates (see Using Mailbox Templates, later in this chapter). (If you need to look up the exact name of a hidden mailbox, choose **H**idden Recipients from the **V**iew menu in the Administrator's window.)

A hidden mailbox can receive mail if the sender knows the exact e-mail address and enters it in the To: box of a message, instead of selecting it from the address book list. That's useful for executive mailboxes or for other mailboxes in the organization where the owner prefers not to get mail except from those users to whom the owner has given an e-mail address.

It's also sometimes more politically correct to hide the mailbox instead of using the reject mail feature. With the hidden mailbox, mail from the unwashed masses won't come back from an executive mailbox marked "rejected."

Container Name

The **C**ontainer name field is informational and cannot be changed. If you use the features in the Microsoft Exchange Server Administrator window to move the mailbox to another container, the field reflects the change.

Administrative Note

You can use this field for comments or notes or anything you can think of that you can express within a 1024-character limit.

E-Mail Address Properties

The **E**-mail Addresses property page displays the current e-mail addresses for the mailbox (see fig. 12.19). The default addresses are those created automatically as a result of the connectors and address types you installed in your Microsoft Exchange Server system. You can create additional addresses, modify the existing ones, or remove any that are not being used.

There are three addresses created automatically by Microsoft Exchange Server:

◆ MS Mail

◆ X.400

◆ Internet (SMTP)

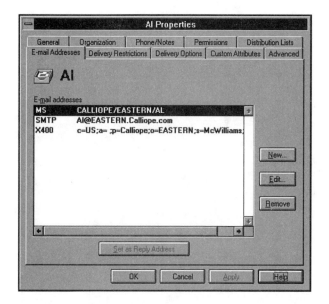

Figure 12.19

The three default addresses handle most e-mail situations, but you can always add new ones for special circumstances.

Create a New Address

If you need other types of address, for instance for PROFS or another e-mail application, you can create one:

1. Choose **N**ew to display the New E-mail address dialog box (see fig. 12.20).

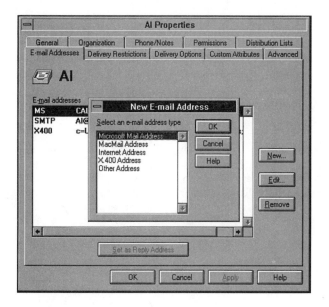

Figure 12.20

To add e-mail addresses to a mailbox, choose an existing address type or use Other to create one.

2. Highlight Other Address, then choose OK to bring up the Other Address Properties dialog box (see fig. 12.21).

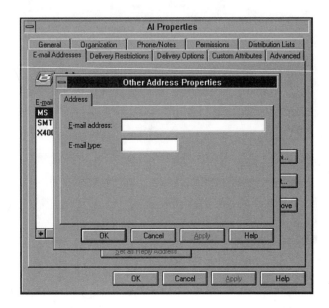

3. Enter the **E**-mail address in the format expected by this address type.

4. Enter the E-mail type so that when you look at the address you remember why you created it.

5. Choose OK to finish and have the new address display on the E-mail Addresses property page.

Edit an Address

If you want to change an existing address, highlight it and choose **E**dit. Then enter the new data or make changes to the existing data.

You need to modify e-mail addresses if you change recipient information, such as a name or alias. The system does not update the e-mail address automatically.

The dialog box that displays for editing e-mail addresses is specific to the e-mail address you're modifying, containing the appropriate fields for the address.

Remove an Address

If you want to delete an address, highlight it, then choose **R**emove.

Editing or removing an address can cause a number of unpleasant ramifications, so don't perform either of these tasks without doing all the necessary follow-up work. This means every messaging unit and reference in the system must be changed. Otherwise, other system tasks can be adversely affected—for example, an address change can affect the efficiency of directory replication, routing tables, or even the delivery of messages.

Distribution Lists Property Tab

Use the Distribution Lists property page to specify all the distribution lists connected to this mailbox. Any list that contains the mailbox user's name can be specified. Information about creating and using distribution lists is found in the section called Managing Distribution Lists, later in this chapter.

Using Templates for Mailboxes

If you're planning to migrate or import an existing mail system into Microsoft Exchange Server, you can create a template or multiple templates to autoconfigure the mailboxes.

The values in your templates are the default values for mailbox properties. The configuration is duplicated in all the new mailboxes created with the Migration Wizard and the Directory Import command. This is extremely useful for fields that don't change from user to user, such as the Company or Site or Trust Levels.

Although it's easy to create a template by using an existing mailbox, all the permissions on the mailbox are part of the template and therefore copied to all the new mailboxes you create with that template. Instead of using an existing user's mailbox, create new mailboxes to use as templates and don't add any user permissions (or any other property that will change from user to user).

Incidentally, even though it's logical and therefore obvious, no matter what mailbox you use as a template, the first name, last name, directory name, and e-mail address are not copied when you create a new mailbox via the template.

To create a template:

1. In the Microsoft Exchange Server Administrator window, select the site object for the site in which you want to place the template.

2. Select the recipient object for the site's recipient container that will hold the template (see fig. 12.22).

Figure 12.22

The left panel of the Microsoft Exchange Server window displays all the components as objects, so it's easy to manipulate components at the appropriate level.

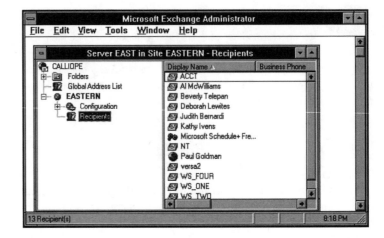

3. Choose New **M**ailbox from the **F**ile menu to bring up a blank mailbox Properties dialog box with the General tab in the foreground.

4. Tab to the **D**isplay field and enter a name for this template. Use a name that's descriptive enough to remind you of its use, or to make its intention clear to any other administrators who might need to use it.

Tip If you're going to use multiple templates, it will be easier to find them if you create a naming protocol that keeps them together in any sorted lists. For example, you might want to start all template names with a number, which ensures that they're displayed at the top of any list. You also can go in the other direction and start them all with the letter z to place them last in displayed lists.

5. Use the property tabs to move through the mailbox properties and enter any data that you want to be duplicated in all the mailboxes you create from this template.

Once you have the template established, you should hide the mailbox so it doesn't get mail accidentally.

Warning There's no link between a template and the mailboxes that are created by that template. If you make changes in a template, they won't be reflected in any mailboxes.

The template(s) you create are used during the installation process when you migrate or import mail information. Details on these tasks are found throughout the installation and configuration chapters in this book.

Using Distribution Lists

It's frequently convenient to prepare lists of recipients for mass-mailing messages, because a great deal of office correspondence is targeted at a specific group. Certainly, having a list for distribution is much easier than sending a message to a group one person at a time.

During your planning for implementation of Microsoft Exchange Server, if you ask users about their correspondence, you'll probably find consistent patterns of inter-office messaging. Perhaps the payroll department distributes time sheets every Thursday, or various department managers distribute monthly reports.

To build a distribution list:

1. In the Microsoft Exchange Server Administrator window, highlight the Recipients object for the site in which you want to work.

2. Choose New **D**istribution List from the **F**ile menu (or press Ctrl+D). A Properties dialog box displays with the General property tab in the foreground (see fig. 12.23).

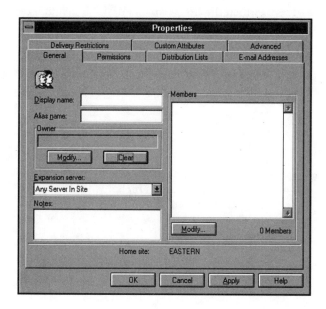

Figure 12.23

Use the distribution list General property tab to establish the basic data that displays—this list will be an item in the address book.

3. Enter the data for the fields in the General Property page:

◆ Use **D**isplay name to enter the name that will appear in the address book listing (you can use up to 256 characters).

 I've found it useful to make sure the word list is in the display name so that a quick glance at the address book listing tells me which addresses are individuals and which are lists.

◆ Use Alias **n**ame to specify a name (up to 64 characters) that will be used to generate other e-mail addresses for this list. When outside mail services use this Alias to send mail, that mail will be redistributed to all names on the list.

◆ Choose the M**o**dify button under the Owner box to see a display of user names, then select one to be the owner of this distribution list. By default, the members of the Global Address List are displayed, but you can change the source of the names in order to pick an owner from another server or site. (If you want to change the owner later, use the C**l**ear button, then redo this step.)

◆ Use the **E**xpansion server field to designate the server on which the distribution list will be expanded (you can choose any server in the site).

Expansion is the process by which the list is expanded into individual recipient names upon receipt of a message. It can be a rather vigorous process, because all recipients have to be verified to make sure they still exist, and a routing plan has to be configured in order to distribute the message. These are processor-intensive tasks and it might be more productive to move them to another server that is less busy, or has a more powerful processor, especially if this distribution list is quite long.

◆ Use the Notes field to enter additional or incidental information about this list. You can use up to 256 characters.

◆ Click on the **M**odify button under the Members list box to display a list of users from which you can choose the ones you want to include in this list (see fig. 12.24). Highlight a user, then choose **A**dd to move the user to the Distribution list **m**embers list box.

Once you create the list by naming it and configuring the rest of the General properties tab, you can move to the other property pages and specify whatever data you believe is appropriate. The information (and the entry procedures) are the same as that for mailboxes, described previously.

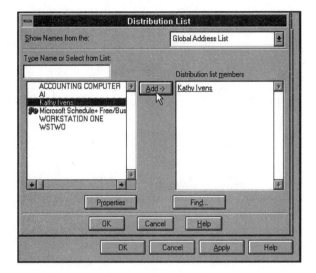

Figure 12.24

The user list from the current address list, or from any address list you want to use, provides the names to select for your new distribution list.

Working with a Distribution List

Once created, a distribution list is just another recipient that can send and receive mail. To work with its Properties dialog box in order to modify its configuration or to add or delete names from the list, double-click on its listing in the Administrator window.

Managing Custom Recipients

A custom recipient is an outsider—a recipient that is not a part of the organization. It might be a user with whom communication is established through the Internet, or someone who is reachable via another host system to which you can dial.

Once you create a custom recipient, it appears in the address book and can send and receive messages.

 If you are going to migrate or import an existing messaging system, the custom recipients are part of that process (see the chapters on migrating, importing, and installation for more information).

To create a custom recipient:

1. In the Microsoft Exchange Server Administrator window, highlight the Recipient object, then choose New Custom **R**ecipient from the **F**ile menu.

2. The New E-mail Address dialog box displays, showing the e-mail address types available (see fig. 12.25). Select the appropriate type and choose OK.

Figure 12.25

*When you create a
custom recipient,
you can use an
existing e-mail
address type or
invent your own.*

The dialog box into which you enter the information about the custom recipient varies according to the type of e-mail address the recipient requires:

◆ For Microsoft Mail recipients, the dialog box requires the **N**etwork Name, the **P**ostoffice Name, and the **M**ailbox Name.

◆ For MacMail address recipients, the dialog box requires the **D**isplay Name, the U**s**er Name, and the Se**r**ver Name. There is an optional selection to require that all mail be sent in MS E**x**change rich-text format.

◆ For Internet recipients, the dialog box requires only the **E**-mail address.

◆ For X.400 recipients, the dialog box asks for full names (there's a field for each part of the name), a Co**m**mon name (nickname), the **O**rganization (and, if needed, additional organizational unit information to help identify and find the recipient), the private management domain name (**P**RMD), the administrative management domain name (A**D**MD), and the **C**ountry.

◆ For other recipients, the dialog box requires an **E**-mail address and an E-mail **T**ype (which you can name according to your own requirements).

Once you complete the Address Properties dialog box, the same Mailbox properties dialog box that is used for your own users' mailboxes is displayed, and you can enter data as described earlier in this chapter.

Moving Mailboxes between Servers

You can move mailboxes from one server to another one in the same site. There are several reasons you might want to do this:

◆ To balance the load between servers

◆ To move mailboxes to the server directly connected to the mailbox owners' computers

◆ To take a server down for maintenance

 Although you can think of them as mailbox users, distribution lists and custom recipients differ from individual users in one important way—they are site-based, not server-based. They are not linked to a server. It doesn't matter which server you were accessing when you created these entities; they belong to the site and are replicated to multiple servers on that site. Therefore, you cannot move their mailboxes from one server to another server—actually, it's not that you can't, it's that you don't have to, so the Move Mailbox process won't let you.

To move mailboxes from one server to another server, both servers must reside in the same site. Follow these steps to accomplish the move:

1. In the Microsoft Exchange Server Administrator window, highlight the Recipient object in the left panel to display the individual recipients in the right panel.

 If you've created a naming scheme for distribution lists and custom recipients, it's easy to identify them and eliminate them from consideration for this task. If you haven't, it can be difficult to determine which mailboxes can be moved. To make it easier to identify mailboxes that can be moved, after you select the recipient object, choose **M**ailboxes from the **V**iew menu. This limits the display in the right panel to mailboxes, eliminating distribution lists and custom recipients.

2. Highlight the mailboxes you want to move. Remember that you can select multiple mailboxes by holding down the control key while you click on each selection, or you can drag the mouse to select contiguous mailboxes.

3. Choose **M**ove Mailbox from the **T**ools menu.

4. The Move Mailbox dialog box displays, listing all the servers in this site. Select a server and choose OK.

If you move some mailboxes to another server, leaving other mailboxes on the original server, try adding up the disk space used by the mailboxes across both servers. The math probably doesn't work—you're probably using more total disk space. This happens because when a message is sent to a group of users, each individual user doesn't get a copy of the message. Instead, one copy of the message is deposited on the server and all the recipients share the message. If some users are on one server and others on another, there are two copies of this group message.

Once a mailbox has been moved, you have to change the configuration for the home server for that mailbox. Open the mailbox Properties dialog box and move to the Advanced tab, then change the H<u>o</u>me Server field.

 There may be a delay in receiving messages into a mailbox that's been moved, until the routing information for the site has been updated. See Chapter 17, "Maintaining Client Services," for information about routing tables.

CHAPTER 13

Administering the Core Components

The two main components in your Microsoft Exchange Server system are the Information Stores and the Directory. These components track and control the system and all the transactions that occur.

Understanding the Information Store

The *information store* is the container for all messages on a Microsoft Exchange Server computer. Each server has two information stores:

◆ The *public information store*, which holds all public folders. Those public folders can contain documents, messages, forms, or any other information your users want to distribute.

◆ The *private information store*, which holds the private folders. User mailboxes are part of the private folders. Users can also put a personal private information store on their client workstations.

In addition to storage tasks, the information store performs several chores relating to messaging services:

◆ It provides the rules and viewing configurations for displaying the objects that are located in the information store.

◆ It maintains the limits on storage and age for the folders in the information store.

◆ It generates notifications about mail.

◆ It delivers messages that are addressed to recipients located on the same home server as the sender.

◆ It turns over to the Message Transfer Agent (MTA) those messages that are intended for recipients located on other servers and systems.

Understanding the Information Store Databases

Although it is never necessary to manipulate the information store databases directly (nor is it possible), it's a good idea to have an idea of the way your messaging services run.

The database engine in your Microsoft Exchange Server system (Microsoft has named the database engine Jet) manipulates the databases that keep the information that accumulates as messaging services go on. The messages or documents are stored and sent to the correct targets, and all this data is kept in databases on the server computers.

The primary database that Jet manipulates on the server is SYSTEM.EDB. It is, however, made up of two subdatabases, PRIV.EDB (the private database) and PUB.EDB (the public database). These databases are made up of pages, with each page consisting of a 4 KB block of data.

In addition, the Jet-run system also has a cache in RAM and one or more transaction log files. As transactions occur, they are sent to the cache to be moved to the proper target mailbox or folder and also sent to the transaction log. When the activity level permits, a programming thread is dispatched to copy transactions from the log to the database. That is a time-consuming action, because there's some disk-seeking involved in finding pages that have room to hold the data.

Having transactions sent to the log sequentially (the fastest way to write to a file), held in the log, then written to the database, keeps the productivity of your system at a high level. Because Windows NT is a multi-tasking operating system, the actual write to the database can take place in the background with very little disturbance to any current transaction activity.

 You might want to consider putting the transaction logs on a dedicated physical drive to increase performance.

Because sequential writes are the fastest I/O disk process, this drive zooms along, accepting data without having to move the drive heads all over the place—and there is less worry about running out of disk space.

This is even more interesting because, depending on the level of activity, it is possible to receive mail in your mailbox, respond to it, and have that response received and read before the transaction is even written to the database.

Understanding the Transaction Logs

Notice that the preceding section mentions that the transactions are copied from the transaction log to the database, not moved. The transaction log retains the information.

A transaction log is always 5 MB. When you first begin using Microsoft Exchange Server, the transaction log filename is EDB.LOG. When that file reaches a point where the next transaction will cause it to become larger than 5 MB, the file is renamed and a new, empty EDB.LOG begins accepting transaction data. When the 5 MB limit is approaching for the new EDB.LOG file, the process is repeated. The renaming scheme for transaction logs is EDB*XXXXX*.LOG, where *XXXXX* is a 5-digit hex number 00001-fffff and is the lowest unused number so far.

Of course, by now you are asking how you keep from having to buy more and more disk storage space to store all these logs—remember, you cannot manipulate them, which means you can't delete them.

 There's another clever trick invoked—two 5 MB files named RES1.LOG and RES2.LOG are placed on the disk to reserve space so that if your drive does fill up, there is less chance of corrupt data when you get your "out of space" error (Exchange Server knows they are fake files and will take the space to avoid corrupting data).

There are two solutions, and they have different ramifications:

◆ Let the system clean itself out with a backup

◆ Set up circular logging

Cleaning the Logs with a Full Backup

The special features added to your Windows NT Backup software during the installation of Microsoft Exchange Server provide the log cleanup tasks. During a full backup (the NT backup software uses the term "normal" rather than "full"), the log files are compared to the databases. If the contents of the transaction log have been committed to the database, the transaction log is deleted after the backup is completed. Transaction logs with uncommitted data are not deleted after the backup.

If you do an incremental backup, none of the log files are deleted, and if you have a crash and have to restore, you really need to restore only the log files.

Because Jet checks the transactions in the log files against the database, writing to the database if the transaction is not there, the log files can recreate the database.

This means, of course, that you must do frequent full backups to avoid filling up your drive. Detailed information about this, and about backing up your Microsoft Exchange Server system, is found in Chapter 11, "Backing Up and Restoring."

Using Circular Logging

You can, if you are worried about disk space, use a feature called circular logging. This means that as transactions are committed to the database, they are removed from the log. The log does not have any size limit, but it shouldn't grow huge, because it's constantly being cleaned out. You can probably estimate that it will stay under 100 MB. If you enable circular logging, the Backup Software will not permit incremental backups.

Circular logging may make your system slower because you're losing the advantage of writes to the database whenever there's a split-second lull in transactions. You have to make sure you are running a full backup at least once a day in order to keep your data secure.

By default, circular logging is turned off. If you want to enable it, use these steps:

1. Open the Microsoft Exchange Administrator and select the Server object for the server you want to change to circular logging.

2. Choose **P**roperties from the **F**ile menu (or double-click on the server object) to bring up the server Properties dialog box. Then click on the Advanced tab (see fig. 13.1).

3. Select Information **s**tore in the circular logging section of the property page.

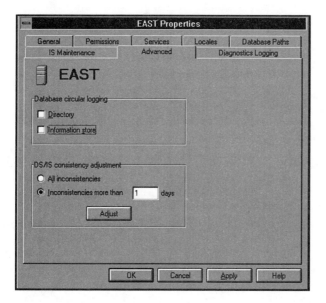

Figure 13.1

Use the Advanced property page to configure the database files for circular logging and to keep the information store files consistent with the Directory data.

The system will stop and restart the service in order to change the settings, which may result in the loss of some in-progress transactions.

Understanding the Directory

Directory components, or records, manage all the objects in the organization and make information about the organization available to users, administrators, and system processes.

When these directory objects make the information available to users and administrators, the information is displayed in an easy-to-understand graphical manner.

Processes access the directory objects through remote procedure calls (RPCs) to get the information they need to perform tasks. For example, the MTA looks up user addresses in order to route messages.

The directory is implemented as a Windows NT service, and it must be running at all times in order to have your Microsoft Exchange Server components function.

The information elements managed by the directory include the following:

◆ Private folders, which means the mailboxes (including names, addresses, configurations, and so on), distribution lists, and other data needed for messaging.

◆ Public folders

◆ Servers

◆ Sites

The directory itself has two main functional components:

◆ The *directory database* (DIR.EDB), which is a flat database that stores the information about all the directory objects.

◆ The *directory service* (DS), which manipulates the information in the directory database. It processes directory requests from users and applications.

 Note DS is actually an executable file (DSAMAIN.EXE), which launches the services that do the following:

◆ Display the directory objects stored in the directory database in a hierarchical tree structure.

◆ Provide the interface between Microsoft Exchange clients and the directory database.

◆ Enforce the rules that control the structure and contents of the directory.

◆ Send directory replication notifications to directories on other servers and receive directory replication notifications from other servers.

The objects controlled in the directory are not static—there are frequent changes made. New mailboxes are created, permissions are changed, folders are created, configurations of objects are altered, and a host of other administrative actions occur that change the information stored and controlled in the directory.

As with the information stores, you need to back up the directory regularly so that you can resume working with the latest configuration in the event of a disaster.

Keeping Information Store Statistics

Keeping and viewing statistical information about the information stores enables you to plan intelligently for the growth of your Microsoft Exchange Server system.

Private Information Store Statistics

If you check the statistics for the private information store regularly, you see patterns for mailbox use and are able to determine (and predict) the way resources are being used.

To see the statistics for the private information store, use these steps:

1. From the Administrator window, select the server that contains the private information store you want to examine.

2. From the right panel, highlight Private Information Store, then choose **P**roperties from the **F**ile menu (or double-click on the Private Information Store object).

3. Select the Mailbox Resources tab of the Properties dialog box to see the mailboxes contained in this private information store (see fig. 13.2).

4. Use the horizontal scroll bars to view all the information about each mailbox.

5. If you wish to view additional information or to change the order in which information displays, choose **C**olumns to see the Columns dialog box (see fig. 13.3).

6. To add a column (each column displays a specific piece of information), highlight it in the A**v**ailable columns section, then choose A**d**d.

7. To remove a column, highlight it in the Sh**o**w panel, then choose **R**emove.

8. To change the order of columns, highlight the title in the Sh**o**w the following columns area, then choose Move **U**p or **M**ove Down.

 Tip   If you are really fussy about the way things display, you can change the size of a highlighted column by choosing **W**idth and then specifying a value in pixels, or change the column width on the Mailbox Resources property page by dragging the column separator lines in the title header.

Figure 13.2

Check out the Mailbox Resources property page to monitor the activity of the user mailboxes on a specific server.

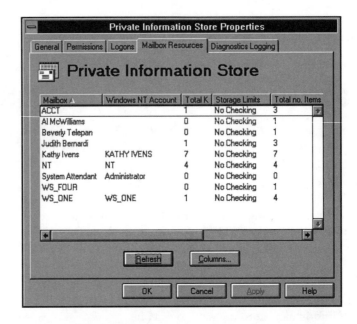

Figure 13.3

You can customize the Mailbox Resources property page to display the specific information you want to see in whatever order you prefer.

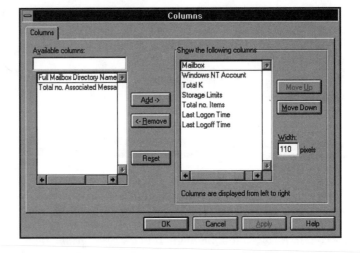

Public Information Store Statistics

The resource use generated by the public information store activity can be viewed so that you have an opportunity to prevent problems and plan for the future. To see the public information store statistics, follow these steps:

1. In the Administrator window, highlight the server you want to view, then select the Public Information Store. Choose **P**roperties from the **F**ile menu (or double-click on the Public Information Store object).

2. Select the Public Folder Resources tab to see a display of all the public folder objects and their statistics (see fig. 13.4).

3. You can choose **C**olumns to add, delete, and change the order of columns in the same way described for the private information store (see fig. 13.5).

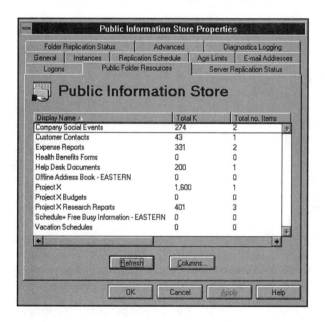

Figure 13.4

Keeping an eye on the size of folders helps you establish and enforce rules and limits about filling and emptying folders.

Don't pay attention only to the number of bytes being used by the public information store—keep an eye on the number of items and the number of contacts that were made (the number of times the folder was accessed). You will begin to see patterns, and my bet is that the primary pattern will be that there are more items in each folder than makes sense. It is not productive to have to scroll through a lot of small documents in order to get to the current, important information. People (or administrators) need to clean data out regularly. If the problem is primarily disk real estate being used up by big documents, you might want to set limits on message sizes.

Figure 13.5

Configure the display of Public Folder Resources by deciding the information categories you want to watch.

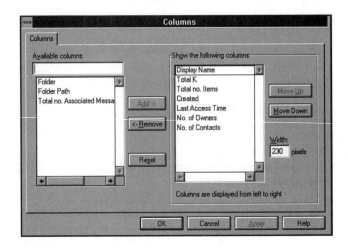

Scheduling Information Store Maintenance

The system performs a maintenance routine on the information store automatically, according to a schedule you configure. The maintenance routine defragments the public and private information stores, which makes the system perform faster.

You can schedule maintenance at regular intervals, the default setting being daily. Set up an automated maintenance schedule as soon as your Microsoft Exchange Server system is up and running. You can always adjust the schedule after you run Microsoft Exchange Server a while and can see the needs more clearly.

To set up a maintenance schedule for the information store, follow these steps:

1. From the Administrator window, select the server you want to work on, then choose **P**roperties from the **F**ile menu.

2. Click on the IS Maintenance tab to move to the Maintenance property page (see fig. 13.6).

Make sure you start by running maintenance once a day—it's probably easiest to use the times established as the default.

If the occurrence of transactions in your system is very high, you may want to perform maintenance more frequently and schedule another occurrence during the day. However, while the maintenance tasks are being performed, response times for users are slower than normal.

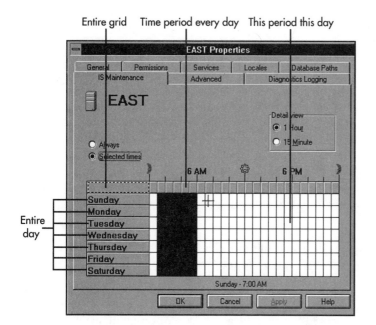

Entire grid   Time period every day   This period this day

Figure 13.6

*The default
maintenance
time is 1 AM
to 6 AM, but
the graphical
interface makes
it easy to select
your own
schedule for
maintenance
of your
information
store.*

You have to work out this formula by weighing the benefits against the advantages. If you are running a large system with lots of users and lots of messaging, it might be better to have a small slowdown during the day while you run another maintenance routine than to let the system bog down in the afternoon and continue to perform slowly throughout the rest of the day.

If you need to schedule a maintenance event during the day, in addition to one run in an off-time, choose a time of day that is less inconvenient. Some companies that need to perform maintenance or backups more than once every 24 hours choose the lunch hour. It's a good idea to issue a notice to users (isn't it nice to have a messaging system that makes it easy to do this?) that they should expect performance slowdowns at 12:30 PM daily because of maintenance tasks. You might want to add the fact that if they stay off the system for a while at that time, the tasks will end sooner and productivity levels will get back to normal more rapidly.

Using the IS Maintenance Property Page

There are a number of options and selections on the property page that make it easy to configure a schedule.

Select Always to have maintenance performed constantly. Actually, it isn't really constant, the maintenance tasks are performed every 15 minutes. This means that the maintenance is quick and easy, because there is no period of time where a lot of messaging is performed and therefore a lot of maintenance is needed.

Select the Selected times button to use the schedule grid for setting the time(s) for maintenance.

Choose the 15 Minute button to change the grid display so that it displays a grid square for every 15-minute period in the day. In this mode, the individual times are not noted at the top of the grid, so as you move your mouse pointer around, the times are displayed beneath the scroll bar.

Administering Public Folders

Public folders are containers for information that can be shared by the users in the system.

Public folders are created by the client software, working at a client workstation. Once they are established, however, they can be administered at either the workstation by the folder's owner or at the server by the administrator.

Public folders reside in the public information store of a Microsoft Exchange server computer and can be configured through the administrator program, including the configuration of replication schemes. Because public folders are usually replicated throughout the organization, any changes you make are also replicated. More information about replicating folders is found in Chapter 9, "Managing Replication and Synchronization."

To make administrative changes to the configuration of a public folder, use these steps:

1. In the Administrator window, select Public folders, then choose the folder object you want to manipulate.

2. Choose Properties from the File menu to display the folder's properties dialog box, which opens to the General property page (see fig. 13.7).

The property tabs dealing with replication are discussed in Chapter 9. For most configuration tasks, you will be interested in configuring only the General properties page and the Advanced properties page.

Configuring the General Properties Page

The following are configuration specifications you can change on the General properties page:

◆ Folder name appears the way it was entered when the folder was created in the Microsoft Exchange Client. There is rarely a reason to change this.

◆ The Address Book displays name defaults to <u>S</u>ame as folder name. If you think that users might not understand the meaning of the folder name when they view the address book, you can change the way the folder name appears there. Select <u>U</u>se this name and specify a name for the folder that will display in the address book, which users display when they want to post information to a folder.

◆ The Alias <u>n</u>ame is the name that is used in the TO: section of a message that is being sent to this folder. You can enter the same name as the folder or specify a different alias (for example, if you want to use a shortcut version of the name).

◆ Select Age limit for all <u>r</u>eplicas and then specify a number of days before messages in this folder are automatically deleted. The age limit applies to the original folder and all replicas.

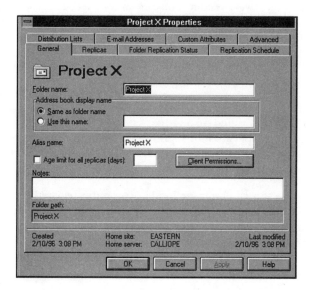

Figure 13.7

Client Permissions, Age limit, and other General properties of public folders can be changed through the Administrator program.

 Sometimes there are reasons to leave messages for a longer period on certain servers. You can override an age limit for a replica on a specific server by using the Public Information Store Age Limits property page on that server.

◆ Choose the <u>C</u>lient Permissions button to define or modify permissions for users who have access to this folder. The original permissions and roles were established when the folder was created, but you can add, delete, and modify permissions and roles. Detailed information about manipulating the permission levels and roles for a public folder can be found in Chapter 3, "Ascertaining Needs."

◆ Use the Notes section to enter additional information about the folder. Your notes will display in the address book.

◆ The Folder path is entered when the folder is created by the client and cannot be changed by the Administrator program.

Configuring the Advanced Property Page

There are some important options on the Advanced property page, and you will probably want to use it to add to or modify the folder's configuration (see fig. 13.8):

◆ The Simple display name is the folder's name as it will appear to foreign systems when messages are sent to the folder. Some foreign systems have rules about length and permitted characters, so you should specify a name in this entry that will work everywhere, with every system your users might access. If you want to cover every possible foreign system, it's safest to limit the name to eight characters with no spaces.

◆ The Directory name was established when the folder was created and cannot be changed.

◆ The Trust level entry is related to replication and determines whether or not the public folder will be replicated on another server. If the trust level you set is higher than the trust level specified for replication, the folder will not be replicated. Information about establishing trust levels while setting up replication schedules is found in Chapter 9.

◆ The Public folder store storage limits section lets you indicate whether you want to Use information store defaults (which are set in the General properties page of the public information store) or override those limits for this particular folder. To change the limits, select Issue warning and then specify a value (in KB) that represents the size at which a warning message is sent to the folder's owner (it's assumed that having received the warning, the owner will clean out the folder).

◆ Replication msg importance enables you to select a priority during replication for messages that are sent by this folder. Messages are delivered in priority order by Microsoft Exchange Server. The choices are Not Urgent, Normal, and Urgent.

◆ Hide from address book is selected if you do not want the folder to appear in the address book. This is useful if the folder is for very specific use and you want to limit its access without creating a distribution list. Users who are given the exact e-mail address can send messages to the folder by entering it in the TO: section of the message window.

◆ The **C**ontainer name represents the container object in which this folder is stored and cannot be changed.

◆ The Administrative **n**ote field is available for you to make notes to yourself about this folder. These notes are displayed only in the Administrator window.

Figure 13.8

The Advanced properties page for a public folder contains configuration options related to the folder's access and replication.

Moving Public Folders

There are times when it makes sense to change the server on which a public folder resides. For example, if a user on one server established a public folder that is used almost exclusively (or primarily) by a group of users connected to another server, move the folder to the server used by those users. Moving the folder means a more direct traffic pattern for the majority of the users, and the server of the original user can be a replication target for this folder.

Many public folders do not have to be replicated all over the organization, but only to certain servers where there is interest in the content. As you learn the messaging patterns of your users—and as the number of public folders swells—it is worthwhile to spend time creating specific replication schemes. Sending everything everywhere unnecessarily is time-consuming, and the total disk space you use can get enormous.

To move a public folder, follow these steps:

1. Go to the Replicas tab of the Properties dialog box.

2. In the **S**ervers panel, select the server you want to receive the folder, then choose A**d**d.

3. In the Replicate **F**olders To panel, highlight the server the folder is currently on (the server you want to remove the folder from). Choose **R**emove.

After the next replication event, the folder will be moved to the new server.

Maintaining the Directory

There are some maintenance tasks for the directory that you should perform regularly. Mainly, you should take a look at the event logs to make sure that the directory, directory replication, and directory synchronization processes are working properly.

Checking the Event Viewer

The directory services provide reports to the Windows NT Event Viewer from different sources. There are two sources you should check frequently to see whether any problems have been reported:

◆ MSExchangeDS for directory service and directory replication events

◆ MSExchangeDX for directory synchronization events

To check directory events, follow these steps:

1. From the Windows NT Administrative Tools program group, open the Event Viewer.

2. Choose Fi**l**ter Events from the **V**iew menu to display the Filter dialog box (see fig. 13.9).

3. Click on the arrow to the right of the Sou**r**ce field to see a listing of all applications and system components that log events. Choose one of the two Microsoft Exchange Server sources mentioned previously.

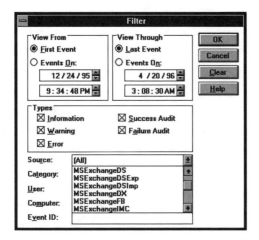

Figure 13.9

You can choose the type of events you want to examine in order to check on the performance of the directory services.

The events logged by the specified service are displayed in the Event Viewer (see fig. 13.10).

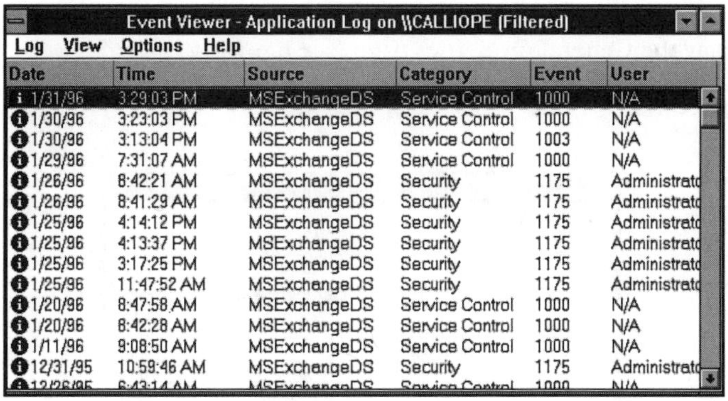

Figure 13.10

Choosing all events enables you to look at everything the application did, even the things that went smoothly.

4. To see the details of any event, highlight it and choose **D**etail from the **V**iew menu (or double-click on it). The Event Detail dialog box shows all the details of the event (see fig. 13.11).

5. You can use the **P**revious and **N**ext buttons to move through the list of events.

You should periodically clean out the logs in the Event Viewer (do not delete anything if you are in the middle of troubleshooting a problem, however).

You can use the features in the Windows NT Event Viewer configuration options to determine a maximum size for your logs (source by source). You also can specify that you do not want events overwritten because you want to clear the log manually.

Configuring the Event Viewer is straightforward and self-explanatory as you go through it. Check your Windows NT documentation for any questions about configuring the Event Viewer.

Checking Directory Consistency

Directory information is replicated to other servers. If you have multiple servers in the same site, the replication is automatic and takes place as a background process. Replication between servers on different sites is established and accomplished as part of your Microsoft Exchange Server configuration.

If a server is added to the system, or if a server crashed and the information was restored from a tape backup, or if there was an error message during replication, there may be inconsistencies between server directories. You can check the consistency of a server by following these steps:

1. In the Administrator window, highlight the server, then choose Directory Service from the right pane of the window.

2. Choose Properties from the File menu (or double-click on the Directory Service listing) to display the General properties page (see fig. 13.12).

3. Click on Check Now.

Figure 13.11

You can see that the security attributes for a mailbox were altered.

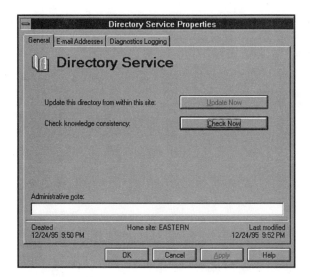

Figure 13.12

Use the General properties tab to check consistency and force a manual replication if necessary.

The consistency check looks for other connected servers within the site and for new sites in the organization. If a server was added to the local site or if a site was added, while this server was down, that fact is recognized.

 It is not always the fact that a new server was added that makes a server appear new. If there was a server crash and the last tape did not have information about a server, it will appear to be new after the restore. This is less likely to occur if you perform full backups every day.

If a new server or site is discovered, you should then choose **U**pdate Now from the General properties tab. This brings everything up to date.

Rebuilding the Routing Table

If you had to perform the operations described previously, it means that the server you are working on was missing knowledge about another server in the organization. To make sure that future replications include the new server, you have to rebuild the routing table:

1. From the Administrator window, highlight the server, then select Message Transfer Agent from the right pane.

2. Choose **P**roperties from the **F**ile menu (or double-click on the listing) to display the General properties tab.

3. Choose **R**ecalculate Now.

It takes a few minutes to rebuild the routing table, and henceforth the new server is included in mail routing.

CHAPTER 14

Installing and Maintaining the Key Management Server

Microsoft Exchange Server has the capability of imposing some very advanced security features on your system, giving you a higher level of data security and integrity. Users will be able to seal (encrypt) messages and sign (use digital signatures), raising the level of confidentiality available in your organization.

All this is provided by an Exchange Server component called Key Management.

Installing Key Management Services

The ideal way to install the Key Management (KM) component is to dedicate a server to it. However, even if you use an administrative server, you can only have one KM server (multiple KM servers would wreak havoc with encryption and authentication errors). To pick a server for this purpose, you have to consider these needs:

◆ The Administrator program you use to administer the system must be located on a computer that has Remote Procedure Call (RPC) connectivity to the KM server.

◆ The server should have the NT File System (NTFS) installed because of the additional security features that accompany that file system.

◆ The server should be situated in a place where it can be physically secured.

Getting Ready to Install Key Management

Although the installation of the component itself is very straightforward, there are a number of steps to take during and after the installation procedure:

1. Install the KM software.

2. Configure the necessary passwords for access and administration.

3. Start the KM services in the KM computer.

4. Configure all sites to use the new features.

5. Configure individual user security features.

Installing the KM Component

Before you start the installation process, you need to have a formatted floppy disk available. During the installation process, the system configures a password that is copied to the floppy disk during Setup. (You can choose not to copy the password to the floppy disk and the password will be displayed on the screen—but you'll have to enter it each time you want to start the KM services).

This password is the one needed to start the Key Management services (from the Services icon in the Control Panel).

There is a second password needed to gain access to some of the administrative tasks in the KM component. This administrative password is chosen by you. During Setup, it is preset to password, and one of the steps you'll take after installation is to change that to a password of your own invention.

To install KM services:

1. Put the password disk into the floppy disk drive so that Setup can copy your password.

2. Run SETUP.EXE from the \EXCHKM subdirectory (of your installation directory) on the Microsoft Exchange Server CD. For example, if you used \SETUP\I386 to install Microsoft Exchange Server, look for \SETUP\I386\EXCHKM.

3. When the Setup program starts, choose **T**ypical (see fig. 14.1).

4. Fill in the **C**ountry code if you do not want to use the default of US, and select or deselect the option to C**r**eate the startup floppy disk (see fig. 14.2).

Figure 14.1

The only choice for Setup is to install all the options of the Key Management Server component.

Figure 14.2

It's advisable to select the option of creating a KM Server floppy disk during Setup so that you don't have to type in the password that is generated.

Starting the KM Services

Once installation is complete, you have to start the KM services in order to use the features:

1. Open Main, then open the Control Panel.

2. Double-click on the Services icon.

3. Double-click on Microsoft Exchange Key Manager to display the Service dialog box (see fig. 14.3).

Figure 14.3

Before you can start the services, you have to configure the logon account for KM.

4. In the Log On As section of the dialog box, select **T**his Account and select the account that will service the KM component. Usually, it's the Administrator account, but you should check the primary permissions account under Directory Services and duplicate that account (both DS and KM are part of the Configuration container).

5. **S**tart the service (you have to place the disk with the password into the floppy disk drive or type the password into the **P**assword box).

Changing the Administrative Password

The first thing you should do is create a new password to admit you (and other administrators you designate) into the administrative windows of KM services.

1. From the Exchange Server Administrator's window, choose the Configuration object.

2. Choose Encryption.

3. Select the Security tab.

4. Select **K**ey Management Server Administrators, which brings up the Key Management Server Password dialog box (see fig. 14.4).

Figure 14.4

You must enter a password in order to access any of the advanced security features.

5. If this is the first time you're seeing this dialog box, use the supplied password, password. Then choose OK.

If you don't want to have to reenter the password every time you want to configure an option, select the **R**emember this password box so you can have five minutes to work before the system insists you reenter the password.

However, if you are going to leave the computer during the five minutes, be sure to choose **F**orget Remembered Password—otherwise anyone can sit at your computer and gain access to the Security tab of any mailbox.

6. Choose **C**hange Password to see the Change Password dialog box (see fig. 14.5).

7. Enter the **C**urrent password, then enter the **N**ew password. You also have to reenter the new password in the **V**erify password box.

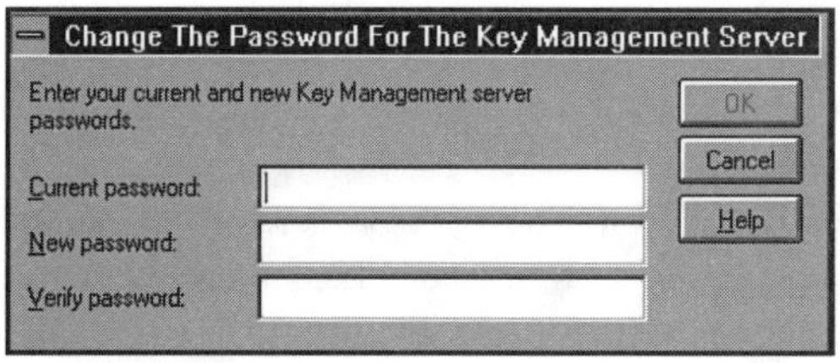

Figure 14.5

Change the default password to keep the administrative functions secure.

Adding Administrators

Once you gain access to the Key Management Server Administrators dialog box (see fig. 14.6), you can configure additional administrators for the KM system.

Figure 14.6

The Administrators dialog box is where you add and remove administrators for this component.

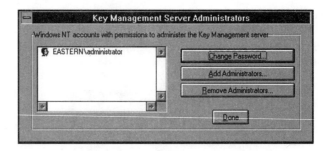

To establish another administrator:

1. Choose **A**dd Administrators. The Add Users dialog box is displayed, listing all users (see fig. 14.7).

Figure 14.7

Choose as many additional administrators as you think you'll need to help run the security component.

> **Tip**
>
> This Add Users dialog box is a bit different than it is when you're adding users to other parts of Exchange Server. Only users are listed in the KM component when you're specifying additional administrators. Most of the time, this dialog box also displays all the groups in the system.

2. Select a user, then choose **A**dd. Continue to add users as needed, and choose OK when you are finished.

3. If you want to change the password for each administrator, highlight the administrator, then choose **C**hange Password. The current password is the one you used (assuming you changed the default).

4. When you finish adding administrators, choose **D**one.

Selecting an Encryption Scheme

Encryption is a security feature provided through the KM component, which permits the encryption of data that is on a disk or traveling through the messaging system.

It's important to note that the Key Manager service does not get involved in the encryption process itself. Encryption is performed by the Microsoft Exchange Client.

The Security tab of the Encryption dialog box displays the current encryption algorithm, which you can change if you want (see fig. 14.8).

Figure 14.8

You can change the encryption algorithm your messaging system uses—the changes can be by location if your organization has offices outside North America.

◆ For North America, Microsoft Exchange Client can use CAST-64 or the U.S. Federal Data Encryption Standard (DES).

◆ For all locations outside North America, Microsoft Exchange Client supports the CAST-40 algorithm.

Setting Up Advanced Security for Users

When you establish advanced security features for the users in your organization, they will be able to sign and encrypt their messages digitally. Each user must be individually configured for this feature.

To establish advanced security for users, follow these steps:

1. From the Microsoft Exchange Administrator window, choose Recipients.

2. Double-click on the mailbox you want to configure for advanced security to bring up the mailbox Properties dialog box.

3. Choose the Security tab. The Key Management Server Password dialog box displays, and you have to enter your password. This is the administrative password, the one you configured when you changed the default password to your new password.

4. The Security property page is now available for configuration (see fig. 14.9).

5. Choose **E**nable Advanced Security.

Figure 14.9

The Security property page enables advanced security and provides other security options.

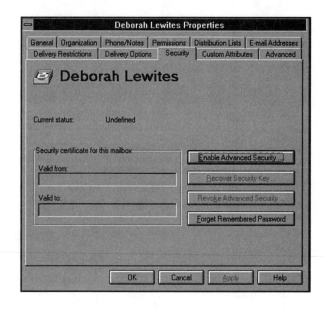

Understanding the Security Token

As soon as you enable advanced security for a mailbox, the KM server generates a temporary token that the mailbox user needs to establish advanced security back at the workstation (see fig. 14.10). Choose OK to generate the token.

Figure 14.10

A one-time token is displayed for a mailbox that has just had advanced security enabled—the token must be passed to the mailbox user.

In order to permit the user to complete advanced security configuration, you have to give the token to the user. Choose a secure method for passing the token—don't ship it through the messaging system to a mailbox that is accessible by multiple users.

When the user begins to configure advanced security at the workstation, that process sends the token back to the server.

Meanwhile, Back at the Workstation

In order to configure advanced security, the user has to open the client software and follow these steps:

1. From the Microsoft Exchange Client software window, choose **O**ptions from the **T**ools menu.

2. Click on the Security tab, then choose **S**et Up Advanced Security. The Setup Advanced Security dialog box requests the token (see fig. 14.11).

3. Enter the **T**oken.

4. Confirm the location of the **S**ecurity file.

Figure 14.11

*To enable
advanced
security, a user
needs the token,
then must create
a password.*

 The security file contains your advanced security profile. It can be stored on your computer or a floppy disk. If you access your mailbox remotely, take a copy of the file with you. Security files can be placed in any folder you wish. The format of the file is name.epf.

5. Enter a **P**assword, then **C**onfirm it. The password must have at least six characters; there is no option of *not* having a password.

 It's a good idea to have a different password for your mailbox security features than the one you use for logon.

6. Choose OK. The request for advanced security is sent to the KM server (which matches up the tokens). Choose OK to acknowledge the sending of the token.

Later That Day...

After the request for advanced security, along with the token, has been sent to the KM server, the request is processed. Then, a message is sent to the user (see fig.14.12).

Completing the Client Advanced Security Configuration

To continue setting up security on the workstation, the mailbox user has to open the message from the System Attendant—the new user password is needed to open the message.

If the request for enabling advanced security was successful, the message announces that fact (see fig.14.13).

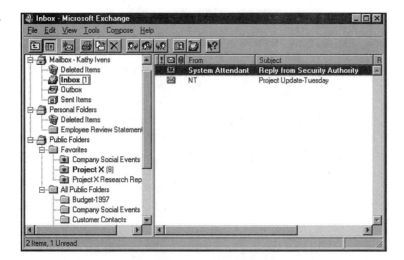

Figure 14.12

*There's mail in
the Inbox from the
System Attendant;
it's a reply to the
request for
advanced
security.*

Figure 14.13

*The request for
advanced security
features for this
mailbox was
successfully
received.*

If the request did not contain the correct token, the message suggests contacting the administrator and trying again.

To set up the capability of signing and sealing messages, return to the Options dialog box and choose the Security tab. The following options are now accessible (choose any or all):

◆ **E**ncrypt message contents and attachments.

◆ Add **d**igital signature to message.

◆ Change Password.

Sending a Sealed and Signed Message

A user with advanced security available composes a message in the usual way. When the Send button is clicked, the security features kick in (see fig. 14.14).

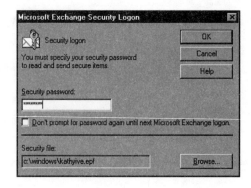

Figure 14.14

*Your password is
necessary in order
to send a
message—
this means the
recipient can be
sure it came
from you.*

The Security Logon dialog box offers several options in addition to insisting on some
required information:

◆ You must enter your password.

◆ Select **D**on't prompt for password if you want Microsoft Exchange Client to
remember your password throughout this session. You can read and send
secured messages without reentering the password, but when you close the
Exchange software, the password is forgotten.

◆ You can **B**rowse to change the security file (if you renamed it or moved it to a
floppy disk).

Sending Mail to an Unsecured Recipient

When you attempt to send a secure message, Microsoft Exchange Server checks the
security status of the recipient. If the recipient hasn't been granted advanced security
(or hasn't yet returned the token to begin configuration of advanced security), the
signed and sealed message cannot be sent. A dialog box appears to tell you the
recipient is not secured, and you can choose either to unencrypt the message or
cancel it.

 When a secured recipient receives a signed or sealed message, it cannot be
opened until the recipient's password is entered. This assures the sender that only
the recipient will see the message.

Enabling Security for Everyone at Once

There is one function that can be performed as a bulk process—the generation of tokens. However, after you've accomplished that, you still have to distribute the tokens one at a time to users. Until the users receive and use the tokens, they are security-enabled only up to the point of having advanced security rights enabled, but not yet installed and therefore not working.

To generate a security token to all users, follow these steps:

1. On the drive where the Key Management component is installed, go to a command prompt.

2. Move to the \BIN subdirectory of the KM software directory (usually \SECURITY).

3. Enter SIMPORT (the program is SIMPORT.EXE). The program begins by binding to the Microsoft Exchange Server directory service.

4. Enter the appropriate data as prompted.

5. The program processes all the users on the selected server and reports back (see fig. 14.15).

6. Exit the command prompt.

```
                          Command Prompt
C:\security\bin>simport
SIMPORT is binding to the Microsoft Exchange Directory service on this computer
..
Enter the site for the mailboxes you want to security enable :eastern
Enter the name of the home server of the mailboxes you want to security enable
east
Enter the Key Mangement Server administrator password:
Enter the computer name of the Exchange Key Management Server: east
Processing mailbox /o=calliope/ou=eastern/cn=recipients/cn=acct
Processing mailbox /o=calliope/ou=eastern/cn=recipients/cn=us_one
Processing mailbox /o=calliope/ou=eastern/cn=recipients/cn=kathyi
Processing mailbox /o=calliope/ou=eastern/cn=recipients/cn=nt
Processing mailbox /o=calliope/ou=eastern/cn=recipients/cn=deborah
Processing mailbox /o=calliope/ou=eastern/cn=recipients/cn=aln
Processing mailbox /o=calliope/ou=eastern/cn=recipients/cn=us-two
Processing mailbox /o=calliope/ou=eastern/cn=recipients/cn=us_four
Processing mailbox /o=calliope/ou=eastern/cn=recipients/cn=beverly telepan
Processing mailbox /o=calliope/ou=eastern/cn=recipients/cn=judith bernardi
Processing mailbox /o=calliope/ou=eastern/cn=recipients/cn=versa2
11 users processed successfully. 0 failure(s) occurred.

C:\security\bin>
```

Figure 14.15

Every mailbox has been assigned a token.

Once the tokens have been issued to all the users, you can retrieve them and pass them along. Open each mailbox, move to the Security tab, and choose **R**ecover security key. Each mailbox will display the user's token so you can note it and pass it to the user (see fig. 14.16).

Figure 14.16

This mailbox user's token has been generated and is being displayed for the administrator— now it has to be passed to the user.

 If you make sure you tell the system to remember your password for five minutes when you enter the password in order to access the first mailbox, you can probably retrieve all the tokens before the time is up. Otherwise, you have to enter the administrator password every time you move to a new mailbox.

Setting Up Security for Other Sites

You can enable all the security features in the KM server at other sites in your organization without setting up a separate KM server (remember, you should have only one KM server in an organization).

You install the KM software at all the other sites, using a built-in "trick" that prevents that installation process from becoming a KM server installation.

For this to work, you have to make sure there is a connection between the new site and the Primary Domain Controller (PDC) on the site that is already set up for KM services.

The reason for the connection is that when you installed KM services at the original site, a new object was installed in your Microsoft Exchange Server hierarchy. The new object is named CA, and it is visible in the right pane of the Exchange Server Administrator window when you highlight Configuration in the left pane.

During installation, the KM services installation program looks at connected servers in order to ascertain whether the CA object exists. If so, it does not set up a new server. Therefore, it's important to make sure the CA object is visible from the new site.

Now, when you run the KM installation program, the services will be available at the new site but you will not have installed a KM server.

Enabling User Security at Remote Sites

Setting up advanced security for users in remote sites requires a slightly different approach.

Generating Tokens for Remote Users

The generation of tokens takes place through RPCs, which, of course, is not possible from remote sites. Therefore, you have to take the following steps:

1. From the remote site, provide the names of users to the administrator of the site where the KM server exists.

2. Generate the tokens for the remote users at the KM site.

3. Send the tokens to the administrator of the remote site (or directly to the users at the remote site).

 Because the administrator and users at the remote site do not yet have advanced security, sending the tokens via regular e-mail misses the whole point. Tokens should be transmitted in a way that does not store the information on a disk. Use either voice or direct connection (dial in to the administrator's computer by using Microsoft's RAS or some other workstation-to-workstation technology) and deliver the tokens. If the receiving workstation is secure, the data can be stored on disk. If the receiving workstation is not secure, the tokens should be distributed immediately and then deleted from disk.

Enabling Security for Remote Users

The request for advanced security takes place through e-mail, which doesn't require RPCs. Consequently, the procedure for enabling advanced security at the workstation is identical for all clients.

Viewing the Security Log

Any unusual occurrence in KM services is logged and available for examination in the Event Viewer. Even in the absence of error messages (at the KM server or at client workstations), you should periodically check the log to see whether there's a potential problem brewing:

1. Open the Administrative Tools program group, then double-click on the Event Viewer.

2. Choose **A**pplication from the **L**og menu to display the events recorded from running applications.

3. Check any events from the source named MSExchangeKMS.

Of course, not just errors or problems are logged—all significant events are recorded. For instance, you can check on the status of token generation or whether a revoked certificate was processed (see fig. 14.17).

Figure 14.17

The Application Event Log displays significant events for the KM services—here we see that a user successfully received a token after bulk-generation.

Viewing Mailbox Security Status

You can check on the status of advanced security for any mailbox (usually as a result of a query from a user) by opening the mailbox and clicking on the Security tab. You will probably have to enter a password (unless you were working in KM services and your five minutes aren't up).

The current status of the mailbox security is displayed under the mailbox name, at the top of the property page (see fig. 14.18):

◆ Undefined means no steps for enabling security have been taken for this mailbox.

◆ New means the token has been issued, but the user has not yet returned it as part of the process of enabling advanced security at the client workstation.

◆ Active means security has been enabled and the user has returned the token and established advanced security at the workstation.

◆ Disabled means that previously enabled security is now disabled for this mailbox.

◆ Key recovery in progress means a new token has been issued (or a previous token reissued) but not yet received back; or, a security that was previously disabled is in the process of being enabled again.

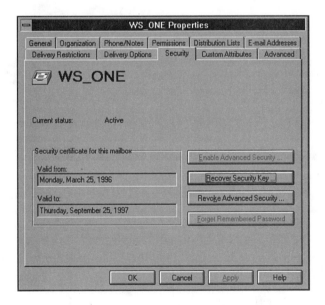

Figure 14.18

The KM server and the user have completed all the necessary steps and security because this mailbox is Active.

Recovering Security Keys

One of the absolute laws of nature for administrators is that users forget their passwords. (Sometimes it seems as if the only users who don't forget their passwords are the ones who write them down and paste the paper on the monitor, which makes the whole idea of the password kind of useless.)

Users also think that you can find their passwords for them, as if there were some secret button to click on in the administrative software that would reveal this information—they don't seem to realize that if administrators could see passwords, the secrecy would be compromised and the whole point of having passwords is lost.

Clever users, who are comfortable with the way the system works, try using Explorer or File Manager to get into the epf file (the file that's created when they enable advanced security). This file provides very little valuable information, and it is no help at all for password memory-jogging (see fig. 14.19).

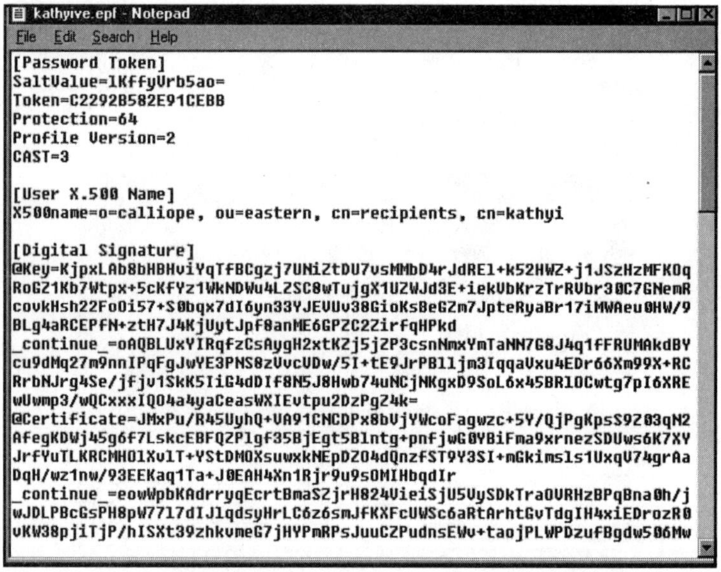

Figure 14.19

The encryption features of KM services apply to everything—the epf file is chock-full of information you can't read or understand.

Because you can't give users their passwords, the only available solution is to start over and let the forgetful user devise a new password (and then, of course, probably return in a few weeks with the same problem).

To accomplish this, follow these steps:

1. Open the mailbox and move to the Security tab (enter your administrative password if prompted).

2. Choose **R**ecover Security Key.

3. If the original key can be recovered, it is displayed. Otherwise, a new token is displayed.

4. Pass the token to the user along with instructions to perform all the steps for advanced security once again. This provides an opportunity to enter a password.

Although this is basically an identical procedure to that performed when you first began the process of enabling security through KM services, there are two differences:

◆ The **E**nable Advanced Security button is greyed out and inaccessible on the mailbox because that step was already performed.

◆ Until the reenabling of advanced security is complete, the mailbox status is Key recover in progress.

Revoking Security

If you have reason to suspect that security for a mailbox has been compromised (or you have some other reason for taking away a user's ability to sign and seal messages), click on the Revoke Advanced Security button on the mailbox Security tab. When security has been removed (it takes only a few seconds), the system notifies you that the operation was successful (see fig. 14.20).

Figure 14.20

This user mailbox no longer has the capability of signing and sealing messages—the security status will be changed to disabled.

CHAPTER 15

Monitoring Events

Built into your Microsoft Exchange Server system is the capability of monitoring certain events, getting an early warning when things aren't functioning properly, and even notifying the appropriate person to fix the problem.

There are three tools in your Windows NT/Microsoft Exchange Server system that are used for monitoring activities:

- ◆ The Link Monitor
- ◆ The Server Monitor
- ◆ The Windows NT Server Performance Monitor

Monitoring services are not the same as logging services or logging events. For example, directory and public folder replication events are logged, but you receive no alerts or offers to fix things if there are errors. In order to check the condition of a logged service, or see whether there are any problems, you have to open a program and look at a file. Monitoring services don't require you to perform a task in order to check on your system's behavior or general health—they're activist programs.

Configuring Link Monitors

Link monitors check the messaging services to ascertain whether or not messages are sent within a specified period of time. The link monitor checks messages that are sent to other servers in the organization (either on the same site or a different site) and messages that are sent to foreign systems. The test measures a round trip by sending a test message, called a *ping message*. At specific intervals a ping message is sent to every server and system that you include in your configuration of the link monitor.

To create a link monitor, follow these steps:

1. From the Microsoft Exchange Server Administrator Window, select the Monitors object in the configuration container of the site object.

2. Choose **N**ew Other from the **F**ile menu, then choose **L**ink Monitor. The General tab property page for a link monitor displays (see fig. 15.1).

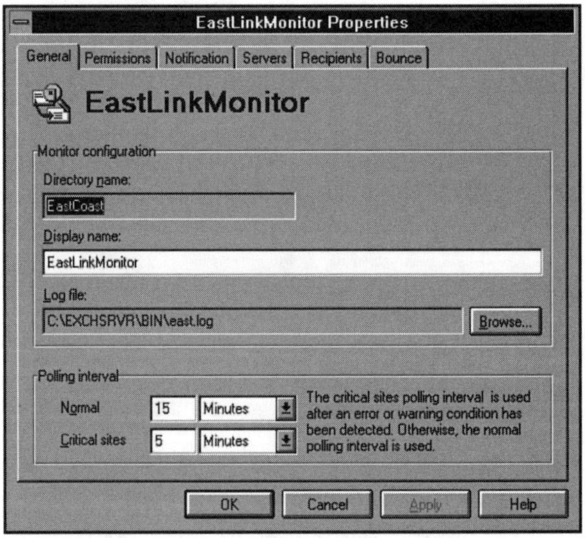

Figure 15.1

All the basic configuration options for a new link monitor are selected on the General property tab.

Configuring the General Property Page

The fields in this property page are used to establish the link monitor and set the conditions under which tests are run.

Directory name is the name of the link monitor—it is not a directory in the way we usually use that word. It's really the name of this link monitor. The name can have up to 64 alphanumeric characters (spaces are permitted). The name cannot be changed. If you do not fill in this field, when you want to run a link monitor the system will prompt you for a name and run/report under that name. The name should be descriptive, explaining the monitor you are configuring. For example, you might have a link monitor called Measure all U.S. sites on rainy Tuesdays.

Display name is the name that appears in the Administrator window. You can use up to 256 alphanumeric characters. If no name is specified, the system prompts for one when you run the monitor. This name can be modified at any time.

> **Tip** Be fairly descriptive in the Display name field because the list of monitors in the Administrator window lists all monitors, of all types. Make sure the word link is in the display name so you can tell which monitors are link monitors, which are server monitors, and so on.

Log File specifies the name of the file, which will be a log containing information about the status of the link monitor, along with notifications of events. You can look at (and edit, to save space) the log with any text editor. It makes sense, of course, to establish a log file name that is similar to the name of the link monitor. You can use the Browse button to choose the path for the log file.

You specify the conditions for polling in the Polling Interval section. You can choose any number of seconds, minutes, or hours that seems reasonable for your particular circumstances:

◆ Set a Normal interval for sending ping messages in order to poll servers.

◆ Specify a Critical Sites interval for those servers that are not responding normally.

> **Note** Once a server fails to return a ping message in the length of time you specify (see the section on the Bounce property page later in this chapter for setting return times), that server is considered to be in a warning or alert state. At that point, the Critical interval becomes active.

continues

A warning state means that a server failed to return a ping message in the specified amount of time.

An alert state occurs when the amount of time specified for that level of worry elapses without a return ping.

Configuring the Bounce Property Page

The Bounce property page is the place to set the maximum elapsed times for round-trip ping messages. (A message returning to the sender is called a *bounce*, and link monitors force the return.)

There are two settings available on the Bounce property page (see fig. 15.2). For both these settings, enter a value and a unit of time (seconds, minutes, or hours):

◆ Warning State, which is a maximum time period that is acceptable for a round-trip message. If a ping message exceeds this maximum, the connection between the servers should be considered to be in a warning state.

◆ Alert State, which is a maximum time period (longer than that entered for a warning state) after which the connection between the servers is deemed to be in an alert state.

Figure 15.2

Specify a period of time for a round-trip message so that if that time is exceeded, you know there may be a problem between connected servers.

If the times you enter are exceeded, and the connection is considered to be in either a warning state or an alert state, you can specify what should happen in order to remedy the situation (see the next sections).

Tip   Servers that are connected in different ways will have different "normal" elapsed times. For example, you may have servers that are dialed up and other servers that are directly cabled. You should create different link monitors for each type of connection so that the elapsed time specifications will be reasonable for the situation. After your system has been running a while and you have an idea of what a normal time duration is, you may want to change the specifications.

Configuring the Notification Property Page

You can establish a notification process so that an administrator is told when a server is in an alert state or a warning state. This notification can be a message, or you can use application software and create a set of conditions that will launch that software in order to perform some type of notification process (perhaps you have software that will issue a message to a cellular pager).

You can also establish a second tier of notification so that additional personnel are notified if the problem worsens or the administrators who are in the first tier do not respond (either because they cannot be reached or they could not fix the problem).

To add a Notification to the system:

1. Move to the Notification tab to display the Notification property page.

2. Choose **N**ew to establish a new notification. The New Notification dialog box displays (see fig. 15.3).

Figure 15.3

The type of notification can vary from a simple mailbox message to the lanching of a software application that will set a chain of events into action.

There are three choices in the **N**otification Type list box in the New Notification dialog box. The process for configuration varies depending on your selection. Highlight the selection you want and choose OK. An Escalation Editor dialog box displays with the appropriate choices, described next.

Launch a Process

Choose Launch a Process to notify personnel who are not logged on and will therefore not receive an alert message through their computers. Choosing this option displays the Escalation Editor (Launch Process) dialog box (see fig. 15.4).

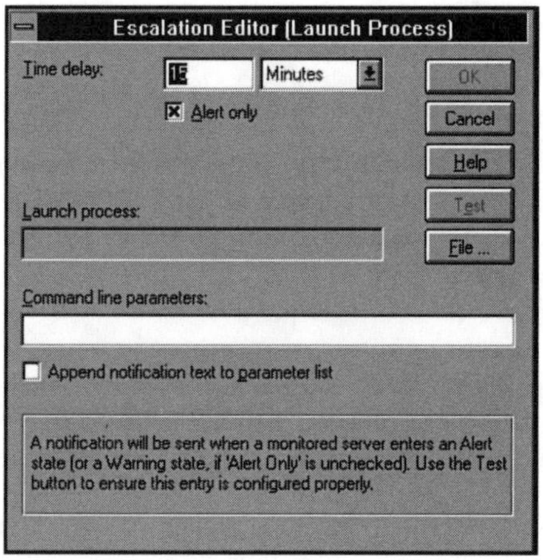

Figure 15.4

You can configure an application that will notify a help desk person or administrator who is away from the office.

The configuration options on this Editor dialog box are the following:

◆ **T**ime Delay, which is the amount of time that must elapse after the warning or alert state is in effect. At that point the software is launched. Enter a number, then choose whether that number specifies seconds, minutes, or hours.

◆ **A**lert Only, which means that the notification will be sent only if a server goes into an alert state. If you want to send the notification when a server is in either an alert state or a warning state, deselect this choice.

◆ **L**aunch Process, which is the name of the executable file that you want to run. You can choose the **F**ile button to browse for the file.

◆ **C**ommand Line Parameters, which can be entered for the executable file. If you are configuring multiple link monitors, you might want to use different parameters to distinguish them (if the software permits).

◆ Append Notification Text to **P**arameter List, which you can select (if the software permits) in order to attach text to any parameters you entered. If additional text will cause the software to return an error message, be sure this box is clear.

After you configure the Launch Process dialog box, use the T**e**st button to initiate an immediate launch. Be sure to tell the recipient it is a test and also have that recipient call you to report the results.

Send a Mail Message

The Escalation Editor (Mail Message) dialog box lets you establish parameters for notifying an administrator or help desk attendant via e-mail (see fig. 15.5).

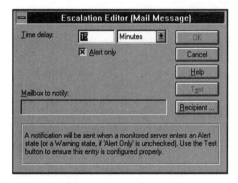

Figure 15.5

Your e-mail system can be the device for notifying the appropriate personnel of a problem on a server, and the inbox of the recipient creates a paper trail for tracking the time the link monitor reported a problem.

The configuration options are similar to those described for Launch Process, except that instead of a software application you have to enter a **M**ailbox to Notify. Enter the mailbox name(s) of the users that need to be notified. You can choose **R**ecipient to see a listing of all the mailboxes available.

Once configuration is complete, use the T**e**st button to send a test message.

Send a Windows NT Alert

Instead of sending e-mail to a user mailbox, you can send a message to a computer so that the person using that computer sees an alert. When you choose this option, the Escalation Editor (Windows NT Alert) dialog box is displayed (see fig. 15.6).

Figure 15.6

Send a message to a computer to notify the user on that computer that there may be a problem between connected servers.

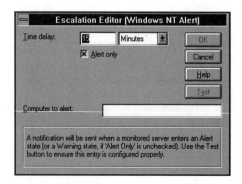

Again, the configuration options are the same as those described previously, but you must specify a name in the **C**omputer to Alert text box.

 Although it's logical to send a message to a user who is on-site at the computer having a problem, or send an alert to a computer connected to one that seems to need maintenance, message alerts do not work if the receiving computer or user is at the other end of a connection that is down. You should also be sure to send a message or alert to an entity on your own LAN so that someone knows to pick up a telephone and have a person on-site where the problem exists investigate.

 You might want to create an escalation path for your notification system. Perhaps you will notify the primary support person when the monitor enters a warning state and then notify a secondary tier of people if the monitor enters an alert state. You could establish staggered notifications for support personnel, with the primary support person being notified immediately, and additional support personnel being notified at varying intervals. If you choose staggered notification, you need to configure separate notifications for each person.

Once you have configured the notifications, the Notification property page will display them, using symbols in the left column that indicate whether the notification is for an alert state (red down arrow) or a warning state (red exclamation point).

Configuring the Recipients Property Page

The round-trip message the link monitor sends in order to test your server connections has to be sent and returned, which means you have to have a recipient.

There are two approaches you can use to carry out a round-trip message:

◆ Specify an existing user and configure an automated program to respond to the message.

◆ Specify a nonvalid address so the message is rejected and returned to the sender.

Use the Recipients property page to list the recipients for your ping messages (see fig. 15.7).

Figure 15.7

Pick a recipient or an invalid address to force a round-trip message so your link monitor can time the trip.

You must tell the link monitor how to find the subject of the original message when it is returned:

◆ If the recipient is configured for an automatic reply program that keeps the original subject text in the reply subject field, use the Message **S**ubject Returned box to list recipients.

◆ If you do not know (or cannot control) how the recipient will handle the text in the original subject field, use the Message Subject or **B**ody Returned box to list recipients.

To place real recipients in either box, enter a valid mailbox or choose the appropriate Modify button to see a list of available mailboxes.

To place invalid addresses in either box, select the appropriate List radio button and then enter data that will cause the message to bounce back as undeliverable.

If you configure your link monitor for multiple servers (see the later section Configuring the Servers Property Page), and you use invalid addresses, you may have a problem. A nondelivery report does not have a name attached to it, so it could have been sent from a computer anywhere along the connection path. You might want to set up separate, specific link monitors for each site/server in your organization.

Configuring the Permissions Page

First, make sure you can see the Permissions property page, because it's hidden by default. To view it, choose Options from the Tools menu, then select Show Permissions Page For All Objects.

This property page enables you to specify users or groups that have rights and permissions to modify and manipulate this link monitor (see fig. 15.8).

Figure 15.8

Use the Permissions property page to give users permission to manipulate the monitor, assigning specific roles to each user or group.

The top section of the page displays the Windows NT accounts that have inherited permissions. This section is read-only and lists the Administrator by default.

To give additional users or groups permissions:

1. Choose Add to see the Add Users and Groups dialog box, which lists all groups and individual users.

2. Highlight the name you want, then choose **A**dd to add the name to the A**d**d Names list (see fig. 15.9). Use the **L**ist Names From box to display names from other servers, sites, or domains.

3. When you finish adding names, choose OK.

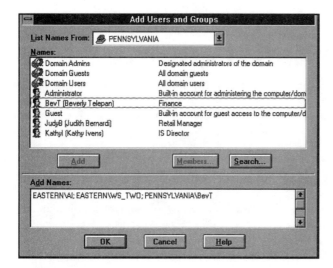

Figure 15.9

Each additional user you select is listed—the domain precedes the user name.

Once you add the new users to the Permissions property page, you can configure each user for specific rights and roles by highlighting the name and choosing a selection from the Ro**l**es list box. Each Role has one or more specific rights attached to it.

The following are the available rights:

◆ Modify User Attributes, which permits modification of the user attributes for this monitor

◆ Modify Admin Attributes, which permits modification of the attributes given to administrators

◆ Delete, which gives rights to delete objects

◆ Modify Permissions, which gives rights to change the permissions on this monitor

You can select or deselect any right(s) attached to a particular role. If you choose a selection of rights that matches another role, the name in the Ro**l**es box will change to that one. If you select a group of rights that do not match a specific role, you have configured a Custom role and the Ro**l**es box will display that fact.

The Roles and their rights are the following:

◆ Admin, which has all rights except Modify Permissions

◆ Permissions Admin, which has all rights

◆ User, which has only the right to Modify User Attributes

Configuring the Servers Property Page

Once you configure all the parameters for this link monitor, it's time to specify the servers that will be monitored. The Servers property page lists all the sites and servers to which you can connect. Choose the servers you want this link monitor to test.

Running a Link Monitor

You can have your link monitor start automatically, or you can start it manually.

Running the Monitor Automatically

To start the link monitor automatically, you have to place a command in the Startup program group:

1. Open the Startup program group.

2. Choose **N**ew from the **F**ile menu, then select Program **I**tem and choose OK to display the Program Item Property dialog box.

3. Enter a **D**escription—what you are doing is starting the Microsoft Exchange Server Administrator program along with the link monitor.

4. In the **C**ommand Line box, enter the command needed to launch the Administrator program and the monitors. The syntax is the following:

```
path\admin.exe /mSite\Monitor\Server
```

where the following is true:

◆ Path is the drive and directory where ADMIN.EXE resides (usually in the \BIN directory below the directory that holds Exchange Server).

◆ Admin.exe is the executable file that starts the Administrator program.

◆ MSite is the name of the site where the link monitor is defined. This is optional, and if it is the current site, it can be omitted.

◆ Monitor is the Directory Name you gave the link monitor.

◆ Server is the name of the server you must be connected to in order to read the monitor.

The first logon to the NT Server will launch both the Administrator program and the monitor.

 You can start multiple monitors in this fashion—just append additional *\monitor\server* entries to the command line.

Running Monitors Manually

There are situations in which it might be preferable to start your link monitor manually. For example, if servers are shut down for maintenance at certain periods (especially if there are sites in different time zones), you might want to test connections only when you know everything is up and running. If your server has had a problem—perhaps it crashed or went to sleep for no apparent reason, or somebody pulled the plug—you might have to restart the monitor.

To start the link monitor manually, choose Start M**o**nitor from the **T**ools menu. If you have multiple monitors or if you did not name the monitor, you are asked to specify the monitor you want to run.

Stopping Monitor Actions

If you need to take a server down for maintenance, you can stop the actions that ensue when a monitor does not receive normal responses. This is necessary for any monitors running from the affected server or any monitors from another server that are polling this server. This stops the notifications that would normally take place when an unexpected problem arises.

To suspend notifications temporarily, enter `admin /t` at a command prompt. To resume normal operations, enter `admin /-t`.

Using Server Monitors

Server monitors are used to check the condition of all the servers that can be reached via remote procedure calls (RPCs). Although this generally means servers that are running on the same site, you can use a server monitor to communicate with any servers that are reached with RPC connections.

Server monitors determine whether servers are up and running, whether the services provided by the servers are running, and they also measure and synchronize the computers' clocks, which is important for all the replication procedures your system is performing.

As with the Link Monitor, you can establish notification procedures when the monitor discovers a problem.

You can use a single server monitor to monitor multiple servers, but if you need to send notifications to different people for different servers, you need to create multiple server monitors.

 The actions you specify will be performed on all servers being monitored by this Server Monitor. If you need different actions for different servers, you have to configure multiple service monitors.

To set up a server monitor:

1. In the Administrator window, highlight the Monitors object in the Configuration container of the site object.

2. Choose **N**ew Other from the **F**ile menu, then choose **S**erver Monitor.

3. Configure each monitor following the guidelines described next.

The configuration schemes for the Permissions and Notification property pages are the same as described for the Link Monitor, so they are not covered here.

Configuring the General Property Page

Use the General property page to establish the name and basic settings for the new server monitor (see fig. 15.10).

Figure 15.10

The General property page is the place to establish the names and action intervals for a server monitor.

Directory **N**ame is the official, unique, name for this monitor. You can use up to 64 characters.

Display Name is the monitor's name as it appears in the Administrator window. It makes it easier to identify this monitor if you make sure you have the word "server" in the name to distinguish it from other monitors you may have established.

Log File (which is optional) is the name of a file where you want status information and problem notification actions kept. Enter the complete path and file name or use the **B**rowse button to point to a directory, then specify a log file name. You can view (and edit, in order to clean out), the log file with a text editor.

In the Polling Interval section, specify the conditions for polling. You can choose any number of seconds, minutes, or hours that seems reasonable for your particular circumstances:

◆ Set a N**o**rmal interval for checking the services running on the servers (that you are monitoring).

◆ Specify a **C**ritical Sites interval for those servers that do not respond normally when polled.

Configuring the Clock Property Page

Use the Clock property page to establish the conditions for an alert state if the servers lack time synchronization and optionally synchronize the server clocks (see fig. 15.11).

Figure 15.11

If a monitored server's clock is off (compared to the sending server), you can choose to issue a warning or alert, or you can synchronize the clock.

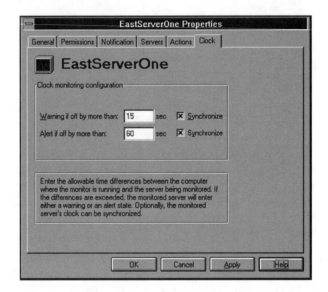

In the **W**arning box, specify a number of seconds by which the two clocks can differ without taking action. If this number is exceeded, a warning notification occurs. You also can select **S**ynchronize to match the target server clock with the monitoring computer's clock instead of issuing a warning.

In the A**l**ert box, specify the number of seconds permitted before an Alert notification occurs, or select S**y**nchronize to match the target server clock with the monitoring computer's clock instead of issuing an alert.

 If you opt to have clocks synchronized, be sure that all servers have been configured properly for time zones, because that is taken into consideration during the synchronization process.

Configuring the Actions Property Page

The Actions property page (see fig. 15.12) enables you to specify actions that should be taken if a server is in a warning or alert state (installed services have stopped or a service is missing). This is not the same as notifications, and you can configure the intervals for notifications so that they take place before, during, or after these actions occur.

Figure 15.12

Use the Actions property page to specify an escalated set of actions when there is a problem at a monitored server.

The **F**irst Attempt action is taken the first time a monitored server is polled and found to have a problem.

The **S**econd Attempt action is taken the second time a monitored server is polled and found to have a problem.

S**u**bsequent Attempt actions are taken after the second time a problem is discovered. Whatever action is specified here will occur continuously, using the interval specification established in the Critical Site Polling Interval on the General property page.

For each attempt, you can specify that one of the following actions be taken (use the arrow to the right of each choice to display and select an action):

Take No Action means that only the notifications you established on the notifications tab will occur.

Restart Service means that the server monitor should make an attempt to restart the missing service.

Restart Computer means that the server monitor should attempt to restart a computer (using the Windows NT Shutdown and Restart feature). If you choose this option, you have to configure two additional fields:

◆ **R**estart Delay, which specifies the number of seconds that must elapse before the computer is shut down. Make sure you give enough time for users to save their work.

◆ Restart **M**essage, which is a message that will be displayed on the server that is going to be shut down and restarted.

 Be sure the Critical Site Polling Interval is sufficiently long enough to enable the specified actions to be taken. For instance, if a server takes 7 minutes to restart and you have selected a **R**estart delay of 60 seconds, the Critical Site Polling Interval should be at least 8 minutes. Otherwise, the server continuously must be restarted.

 If the problem server is providing services over and above Microsoft Exchange Server, it is probably not a good idea to opt for restarting the computer, because that may create problems with open applications.

Configuring the Servers Property Page

You can choose the servers you want to monitor in the same way described for Link Monitors (select a server, then A**d**d it to the Monitored Servers list).

In addition, once you select a server to monitor, you can specify the services you want to monitor:

1. Highlight a monitored server, then choose Ser**v**ices to display the Services property page (see fig. 15.13).

2. The **M**onitored Services section lists the services you are watching with this Server Monitor. By default the directory, information stores, and MTA are monitored.

3. Highlight a service in the **I**nstalled Services section of the property page (which lists all the services installed on the selected server) and choose A**d**d to monitor that service.

4. Highlight a service in the **M**onitored Services section and choose **R**emove if you no longer think it's necessary to monitor a service you added.

   You can also choose **N**one, D**e**fault or A**l**l, which can clear or fill up the Monitored Service sections, in order to make changes with fewer mouse-clicks.

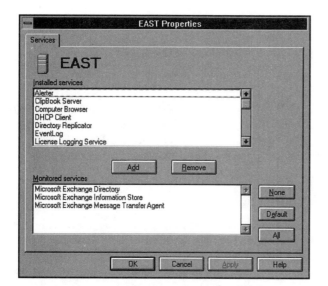

Figure 15.13

Choose the services you want to check on for each server you're monitoring.

Starting and Stopping Server Monitors

The process described for starting and stopping Server Monitors is the same used for Link Monitors. You can start them automatically (using the syntax described previously) or manually.

Using the NT Performance Monitor

The Performance Monitor is a Windows NT tool that you can also use for your Microsoft Exchange Server system. It's used for displaying the performance levels of your computer and any connected computers. It has a graphical interface, so it is easy to see performance levels when you look at the monitor's window.

You can get detailed information about the Performance Monitor from your Windows NT documentation; this discussion is limited to an overview and the use of the performance monitor by Microsoft Exchange Server.

The Performance Monitor is flexible, customizable, and powerful. The tasks it can perform include the following:

◆ Monitoring the hardware

◆ Monitoring the workload

◆ Monitoring the routing of messages between servers

◆ Detecting places where bottlenecks are occurring

◆ Fine-tuning server performance

Configuring a Performance Monitor means choosing specific, individual components of a system to monitor. Then you can see the behavior of those components in real time by watching the monitor's window, or you can open log files at a convenient time in order to see the activity levels that were recorded.

Understanding Counters

Every component, resource, device, and running process in a computer is seen as an object by the Performance Monitor. For instance, a task being performed by an application is an object; the memory it is using is an object. The components it is accessing and the subsystems it calls on (such as the print spooler) are also objects capable of being measured by the Performance Monitor.

The Performance Monitor uses a unit of measurement called a *counter* to track the activity of all the objects in your system. Counters may measure usage, time, lengths, or some other measurement that is appropriate for the object being measured.

You can use these counters to specify the conditions for an alert. Each counter can be set for a limit, either a maximum or a minimum, which determines normal behavior. When the object's counter falls short or exceeds the limit, it indicates that you need to remedy the situation.

The Exchange Server Performance Monitors

The number of objects and counters for any computer is incredibly extensive, so they are not listed here. Within that list is a list of those objects and counters that affect, or are affected by, Exchange Server. That list, too, is much too long to set out here. You can go through all the objects available in the Windows NT Performance Monitor to decide which you should be watching. Then, you need to configure monitors to measure one object or a group of related objects (or a group of unrelated objects, but that wouldn't make a lot of sense).

Before you go through the work involved in accomplishing that, however, take a look at the icons in the program group for Microsoft Exchange. Notice a group of Performance Monitors already configured for you (see fig. 15.14).

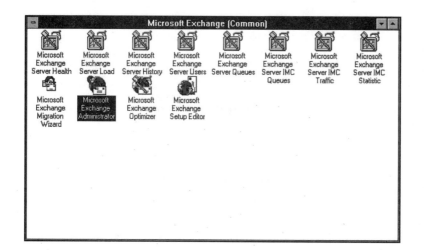

Figure 15.14

Preconfigured Performance Monitors make it easy for you to watch the system's activity without having to go through all the configuration routines.

The Elements of the Microsoft Exchange Performance Monitors

To understand how these monitors are configured, open one—for this discussion, let's open the monitor named Server Health (see fig. 15.15).

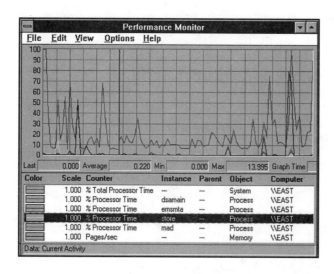

Figure 15.15

The Server Health monitor measures processor time and paging.

If you double-click on a Microsoft Exchange monitor and do not see the title bar or menu bar, double-click on the monitor window.

The central part of the monitor window is the chart, which is a line chart that changes as you watch it. There are several lines in the chart, each a different color.

The bottom of the window is the legend, where the details for each object being measured are displayed, including the following:

◆ Color, which is the color of the chart line for the object.

◆ Scale, which is the way the count information is displayed. It's really a percentage factor—you can choose 1, .1, .01, .001, and so on.

◆ Counter, which is a type of monitoring about the object that is being displayed. Some objects have multiple counters that can be measured.

◆ Instance, which is the description of the particular object being monitored. For example, if you have two processors in your computer, you have two instances of processors. You can also have multiple instances of physical hard disks. There are some objects that cannot have multiple instances, such as memory or server.

◆ Parent, which is the parent process if the object being monitored is a thread.

◆ Object, which is the object being monitored.

◆ Computer, which is the computer being monitored. You can configure a monitor for any computer attached to your network.

Displaying the Configuration Details

You can get a detailed look behind any line in the legend by double-clicking on it. For example, if you double-click on the dsamain instance of the process object, you can see the configuration of the chart line (see fig. 15.16).

For the counter being measured in figure 15.16 (percentage of processor time), there are multiple instances, and this chart line is configured for dsamain. Choose **E**xplain to see an explanation of the counter (see fig. 15.17).

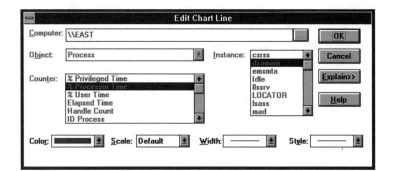

Figure 15.16

The details of the chart line indicate the specifics of the object being measured as well as the appearance of the chart line.

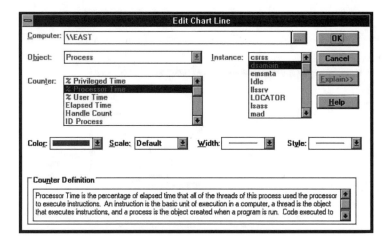

Figure 15.17

The Counter Definition window tells you more than you probably need (or want) to know about the counter being monitored.

Editing the Chart Line

You can use this dialog box to edit the chart line if you wish. The following items are part of the chart line:

◆ Color

◆ Scale

◆ Width

◆ Style

Click on the arrow to the right of any of the parameters to edit the selection. Choose OK when you are finished or Cancel if you do not want to make any changes.

Changing the Monitor's Configuration

You can change the other configuration elements from the monitor's main window. Without going into all the details (which are available in your Windows NT documentation), here are the basics:

Make sure you are in Chart mode (choose **C**hart from the **V**iew menu).

Choose **A**dd to Chart from the **E**dit menu to configure additional counters for this monitor.

Highlight a counter and choose **D**elete From Chart from the **E**dit menu to remove a counter from the monitor.

Choose **C**hart from the **O**ptions menu to change the type of chart this monitor displays. The Chart Options dialog box presents a variety of choices (see fig. 15.18).

Figure 15.18

You can change the look of the chart as well as the interval for updating information in the Chart Options dialog box.

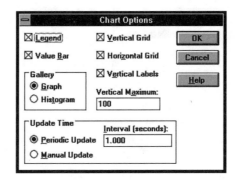

You can save the new settings by choosing **S**ave Chart Settings from the **F**ile menu (charts have a file extension of PMC).

Configuring Alerts

You can configure a performance monitor to alert you when certain objects, which you define, reach a measurement outside the parameters you select. The alert is displayed in an alert window log, and you can monitor multiple counters in the alert configuration. To set up an alert:

1. Move to the monitor's Alert window by choosing **A**lert from the **V**iew menu. The Alert window is blank until you create an alert configuration or open a file that contains a previously created one.

2. Choose **N**ew Alert Settings from the **F**ile menu.

3. Choose **A**dd to Alert from the **E**dit menu. The Add to Alert dialog box is displayed, showing the existing or default settings for a counter.

4. Configure the options the way you want them:

   ◆ **C**omputer is the workstation or server you want to monitor. By default, the current computer is chosen. To change computers, enter the name of the new computer or click on the button to the right of the Computer field to choose one from the list of attached computers.

   ◆ Ob**j**ect is the object you want to monitor. Changing the object changes the counter and instances listings.

   ◆ Coun**t**er is the process you want to monitor for the chosen object. (Click on **E**xplain to see a definition of the highlighted counter.)

   ◆ **I**nstance is the particular instance of the counter (if there are multiple instances).

   ◆ The Alert If box enables you to choose **O**ver or **U**nder as the direction for monitoring the threshold for the value you enter.

   ◆ Run **P**rogram On Alert, an optional choice, is the place to enter the path and file name for a program you want to launch when an alert condition exists. You must also indicate whether you want the program to run the **F**irst Time an alert occurs or E**v**ery Time.

5. Choose a Colo**r** to attach to this counter.

6. Choose **A**dd when you have configured the counter.

7. Repeat the process for each counter you want to put into this Alert configuration.

8. When you complete all your entries, choose **D**one.

As soon as you complete the Alert, it's displayed for you (see fig. 15.19).

You can edit the configuration for the Alert by highlighting it and then choosing **E**dit Alert Entry from the **E**dit menu (or by double-clicking on it).

Figure 15.19

Choosing a low maximum percentage for the use of processor time generates continuous alerts.

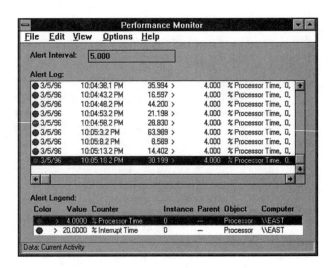

Saving the Alert Settings

You can save your alert log selections so that you can open the file later and see whether the conditions have improved. Choose **S**ave Alert Settings from the **F**ile menu, then enter a file name. Alert files have an extension of PMA. Use **O**pen from the **F**ile menu to view the file later.

If the monitor is open but you are not in the Alert view when an alert occurs, the bottom of the monitor's window will display a symbol (color-coded for the counter) along with the number of occurrences for that alert since the last time you were in the Alert view (see fig. 15.20).

Configuring Logs

Logging enables you to record data for later viewing, so you do not have to open (and watch) a performance monitor. The log records information about the performance of counters from your computer's activities, and you can combine data from multiple computers into a single log.

If you are planning a system upgrade, either for more computers, more disk space, more RAM, or any other hardware, the information contained in the performance monitor logs can be helpful.

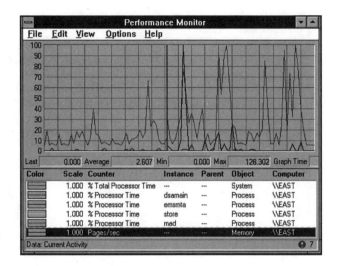

Figure 15.20

Even though the Chart view is displayed, you are notified about Alerts.

To work with logs on any monitors, you must first choose **L**og from the **V**iew menu.

To create and configure a log:

1. Choose **N**ew Log Settings from the **F**ile menu.

2. Choose **A**dd To Log from the **E**dit menu to display the Add To Log dialog box (see fig. 15.21).

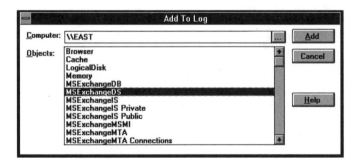

Figure 15.21

Create a log that's useful for troubleshooting and planning by choosing objects to track over a period of time.

3. Select a **C**omputer and an **O**bject and choose **A**dd. Repeat for all the computers and objects you want to track.

4. Choose **D**one when you have finished adding objects to the log. You are returned to the Log view of the monitor, which now displays your selections (see fig. 15.22).

Figure 15.22

This log file was configured to track suspected bottlenecks that might be the cause of occasional slowdowns of the system.

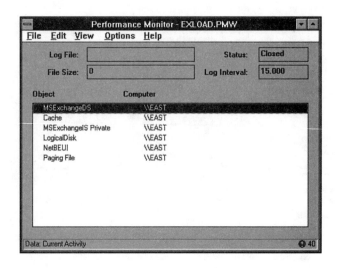

To save the log, choose **S**ave Log Settings from the **F**ile menu and enter a file name (logs have a file extension of PML).

Starting and stopping performance monitors works the same as the other monitors described earlier in this chapter.

PART V

Using Microsoft Exchange Server

CHAPTER 16

Using Client Software

Throughout your organization, users get mail, send mail, and work with files and folders using the Microsoft Exchange Server client software installed on their workstations. Across the variety of platforms supported for client workstations (Windows NT Workstation, Windows 95, Windows 3.*x*, and MS-DOS), the features and procedures remain pretty much the same.

Using the Viewer

The main window for the Microsoft Exchange Server client is accessed differently, depending upon the client platform:

◆ For Windows 3.*x* and Windows NT clients, open the Exchange program group, then double-click on the Exchange program icon.

◆ For Windows 95 clients, double-click on the Inbox icon on the desktop.

◆ For DOS clients, go to the directory in which the DOS version of Exchange client software is installed, and enter EXCHANGE at the command line.

The DOS client software provides only mail and message capabilities; Schedule+ cannot be accessed. It is, of course, a nongraphical application, although there is a menu bar of sorts at the top of the screen (use Alt+menu letter to access the menu items).

This chapter focuses on the Windows clients. The messaging discussion assumes the DOS functions (which have the same features), but any figures or illustrations will represent the various Windows platforms.

The program launches and displays the Exchange Viewer, which looks pretty much the same regardless of the Windows platform (see fig. 16.1).

Figure 16.1

The Windows 95 viewer showing the entire hierarchy—the viewers for Windows 3.x and Windows NT are almost identical.

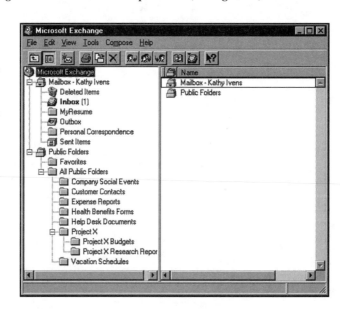

Understanding the Viewer Window

The viewer window contains the elements commonly found in Windows software applications. There is a title bar, a menu bar, a toolbar, a status bar, and the main window.

The Microsoft Exchange Client main window has two panes, and they behave much like Explorer or File Manager. When an object in the left pane is selected (highlighted), the right pane shows the details for that object. If you see only one pane, choose Folders from the **V**iew menu.

The left pane contains a hierarchy of Microsoft Exchange Server folder objects:

◆ Mailbox, where your incoming and outgoing mail is delivered. Mail can include messages, forms, and files.

The mailbox contains an Inbox folder, an Outbox folder, a Sent Items folder, and a Deleted Items folder. You can create additional mailbox folders if you want to store messages and other items in specific folders.

◆ Personal folders, which are folders you created to store on your local drive (although it's possible to store them on the server, it reduces the privacy). You can configure your mailbox operations so that your personal folders receive your incoming mail.

◆ Public folders, which are folders that you and other people in your organization can use to share information.

◆ Favorites folder, which is a place to list the public folders you access most often. Then, to go to one of your favorite public folders, you can use the objects you placed here. Because the number of public folders in an organization can grow quite large, this is a productive feature.

◆ All public folders, which is the parent folder of all the public folders in the system.

 If you are using Microsoft Exchange Client on a Windows NT 3.51 Workstation, while you are using the software you have right mouse button functions just as Windows 95 and NT 4.0 users do.

Using the Address Book

The Address Book is a directory of lists that contains user names, distribution lists, and public folder names. By default, there are two separate lists in your Address Book:

◆ A Global Address List, which has the names of all Microsoft Exchange users and distribution lists to which you can address messages.

◆ A Personal Address Book (PAB), which you create for yourself. In it you can put any type of address you want, such as the people to whom you frequently send messages, any personal distribution lists you create, or custom addresses for people on outside mail systems such as the Internet.

 There may be additional address lists, depending upon the way Microsoft Exchange Server is configured. For instance, if the organization has access to another mail system through a gateway, there may be a separate list for those addresses.

Most of the time, you access the address book as part of the process of composing a message. However, you can display it by clicking on its icon on the toolbar or choosing **A**ddress Book from the **T**ools menu (see fig. 16.2). When you access the address book in this way, it's called the viewer display, and this format enables you to view detailed information about the names on the list.

Figure 16.2

The Address Book window defaults to a display of the Global Address List.

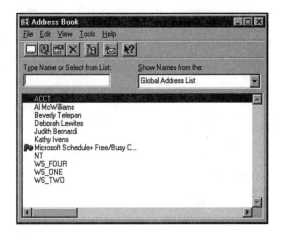

To change the address list that displays, click on the arrow in the **S**how Names box to view all the available lists (see fig. 16.3) and choose the one with which you want to work.

Figure 16.3

The Address Book lists the organization and available sites in addition to the default user lists.

Using the Personal Address Book

Your Personal Address Book (PAB) is a customizable list that exists as a file, so it's easy to copy it to a disk and use it on another computer (your home or portable computer). The file resides in the directory where Exchange is installed, and its extension is PAB.

To work with the PAB, choose it from the **S**how Names box in the Address Book window.

To add a name to the PAB, choose New **E**ntry from the **F**ile menu or click on the New Entry icon on the toolbar. The New Entry dialog box displays (see fig. 16.4). Pick the type of address you are inserting and choose OK.

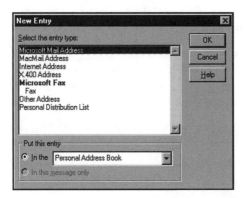

Figure 16.4

To add a new entry to your PAB, you have to specify the address type.

The entry types that display reflect your configuration. If you haven't installed one or more of the services, the entry type won't be offered.

 A quick way to add names from the global list to your personal address list is to display the global list, then right-click on any entry and choose **A**dd to Personal Address Book.

The dialog box that displays to receive the data for the new entry differs depending on the entry type. Besides the e-mail address, you can enter optional information such as voice line numbers, addresses, and even notes to yourself.

Creating a Distribution List

You can create personal distribution lists (PDLs) so that when you address a message to one of them, every individual on the list will receive the message. (There are also global distribution lists, created by an administrator, that are kept on the server.)

When you select PDL as the entry type, the New Personal Distribution List Properties dialog box displays (see fig. 16.5):

1. In the **N**ame box, enter a name for the list.

2. Choose Add/Remove **M**embers to see a list of all the users in your system (see fig. 16.6). You can select any existing list to display those names.

3. If there are lots of address lists and lots of names, use Fin**d** to speed your search. You can hunt by **D**isplay name, **F**irst name, **L**ast name, **T**itle, and even by Cit**y**.

4. To move a name into your PDL, highlight it and choose **M**embers to transfer it to the Personal Distribution **L**ist section or double-click on the name. You can move an existing PDL into a PDL you're currently creating.

5. To add a name to your PDL that is not already on one of the available lists, choose **N**ew. The process for adding the name is the same as described previously for adding names to your address book.

6. When you finish adding names to your PDL, choose OK. This returns you to the PDL Properties dialog box. At this point you can add notes about the list. Then choose OK.

The PDL is listed in your PAB, and its object is displayed differently than user names: the title text is bold and the icon shows two people.

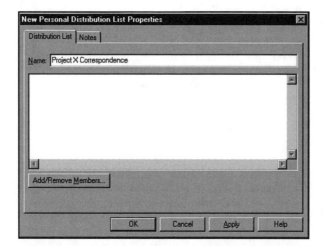

Figure 16.5

Create a PDL to hold names that should receive copies of certain messages; then send one message to reach all the members of the list.

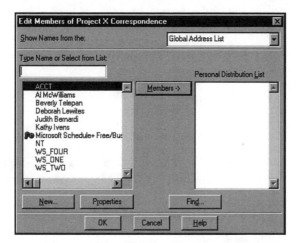

Figure 16.6

As you add names to your PDL, all the address lists in the system are available and you can choose from any of them.

Transferring Names to Your PAB

You can place users who are listed in the Global Address List into your PAB very easily:

1. Display the Global Address List in the Address Book dialog box.

2. Select (highlight) the name you want to transfer and right-click on it.

3. Choose **A**dd to Personal Address Book from the menu.

Sending Messages

Messages are easily composed and sent by using the viewer. To send a message:

1. Click on the New Message icon, or choose **N**ew Message from the Co**m**pose menu. The New Message dialog box displays (see fig. 16.7).

2. Click on T**o**, which displays the Address Book window so you can choose a recipient or multiple recipients.

3. If you want, you can click on **C**c to choose a user who will receive an indicated copy of the message.

4. Enter a subject for this message. You should carefully consider what you place in this entry box, because the Subject text can be used to filter messages (by you and by the recipient) when you want to search through messages.

5. Enter the message text. You have a robust range of formatting options and other word processing features at your disposal:

   ◆ You can change the font, the size, and the attributes (bold, italic, color, and so on) of any text.

   ◆ You can center, right-justify, indent, and tab.

   ◆ You can create bullet lists.

Figure 16.7

The New Message dialog box works like a mini word processor as you compose a message.

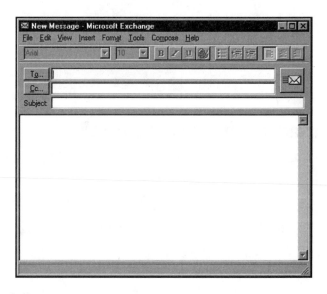

◆ You can spell-check the document or any part of it.

◆ You can use the usual Edit functions (cut, copy, paste, find, replace).

6. When you finish, click on the Send icon or choose Se**n**d from the **F**ile menu. You are returned to the Exchange viewer (the message is listed in the Sent Items object).

Options for Sending Messages

You do not have to send the message immediately; you can delay it. To see the options, choose Send Options from the **F**ile menu:

◆ Send this item I**m**mediately (the default).

◆ Send this item **I**n—specify a number, then choose whether that number indicates minutes, hours, days, or weeks. The message is sent to the server, which holds it until it is time to ship it to the recipient.

You can also save the message by choosing **S**ave from the **F**ile menu. The message is saved in your Inbox folder. Then, later, you can right-click on the message, choose P**r**operties and select Send **O**ptions from the General property page to choose an option for sending the message, as described previously.

You can also choose options for the way the message expires. An expiration affects only unread messages. You can choose to have a message that never expires or one that expires in a time frame that you select. If a message expires, it is deleted by the Microsoft Exchange Server.

Understanding AutoSignature

An AutoSignature is text you create in order to apply it as your signature whenever you send a message. You can have multiple AutoSignatures.

Creating an AutoSignature

To create an AutoSignature, choose Au**t**oSignature from the **T**ools menu, which brings up the AutoSignature dialog box (see fig. 16.8).

Figure 16.8

Use the AutoSignature dialog box to create and edit signatures and to set a default signature.

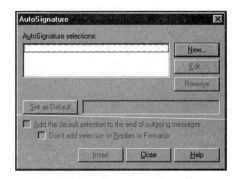

To create a new AutoSignature:

1. Choose **N**ew to display the New AutoSignature dialog box (see fig. 16.9).

Figure 16.9

You can create a signature that is made up of text you want to add to every message —it can be instructional, humorous, biographical, or anything you want.

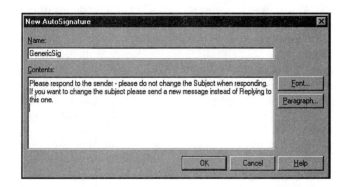

2. **N**ame this AutoSignature.

3. Enter the **C**ontents of the AutoSignature.

4. Choose **F**ont to change the font, size, or attributes of the text.

5. Choose **P**aragraph to change the alignment of text or add a bullet list.

6. Click on OK when you are finished.

You can repeat the process in order to create additional AutoSignatures.

Using AutoSignatures

Once you create one or more AutoSignatures, you can establish the protocols for using this feature from the AutoSignature dialog box (shown in fig. 16.8):

◆ Highlight an AutoSignature and choose **S**et as Default to have the selected item become the AutoSignature when you indicate you want one (otherwise you will be shown a list and can choose the one you want to add to the current message).

◆ Select **A**dd the default selection if you want to automate the process of placing the default AutoSignature at the end of every outgoing message.

◆ You can opt to skip the AutoSignature for **R**eplies or Forwards by selecting that choice. This means that only messages you compose will have an AutoSignature.

Receiving Messages

When you launch Microsoft Exchange Client, if there are any new messages in your mailbox, they are listed in the viewer's Inbox object. The header information that displays is in bold type to indicate it is still unread (see fig. 16.10).

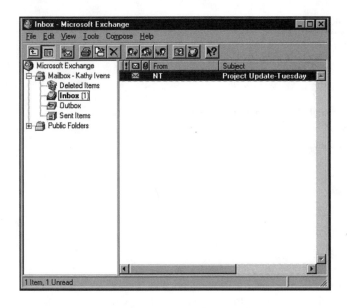

Figure 16.10

Someone has sent me a message—I can see the recipient and the subject so I can decide whether I want to open it right away (lunch invitations have priority).

To open a new message, double-click on it. A message window opens to display the message (see fig. 16.11).

Figure 16.11

When you open a received message, the window title bar contains the text from the message subject field.

Replying to a Message

If you want to send a reply to a message, click on the Reply button on the toolbar or choose **R**eply to Sender from the Co**m**pose menu.

 If you are one of multiple recipients of this message, you can also choose to reply to all the recipients. Choose Reply to **A**ll from the Co**m**pose menu or click on the Reply to All button on the toolbar.

A New Message form opens, with the original message displayed (see fig. 16.12).

You have a number of options available for replying to the message:

◆ You can change the Subject.

◆ You can delete all or some of the original text.

◆ You can insert comments or notes in the original text (it will automatically be formatted in a different font and color so it will be noticed).

◆ You can add additional recipients.

When you finish composing your reply, click on the Send button or choose Se**n**d from the **F**ile menu.

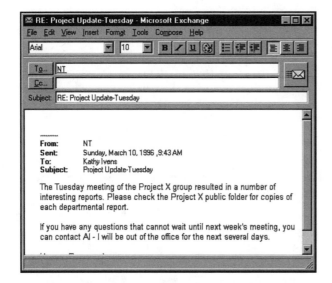

Figure 16.12

The New Message window that opens when you want to reply to a received message contains the original subject and text.

Forwarding a Message

When you receive a message, you can forward it to another user:

◆ If the message is open, click on the Forward button on the toolbar, or choose **F**orward from the Co**m**pose menu.

◆ If the message is not open, select (highlight) it in the Inbox, then use one of the previous options to forward it.

Either way, a message window opens and you can select a recipient by clicking on the T**o** field and choosing a user (or enter a name directly into the T**o** field).

Deleting Messages

You can delete a received message by choosing **D**elete from the **F**ile menu or, if the message is not open, in one of the following ways:

◆ Right-click on the message listing in the Inbox, then choose **D**elete from the pop-up menu.

◆ Highlight the listing and choose **D**elete from the **F**ile menu.

◆ Highlight the listing and press the Del key.

◆ Highlight the listing and click on the Delete button on the toolbar.

There is no confirmation dialog box (the familiar Are You Sure...), but don't worry, all is not lost if you accidentally delete a message. Your Mailbox has a container for deleted messages.

To get a deleted message back, select the Deleted Items object, select the message, then choose Cop**y** or Mo**v**e from the **F**ile menu. The dialog box that opens (see fig. 16.13) presents a display of all your Microsoft Exchange Client objects, and you can choose the appropriate container.

 By default, the ability to get back a deleted message exists only while you are still in this Exchange session. When you exit the software, the deleted messages really are deleted.

However, you can change that configuration by deselecting the **E**mpty the Deleted Items Folder choice in the General tab of the Options dialog box. Choose **O**ptions from the **T**ools menu to display that dialog box.

Figure 16.13

Whew! I can Move a deleted message back into my Inbox and it's as if I never accidentally deleted it.

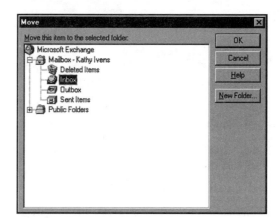

Creating and Managing Personal Folders

You can create personal folders to hold information, messages, or anything else you want to store. Personal folders are stored in your local exchange directory (with a file extension of PST) and are displayed in the viewer's folder list.

Adding Personal Folder Services to Your Profile

In order to have a personal folder, you have to establish it as a service in your Microsoft Exchange profile. If you don't see a Personal Folder in the viewer, follow these steps to add the service:

1. Choose **O**ptions from the Tools menu, then click on the Services tab of the Options dialog box.

2. Choose A**d**d to add a service, then choose Personal Folders from the list and choose OK.

3. Enter a path and name for the personal folder (it's probably best to place it in the Exchange directory). The default extension is PST.

Creating a Personal Folder

Once your profile permits it, a Personal Folder object appears in the viewer. Now you can create as many personal folders as you want:

1. Select the personal folder, then choose New **F**older from the **F**ile menu.

2. Enter a name for the folder.

Creating a Mailbox Folder

You can also create folders for your mailbox. Then you can move mail into those folders in order to separate messages in some logical manner.

To create a mailbox folder, follow the steps for creating a personal folder, except select the mailbox rather than the personal folder as your beginning point.

Using and Managing Personal Folders

Once you create a personal folder (or mailbox folder), you can use and configure it in whatever way is most useful to you:

◆ You can add files to the folder by opening Explorer or File Manager while the viewer is open. Drag the file from its original directory to the viewer.

◆ You can put received messages into the folder by highlighting the message and choosing copy or move, then choosing the personal folder as the target.

◆ You can configure the personal folder properties:

1. Choose Services from the Tools menu to display the Services dialog box.

2. Select Personal Folders, then choose Properties (see fig. 16.14).

Figure 16.14

Once you configure the properties of the personal folders services, the new configuration is inherited by subfolders.

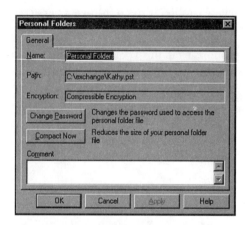

3. You can change the Name, add a Comment, add or change a Password, or Compact the folder file.

4. Choose OK to complete the configuration process.

 Note   Compacting a personal folder file reduces the amount of disk space it occupies. As you add items to personal folders, the file expands. However, when you delete items, the file does not automatically shrink. You must initiate a Compact action to get rid of the blank spots—it's as if you were defragging the file.

Creating and Managing Public Folders

Public folders are generally used to store files and forms that all users can access. Public folders are created at workstations, by users, but they are stored on the server. (Personal folders, covered in the next section, are kept in the user's local exchange directory.)

Public folders can be replicated throughout the organization so that all users have access to the contents of any or all public folders.

One of the most powerful uses of public folders is limiting the type of information that is placed in the folder and specifying ways the information can be accessed and used.

For example, you might want to set up a public folder for vacation requests. The only item in the public folder is a predesigned form that users must fill out in order to request vacation days. Once completed, the form is transferred to the appropriate person. All this occurs because of the power to designate forms for public folders. Information about creating and using public folder forms is found in Chapter 19, "Developing Forms."

Setting Permissions to Create Public Folders

The permissions for public folders are hierarchical:

◆ Administrators set permissions for top-level public folders through the Administrator program.

◆ Owners of top-level public folders set permissions for creating public folders at a subordinate level through their Microsoft Exchange client software. Folder owners are the users who created the folders.

Setting Top Level Public Folder Permissions

Top Level Public Folder Permissions are not given from the Microsoft Exchange Client software. This is a Microsoft Exchange Server function, performed by the administrator. To set permissions for top-level public folder creation:

1. In the Administrator window, select the site's Configuration object.

2. Select the Information Store Site Configuration object, and choose **P**roperties from the **F**ile menu (or double-click on the IS Site Configuration object).

3. Click on the Top Level Folder Creation tab (see fig. 16.15) to add, remove, or modify the permissions entries.

4. Choose A**l**l to give all users permission to create top-level public folders.

5. Choose **M**odify in the All**o**wed section to see a display of all users and groups, then choose those who will be able to create top-level public folders. (The A**l**l radio button will be deselected and L**i**st will be selected automatically.)

6. Choose **N**one in the **N**ot allowed section if you choose not to explicitly exclude users from creating top-level public folders.

7. Choose Mo**d**ify in the **N**ot Allowed section to see a display of all users and groups, then choose those who will be prevented from creating top-level public folders.

Figure 16.15

Any entity in the address list can be given permission to create top-level public folders.

Once a name has been entered in the All**o**wed box, all other users are automatically denied these permissions. To add or delete names from either category, choose the appropriate Modify button.

 If you give a distribution group these permissions, you can exclude any individual user(s) by entering the name(s) in the **N**ot Allowed box. This means that if you want to give a large percentage of a group these permissions, you don't have to enter each name individually.

Setting User Permissions

The person who creates a public folder is the owner, and the owner is the only one who can change the folder's permissions. This is done at the workstation, using the Client software:

1. Right-click on the folder and choose P**r**operties.

2. Click on the Permissions tab to display the Permissions property page (see fig. 16.16).

3. Highlight the Default name and choose a **R**ole. This becomes the permissions level granted to all unnamed users who access the folder.

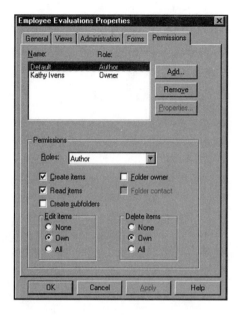

Figure 16.16

If you own a public folder, you can define and modify permissions for the users who access it.

4. Choose A**dd** to add specific users or groups, with specific roles. A list of users and groups displays, and you can select those you want to give specific permissions for this folder. The new name is placed in the **N**ame box and the default Role is assigned.

5. Select (highlight) the new name, then choose a role from the **R**ole box.

The following are the available roles:

◆ Publishing Editor, with permission to create, read, edit, and delete items, and create subfolders

◆ Editor, with permission to create, read, and edit items

◆ Publishing Author, with permission to create and read items, edit and delete your own items, and create subfolders

◆ Author, with permission to create and read items and edit and delete your own items

◆ Reviewer, with permission to read items

◆ Contributor, with permission to create items

You can, if you want, create a set of permissions for which there is no predefined role, in which case the role is named Custom.

Setting Other Folder Properties

There are some other administrative tasks an owner can execute with the folder's Properties dialog box:

◆ Use the General tab to enter a **D**escription of the folder, or its contents, or the way you would like it to be used.

◆ Use the Views tab to change the way the contents of the folder are viewed. More information about folder views is found later in this chapter.

◆ Use the Administration tab to set the options for the way this folder can be accessed and managed.

You can specify whether an item that is dragged to the folder is moved or copied as it was (containing information about the originator of the item, even if the receiver moved it to the folder), or whether it is treated as a posting from the person who moved it into the folder (which really means it was forwarded).

You can add the folder to your personal address book so that you can address messages to it.

You can invoke the Folder Assistant, (see the discussion in the next section).

You can limit access to the folder.

◆ Use the Forms tab to place customized forms in the folder. Once forms are created, you can manage their use from this tab. See the detailed discussion about forms in Chapter 19.

Using the Folder Assistant

The Folder Assistant is a feature that enables you to create rules about processing items that are placed in the folder. These rules first specify the items that are governed and then direct the kind of action that is applied to the item.

To create rules for a folder:

1. From the Administration tab, choose Folde**r** Assistant to display the Folder Assistant dialog box.

2. Choose **A**dd Rule to bring up the Edit Rule dialog box (see fig. 16.17).

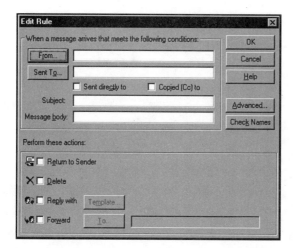

Figure 16.17

The top half of the Edit Rule dialog box is for setting the criteria, and the bottom half specifies the resulting actions for items that meet the criteria.

3. Enter data into the fields to create the conditions for the rule:

   ◆ If you specify multiple conditions, items must meet every condition to have special processing imposed.

   ◆ To specify more than one condition in a field, separate each condition with a semicolon.

   ◆ Use the Che**c**k Names button to verify the names you are entering. If they don't exist in your address book, you are asked to reenter the name.

The fields are self-evident and there is no need to explain them in detail here. However, it is probably useful to point out that the Message **B**ody field does not require you to fill in the total message you are looking for—any string(s) you enter that can be found in the body of the message will create a match.

If you wish, you can narrow the specifications by choosing **A**dvanced and entering data in the Advanced dialog box (see fig. 16.18).

 If you have created Forms that you want to use in this folder, choose **F**orms; then use the Select Forms dialog box to **A**dd them to this folder.

Figure 16.18

Use the Advanced dialog box to narrow the specifications or to indicate that you want to include only items that do not meet a set of conditions.

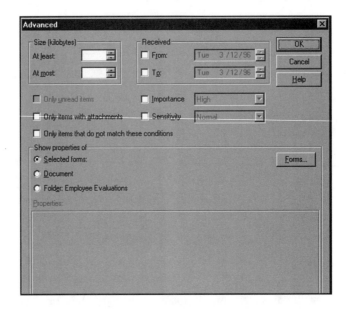

Viewing Public Folder Properties as a Non-Owner

When you display a folder's properties, there is a difference in the view, depending upon your role or the permissions you are given.

For one thing, the Properties dialog box looks different (see fig. 16.19) because the tabs that permit administration and permissions are missing. If there are Forms for the folder, there will be a Form tab. If not, there are only two tabs, General (which displays the folder's name and any optional description the owner added) and Summary (which displays your permissions).

The Summary tab actually changes its view, depending upon who is accessing it:

◆ Users who are not owners can view only their own access permissions when the Permissions tab of the folder's properties dialog box is displayed.

◆ If you have been given specific permissions by the owner, your name is displayed.

◆ If you are given permissions because you are a member of a distribution list that was assigned a role, the distribution list name is displayed.

◆ If you have not been specifically named, you are considered an undefined user and you have the default permissions.

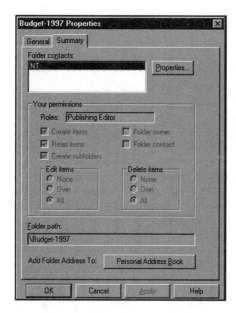

Figure 16.19

This user can see his name and role because the owner specifically added him—any other users who were also added are not displayed for him.

Creating Public Folders

When you create a public folder, it is stored on the server and is accessible to others. You can choose to use it for storing specific types of information if you want, and you can customize its properties to meet your needs.

To create a new public folder:

1. Move to the All Public Folders object in the Microsoft Exchange Client software viewer, then choose New **F**older from the **F**ile menu.

2. Name the folder.

Customizing Public Folders

Customizing a public folder means you can control the way the folder is displayed and used:

◆ You can put forms into the folder.

◆ You can set rules for processing the forms (or other items) that are placed in the folder.

◆ You can set access permissions.

◆ You can design views (the way the folder displays its contents).

If you want to customize a public folder, Microsoft Exchange Client provides a Cue Cards feature to help:

1. Select the public folder you want to customize, then open the **T**ools menu.

2. Choose Applicati**o**n Design, then choose F**o**lder Design Cue Cards.

The Folder Design Cue Cards act as a tutorial to walk you through the customization process. The feature displays in a format similar to Help files, but acts like a Wizard, with the familiar Next and Back buttons (see fig. 16.20). There are ten Cue Cards available, but you don't have to use the functions of every one—you can skip whatever you don't want to use.

Figure 16.20

Specifying configuration properties for a public folder is easy when you let the Cue Cards guide you.

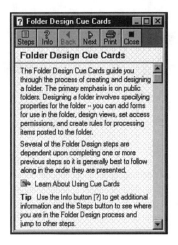

As you press Next to display a property or design feature, you can invoke it, or press Next again to move to the next Cue Card. The permutations and combinations of available configuration properties are quite large. The button bar enables you to maneuver and navigate through the process:

◆ Choose Steps to see the point at which you currently stand in the configuration process—you can jump directly to any step.

◆ Choose Info to see detailed information about procedures and tasks.

◆ Choose Back to move back to the previous Cue Card.

◆ Choose Next to move to the next Cue Card.

◆ Choose Print to print the current Cue Card.

◆ Choose Close to close the Cue Cards.

Using Public Folders

Depending on the way a public folder is configured, you may have to use a custom form for posting information to it or for replying to information that is posted. The folder may be configured so you can use the standard New Post or New Message forms.

The following are the choices for posting to a public folder:

◆ Custom Forms, which are forms that have been designed specifically for this public folder. These forms provide the protocols for entering, viewing, and organizing the information in the folder. When a public folder is open, any forms that have been created for it are listed at the bottom of the Compose menu.

◆ New Post Form, which is usually used in bulletin board folders to post discussion items or reply to existing postings. It's not the same as a message, because there is no recipient (the folder is the recipient) and the Subject is really a Conversation thread. The New Post command is found on the viewer, in the Compose menu.

◆ New Message form, which is the standard message form that you can use to send a message to a folder. New Message is also a command in the Compose menu of the viewer.

◆ Files, which means you send a standard data file that was produced by software, such as word processing documents, spreadsheets, graphics, database reports, and so on.

Sorting and Filtering Folder Items

When you view the contents of any folder, the items in the folder display according to date by default, with the most recent item at the top of the list. If you prefer a different sort order, you can change this, and Microsoft Exchange Client will remember the sort scheme in the future.

By default also, all items are displayed. You can apply a filter to a folder so that only those items that meet your specifications are shown.

Sorting Items

To change the sorting scheme for a folder:

1. Highlight the folder, then choose **S**ort from the **V**iew menu.

2. In the Sort dialog box, display the list in the Sort items by box (see fig. 16.21).

3. Choose the column heading you want to sort by, then select **A**scending or **D**escending. You can choose any column heading for sorting, even if that column heading is not currently being displayed in the viewer.

Figure 16.21

Click on the down arrow to see all the available categories for sorting the folder's contents.

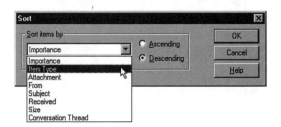

 There is a shortcut for sorting, as long as you choose to sort by a currently displayed category. Click on the column heading you want to sort by, and the items will rearrange themselves in ascending order by that category. Press Ctrl when you click on the column heading to sort in descending order.

A small arrow displays on the column that is the basis of the sort—it points up for an ascending sort, down for a descending sort. You can toggle between ascending and descending by clicking on that arrow.

Filtering Items

To filter the items in a folder:

1. Select the folder, then choose **F**ilter from the **V**iew menu to display the Filter dialog box (see fig. 16.22).

2. Choose the conditions for filtering the items:

   ◆ If you enter multiple conditions, only items that meet all of them will be displayed.

   ◆ If you input multiple entries in one condition, items that contain any of those entries are displayed. Multiple entries are separated by a semicolon.

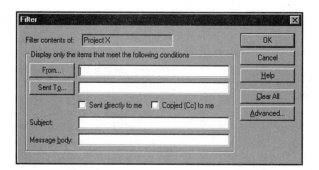

Figure 16.22

Configure a set of criteria to determine whether an article will be displayed.

3. Choose **A**dvanced to set filters based on criteria that will narrow the scope of the filter (see fig. 16.23).

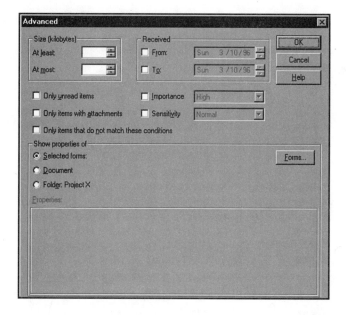

Figure 16.23

You can tighten the conditions for filtering items with the Advanced dialog box.

 You can also reverse the process on the Advanced section—selecting items that do not match criteria. Creating an exclusion filter is sometimes faster.

When you want to remove a filter, choose **C**lear All from the Filter dialog box.

Delegating Mail Functions

You can give someone the authority to handle your mail, letting the delegate send mail on your behalf, read messages sent to you, or both. There are a couple of common reasons that people chose to use this feature:

◆ Users who travel frequently delegate mail tasks so they can call in and get a summary report or can arrange to be notified if something urgent shows up in the mailbox.

◆ Users (usually executives) who normally delegate the opening of snail-mail may very well want to handle e-mail the same way.

 If you are an executive that takes the common executive tactic of having an assistant or secretary open all your mail, including your e-mail, there is no way to exclude confidential or personal items (written mail of this sort usually has a message on the envelope stating the special circumstances).

To remedy this, have the administrator create a second mailbox for you and make it a hidden mailbox, which means it won't be displayed on lists when people send messages or create address lists. Give the hidden mailbox name to those users who might need to send you a message you don't want anyone else to see. If they enter the mailbox name directly in the TO: box of a message, it will get to you.

You cannot perform the configuration for granting a user the permission to send mail in your name; you must have the Microsoft Exchange Server administrator perform that task. You can set all the other delegating configurations yourself.

Giving Others Access to Your Mailbox

To give another user access to your mailbox:

1. Select your mailbox object, then choose Properties from the File menu (or right-click on the object and choose Properties).

2. Choose the Permissions tab of the Mailbox Properties dialog box (see fig. 16.24).

3. In the Name box, choose Add, then select a name from the user list.

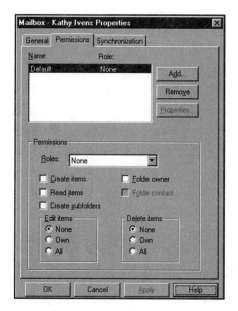

Figure 16.24

Add permissions for other users to access your mailbox and define those permissions to suit your needs.

4. Highlight the new name, then choose a **R**ole:

   ◆ Owners have all permissions.

   ◆ Publishing Editors can create, read, edit, and delete items and can create subfolders.

   ◆ Editors can create, read, edit, and delete items.

   ◆ Publishing Authors can create and read items, edit and delete the items they create, and create subfolders.

   ◆ Authors can create and read items, and edit and delete the items they create.

   ◆ Reviewers can read items.

   ◆ Contributors can create items.

 Tip   When you select a role, the rights for that role are selected automatically in the Permissions section of the dialog box. If you select an additional right, or deselect a given right (or both), a role that matches the new permissions configuration is automatically chosen.

If you choose a combination of permissions that does not match a defined role, the role will be named Custom.

Delegating the Send Mail Function

You can choose a user to send mail on your behalf. The FROM: field of messages sent by the delegate will contain the phrase Sent On Behalf Of followed by your name in addition to the delegate's name.

This is not the same as having a user send mail in your name—only the administrator of your Microsoft Exchange Server service can configure that right.

To authorize a user to send mail on your behalf:

1. Choose **O**ptions from the **T**ools menu.

2. Click on the Exchange Server tab of the Options dialog box (see fig. 16.25).

Figure 16.25

You can choose additional users who will be able to send mail throughout the system on your behalf—the receiver is told who sent the mail and informed that it was sent on your behalf.

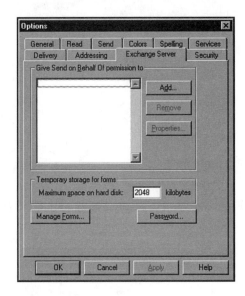

3. Choose **A**dd to place an additional name in the Give Send on **B**ehalf Of box. Select a name from the user list that's displayed, and choose **A**dd to move the name into the Add Users box (or double-click on the name).

4. Repeat this as often as you want. Choose OK when you finish adding names.

Sending Mail for Another User

If you have permission to send mail on behalf of another user, you perform the task from your own mailbox. Everything is performed in the same manner as if you were sending mail under your own name, except you have to take one additional step: place the other user's name in the From box of the message.

By default, the From box does not appear in the message window. You can change that by choosing Fro**m** Box from the **V**iew menu.

 Tip   The ability to view the From box is toggled on and off via the **V**iew menu. Once you select it, it becomes the new default for your message window until you deselect it.

If you don't have the appropriate permissions, when you attempt to send the message, Microsoft Exchange Client will issue an error message and refuse to send the mail (see fig. 16.26).

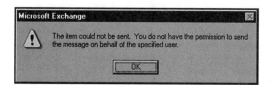

Figure 16.26

You cannot send a message on someone else's behalf unless that person gives you permission to do so.

Configuring Your Client Software

There are a number of configuration options you can change in your Microsoft Exchange Client software—some that affect the appearance of the viewer and the message windows, others that affect the processes you use.

This section presents a brief overview of some of the configuration options with which you might want to experiment. Complete explanations of all the configuration options are found in your documentation.

Configuring the Viewer

There are lots of configuration options that control the appearance of the viewer:

◆ You can use the **V**iew menu of the viewer to show/hide Fo**l**ders, the **T**oolbar, and the Status Ba**r**.

◆ Choose **C**olumns from the **V**iew menu to add and remove columns that display in the viewer, and you can change the order in which columns appear (see fig. 16.27).

◆ If you don't like or need the ToolTips (the little messages that explain what a button on the toolbar does if you hold your pointer over it for a second or two), you can get rid of them. Choose **O**ptions from the **T**ools menu, then deselect Show **T**oolTips on the General tab of the properties dialog box.

Figure 16.27

The Available columns box lists the columns that are not currently displayed—you can display any of them.

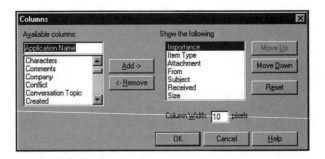

Configuring the Message Windows

You can change the appearance of the message windows by adding a toolbar and other options as described for the viewer.

In addition, you can add or delete fields in the message header by selecting/deselecting them in the **V**iew menu:

◆ Choose Fro**m** Box to add that field. This is really unnecessary unless you're sending a message for someone else.

◆ Choose **B**cc Box to add a field for a blind (not indicated on the message header) copy to another recipient.

Configuring the Toolbar

You can add and remove buttons from the toolbars:

1. Display the toolbar (choose **T**oolbar from the **V**iew menu) if it is not currently displayed.

2. Double-click the toolbar background on a blank spot. This displays the Customize Toolbar dialog box (see fig. 16.28.)

Figure 16.28

There are buttons available for many of the menu functions—add the ones that represent tasks you do frequently.

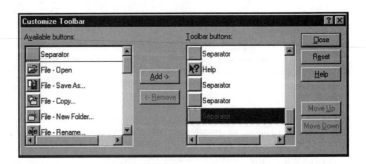

3. To add a button to the Toolbar, highlight a button from the A<u>v</u>ailable Buttons box, then choose <u>A</u>dd to move it into the <u>T</u>oolbar Buttons box.

4. To remove a button, highlight it in the <u>T</u>oolbar Buttons box and choose <u>R</u>emove.

5. To change the order of the buttons, highlight a button and choose Move <u>U</u>p or Move <u>D</u>own.

6. Choose R<u>e</u>set to put everything back the way it was when you first installed Microsoft Exchange Client.

7. Choose <u>C</u>lose when you are finished.

Creating and Applying Views to Folders

A folder's view is the way the items in the folder are displayed. You can change a folder's view, and you can create multiple views so that the items are displayed differently depending upon your needs of the moment.

There are two ways of applying views to folders:

◆ Folder view, which affects only the personal folder upon which you took the action.

◆ Personal view, which applies a view to all folders when you select them. Even if the folder is a public folder, a personal view is seen only by you—it is not attached globally to the public folder.

 Note Microsoft Exchange has four preconfigured personal views for folders: Normal, Group by From, Group by Subject, and Group by Conversation Topic. You can choose among them by selecting <u>P</u>ersonal Views from the <u>V</u>iew menu. Any views you create and apply are added to these; you cannot remove them.

Defining and Applying Personal Views

Before you can apply a view, you must create (define) it:

1. Choose <u>D</u>efine Views from the <u>V</u>iew menu to display the Define Views dialog box. Select <u>P</u>ersonal views (see fig. 16.29).

2. Choose <u>N</u>ew to create a new personal view in the New View dialog box (see fig. 16.30).

3. Enter a View <u>N</u>ame.

Figure 16.29

When you first open the Define Views dialog box, the currently active view is checked, and a description of the view's configuration is displayed.

Figure 16.30

Use the New View dialog box to create a new view of the items in a folder.

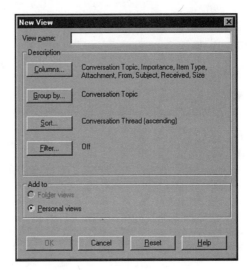

4. Configure the categories shown on the dialog box. As you select each of them, a dialog box opens to display the available choices.

5. When you are finished, choose OK. The new personal view displays on the **P**ersonal Views submenu (on the **V**iew menu).

Tip There is a pecking order to the categories; the order is Filter, Group by, Sort, Columns. You should make changes in this order.

Once you define a personal view, you can apply it instead of using the preconfigured views.

1. Select (highlight) the folder.

2. Choose **P**ersonal Views from the **V**iew menu.

3. Choose the new view, which is listed below the preconfigured views.

Defining and Applying Folder Views

The steps for defining a folder view are the same as those for a personal view, except you have to take some preliminary steps:

◆ Highlight a personal folder before choosing **D**efine Views from the **V**iew menu.

◆ Choose **F**older Views from the Define Views dialog box.

When you are defining a folder view, there is a second method that may be easier—even if it isn't easier, it gives you an opportunity to see how the view will display.

Before taking the steps to define a new view, open the folder and make whatever changes you want. Add/remove columns and change the sort, filter, and grouping configurations. Then, when you open the Define Views dialog box, the current configuration is displayed. Just choose **N**ew and give it a name.

Once you define a folder view, its name appears in a submenu when you choose Folder **V**iews from the **V**iew menu.

Working Offline

You don't have to be connected to a Microsoft Exchange Server to use the Microsoft Exchange Client software. Let's go over the steps needed for a person who uses a portable computer (in addition to the office computer, which is connected to a Microsoft Exchange server).

Install the software on the portable computer you will be using, and when you create the user profile, answer Yes to the question Do You Travel With This Computer? Make sure you include Microsoft Exchange Server in the profile.

When you launch Microsoft Exchange Client while you are offline, the viewer displays only those objects available on your local drive (see fig. 16.31).

Figure 16.31

If you are working offline, you can access only objects stored on the local disk.

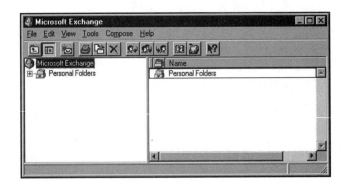

Preparing for Offline Work

If you are going to work at home or on the road, you need to get your offline system ready to work unconnected to the server and also be able to resynchronize everything when you reconnect.

Copying What You Need

Take the following steps while you are connected to the Microsoft Exchange server:

◆ Download the Address Book (use Synchronize from the Tools menu).

◆ Add any public folders you want to work with to your Favorites folder (highlight each folder, then choose Add to Favorites from the File menu).

◆ Make the folders available for offline work (choose Properties from the File menu, select the Synchronization tab, Select When offline or online).

The first time you make a folder available offline, you will probably see a message that tells you to configure an offline folder file first (unless you knew to do this during installation). The message offers to perform the task for you; answer Yes.

A file is created (the default name is EXCHANGE.OST but you can change the file name to whatever you want, keeping the OST extension). You also can place the file in any folder—by default it goes into your Windows directory.

You can copy the offline folder file from your office computer to the portable, rather than hooking the portable into the network.

Configuring for Dial-In Connections

If you want to be able to dial in to the server while you are offsite, you can accomplish that by establishing a dial-up connection. Then you can work offline and, when you need to connect to your server (to send messages you composed offline, to pick up any mail that was delivered to your mailbox), use your modem to connect to the server.

To configure dial-up connection options:

1. Choose Services from the Tools menu.

2. Highlight Microsoft Exchange Server and choose Properties.

3. Select the Dial-Up Networking tab (see fig. 16.32).

Figure 16.32

Specify the information for setting up a dial-in connection to the Microsoft Exchange server— there's a Wizard to help with the details.

4. If no connection is configured in the **D**ial Using box (there probably isn't), choose Ne**w**.

5. Enter the data requested by the Make New Connection Wizard, which will finish by entering the new connection's name in the **D**ial Using box.

6. In the **U**ser Name box, enter the name you use to log onto the network (not necessarily the name for logging on to Microsoft Exchange Server).

7. In the **P**assword box, enter your logon password.

8. In the Do**m**ain box, enter the name of your domain.

9. If you perform this task while you are connected to the server, you should select Do **N**ot Dial. If you are offline, don't select that option, and when you choose OK the dial-in connection will begin.

Going Back Online

When you are back online, you have to synchronize your offline folders with your online folders. Synchronization means that any changes made to any folders on the desktop computer are reflected in the offline computer, and vice versa.

You can perform this task by dialing in or by reconnecting at the network site:

1. Choose **S**ynchronize from the **T**ools menu, then select This **F**older (if you selected a single folder) or **A**ll folders.

2. An information dialog box tells you that the synchronization is proceeding.

3. When the synchronization is completed, highlight the Deleted Items folder in your mailbox. You will find the Synchronization Log, which you can open if you want to examine it (see fig. 16.33). If there is nothing remarkable in it, you can delete it.

Figure 16.33

The Synchronization Log gives a detailed listing of all the tasks accomplished during the synchronization process.

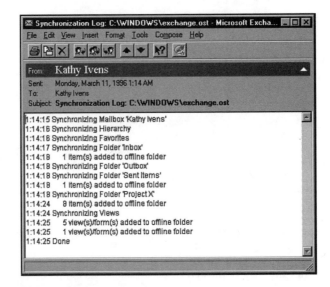

Using the Out Of Office Assistant

If you are going to be out of the office and won't be picking up your messages for a while, you can automate the processing of incoming mail during that period.

The Out Of Office Assistant is a feature that enables you to set rules for handling your mail while you are gone. Each rule is accompanied by a description of the circumstances that must exist in order for the rule to take effect. For instance, you can establish circumstances under which mail is sent to another user's mailbox (perhaps your assistant or a co-worker in your group). You also can have a rule that establishes the fact that under certain conditions a reply is automatically sent to the senders telling them that you are away (this is called AutoReply). The message can include any text you want, such as a promise to take care of things when you return or a notification of your expected date of return.

To set up this feature, select O**u**t of Office Assistant from the **T**ools menu to display the feature's dialog box (see fig. 16.34).

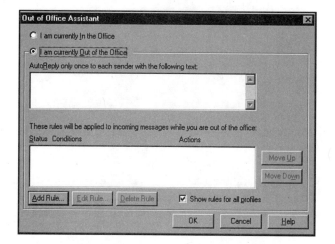

Figure 16.34

You can set up rules for handling your mail while you are not in the office.

Creating an AutoReply Message

If you want to set up an AutoReply to be sent to each person who sends you a message, follow these steps:

1. Select I Am Currently Out of the Office.

2. In the Auto**R**eply text box, enter the message you want to send.

3. Choose OK.

Creating Rules for Mail Handling

To establish conditions for automatic mail handling, follow these steps:

1. Choose **A**dd Rule to display the Edit Rule dialog box (see fig. 16.35).

2. In the From box, select the names of those people whose mail will set off the response you're designing. For multiple senders, separate names with a semicolon.

Figure 16.35

Set up the conditions to enable specific automatic responses with the Edit Rule dialog box.

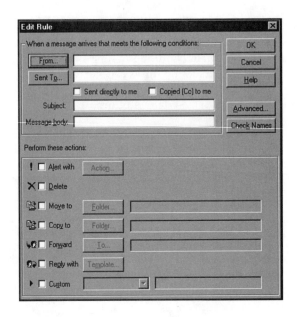

3. In the Sent T**o** box, specify those recipient names that appear in the TO: box in a message for which this rule applies. Use this for messages in which you are one of multiple recipients.

4. Select Sent dire**c**tly to me or Cop**i**ed (Cc) to me (or both) to include these restrictions.

5. Use the Subject box to identify messages with specific subjects. You can type text that is a partial string from the subject matter, but that text must match the subject string exactly. To specify multiple subjects, separate each text entry with a semicolon.

6. Use the Message **b**ody text box to enter a string of text. If that string of text is matched in the body of any message, the conditions will be met.

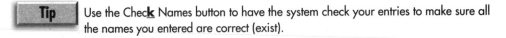

Tip Use the Chec**k** Names button to have the system check your entries to make sure all the names you entered are correct (exist).

In addition to these conditions, you can narrow the specifications for incoming messages by choosing **A**dvanced and selecting additional filters (see fig. 16.36).

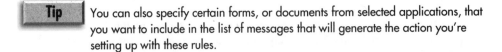

Tip You can also specify certain forms, or documents from selected applications, that you want to include in the list of messages that will generate the action you're setting up with these rules.

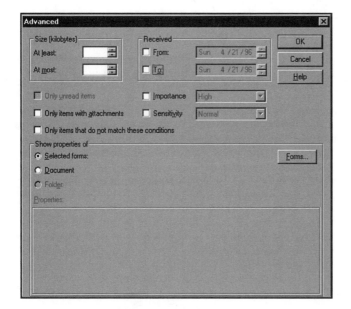

Figure 16.36

You can set stringent rules that must be met by incoming messages or specify that messages that do not meet these criteria should be established as matching messages.

Specifying Actions

Once you have the filters set for the messages, you can tell the Out of Office Assistant what you want to happen when the conditions you established are matched.

Use the Perform these actions section of the Edit Rule dialog box to select the options you want performed:

- ◆ Choose A**l**ert with to get a notification that a message has been received. Then choose an action for specifying the way you want to receive the alert. This is useful for those times when you are working in another office or just want to know when messages are received without having to open them.

- ◆ Choose **D**elete to move the message to the Deleted Items folder in your mail-box.

- ◆ Choose Mo**v**e to (and specify a folder) to move the message to a specific folder.

- ◆ Choose Cop**y** to (and specify a folder) to copy the message to a specified folder.

- ◆ Choose For**w**ard to forward the message to a specified recipient.

◆ Choose Reply with to send an automatic reply to the sender(s) you've specified for this configuration. Choose Template to open a template form so you can compose the message.

◆ Choose Custom to initiate a program or action that is not part of Microsoft Exchange Server.

If you log into your Exchange Server software and the I Am Currently Out of the Office checkbox is in effect, you will see a message to that effect so that you can tell the system you're back.

CHAPTER 17

Maintaining Client Services

T here are some basic maintenance services that administrators have to perform or have to keep an eye on to make sure the system is performing them.

Keeping the messaging system going is the most basic administrative task, and, depending on the size and complexity of the organization, can be the most time-consuming.

Administrators hear about messaging services from users on a constant basis. They hear about the speed with which mail travels from user to user, the mail that doesn't arrive at its destination, the mail that arrives but is corrupted or has some other problem. They hear requests for permissions; one user wants to send mail in another user's name, another user needs to change the properties of some item in the system but doesn't have the appropriate permissions; somebody else has to reach a user on a foreign system for which there is no connector installed.

Understanding and maintaining all the elements that keep the messages rolling along is a full-time job. This chapter presents some of the issues that seem to be paramount for administrators who face this task every day.

Understanding the Routing Table

As messages move through the various layers, sites, and servers, there's a certain amount of order to the process. For each message that leaves one mailbox and has to move to another mailbox, there's a path through the layers, the sites, the connectors, the gateways, and other elements in the system.

The routing table has all the data about the gateways and connectors that are used to route messages anywhere outside the site. Any time you make changes that affect the routing table—for example, adding or removing a gateway—the routing table has to be recalculated. You have several choices for implementing this recalculation task:

◆ Configure a schedule that sets times for the system to calculate the routing table automatically.

◆ Force a manual recalculation whenever you think it's necessary.

◆ Let the automatic system update take care of it, which recalculates the table whenever it detects changes that influence routing.

Configuring a Calculation Schedule

You can create a schedule for calculating (or recalculating) the routing table on a regular basis by following these steps:

1. In the Administrator's window, highlight the Configuration object for the site you want to work in.

2. Open the Site Addressing object and move to the Routing Calculation Schedule tab (see fig. 17.1).

 Select Always to have the recalculation occur every 15 minutes. Select Never if you do not want automatic recalculation and prefer to perform the task manually.

3. Choose Selected times.

4. Fill out the Schedule Grid.

The Schedule Grid is displayed in one-hour increments. As you move your pointer over the grid, the pointer changes to a cross, and the time displays beneath the grid (see fig. 17.2).

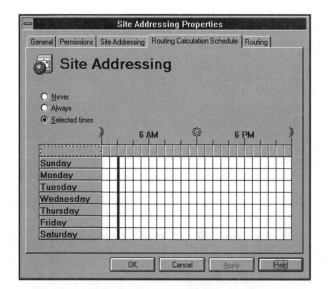

Figure 17.1

Use the Routing Calculation Schedule to establish times for calculating the routing table automatically.

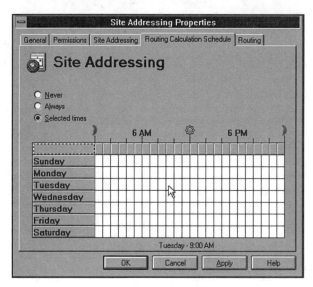

Figure 17.2

As you move through the grid, you can keep track of where your pointer is by checking the time display.

Click and drag to highlight a block of time. For a shortcut, select a time by clicking on the title row—that time is selected for every day of the week.

Forcing a Manual Recalculation

If you add or remove gateways or connectors, those changes impact the routing table. The Message Transfer Agent (MTA) will eventually catch the changes and rebuild the routing table. Because that can take some time, however, you may want to recalculate manually. To do this, follow these steps:

1. In the Administrator's window, highlight the server that is designated to be the routing calculation server for the table you want to recalculate.

2. Open Message Transfer Agent from the right panel, which displays the General tab for the MTA properties (see fig. 17.3).

3. Choose **R**ecalculate Routing.

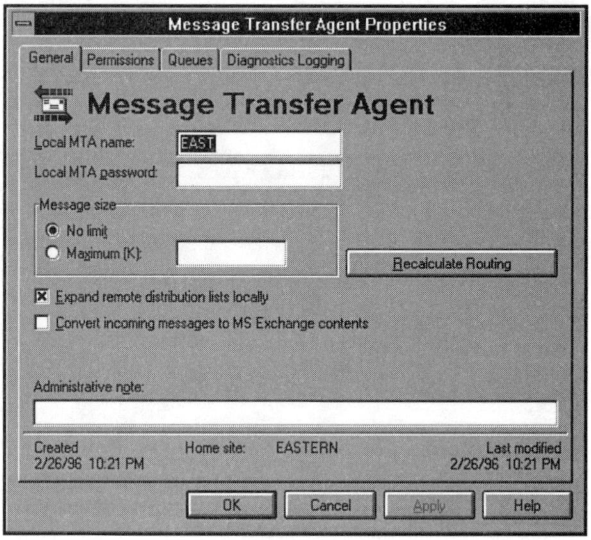

Figure 17.3

The MTA handles messaging and recalculates the routing table itself, or permits you to do it.

Maintaining Message Tracking

You can configure Microsoft Exchange Server to track messages, which is useful if there are any problems in mail delivery. The Message Tracking feature provides more than just the capability of finding a message that seems to have gotten lost—there are a few other chores it can perform:

◆ Connections that have slowed down to a crawl or have ceased to function are identified when you track messages.

◆ If there is a slowdown, you can view each segment of the route and determine if the delay is at that point.

◆ If there is an unauthorized message in the system, you can track it and remove it.

Microsoft Exchange Server does not turn on the message tracking feature by default—it must be enabled by an administrator.

Each component of your system that handles messaging is capable of tracking mail. There is no single message-tracking on/off switch; you must make a decision about whether or not to enable tracking for each individual messaging component. These are the components that have the capability of tracking messages:

◆ MTA

◆ Information Stores

◆ MS Mail Connectors (you must enable tracking on each connector)

◆ Internet Mail Connectors (you must enable tracking on each connector)

Enabling Message Tracking

You can invoke message tracking for one, some, or all the messaging components in your system.

Although the idea of enabling message tracking sounds good, as if it were a way to anticipate problems and be totally prepared to solve them, there is a downside to this feature. Tracking creates traffic on the drive as messages are logged. Writing to the tracking log (which is discussed in detail in this chapter) can slow down a system, especially if there is a lot of messaging.

Once you do enable message tracking, you must restart the service for each component in which you made this change. This is accomplished by opening the Services icon in the Windows NT Control Panel and choosing Stop, then Start for each component.

Message Tracking for the MTA

The MTA routes messages to the other Microsoft Exchange Server MTAs and gateways. To enable message tracking for the MTA, follow these steps:

1. In the Administrator's window, select the site, then select Configuration.

2. Open the MTA Site Configuration object, which displays the General tab (see fig. 17.4).

Figure 17.4

*Enable message
tracking for
the MTA on the
General tab of the
MTA properties
dialog box.*

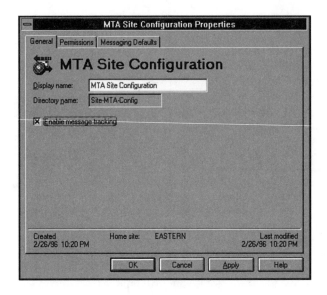

3. Choose **E**nable message tracking.

4. Restart all the MTAs in the site.

Message Tracking for the Information Store

The Information Store contains user mailboxes, as well as public and private folders.
You can enable message tracking to track all messaging on all the information stores
on the site:

1. In the Administrator window, choose the Configuration object for the site.

2. Open the Information Store Site Configuration object, which shows the General
   tab in the foreground (see fig. 17.5).

3. Select Enable **m**essage tracking.

4. Restart the IS service.

Message Tracking for MS Mail Connectors

You can choose message tracking for one, some, or all the MS Mail connectors you
configured for your system. If you are enabling message tracking for more than one
MS Mail connector, you must perform these steps for each of them individually
(there is no master switch you can turn on):

1. In the Administrator's window, click on the plus sign on the Configuration object, then select the Connections object.

2. In the right panel, open the MS Mail Connector object (see fig. 17.6.).

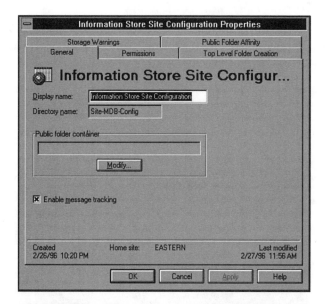

Figure 17.5

Enable message tracking for the Information Stores throughout the site from the General tab of the IS properties.

Figure 17.6

Enable message tracking to trace problems as messages are moved between Microsoft Exchange Server and an MS Mail Connector post office.

3. Select **E**nable message tracking.

4. Restart the service.

Message Tracking for Internet Mail Connectors

You can choose message tracking for one, some, or all the Internet mail connectors on a site. If you are enabling message tracking for more than one Internet mail connector, you must perform these steps for each individually:

1. In the Administrator's window, click on the plus sign on the Configuration object, then select the Connections object.

2. In the right panel, open the Internet Mail Connector object (see fig. 17.7.).

Figure 17.7

Enable message tracking for messages that travel between Microsoft Exchange Server and an Internet Mail Connector.

3. Select Enable me**ss**age tracking.

4. Restart the service.

Understanding the Message Tracking Log

No matter how many instances of message tracking you enable, there is one tracking log. The log is begun daily and is named for the date on which it was created (days begin and end at midnight). The syntax for the filename is *yyyymmdd*.log. The log is in the \EXCHSRVR\TRACKING.LOG subdirectory.

You can use any text editor to display and edit any tracking log. Figure 17.8 is a portion of a tracking log that has been loaded into Notepad.

Each individual step of moving a message from the sender to the recipient is noted in the log. Every component of your system that handled the message is listed, showing each step the message went through.

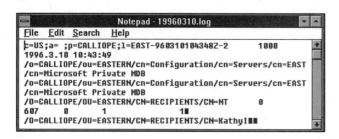

Figure 17.8

You can view the tracking log, search for specific data, edit the log, and print it.

  The tracking log is tab-delimited, so you can load it into other applications. Usually, spreadsheet software will take a tab-limited file and format it perfectly.

Tracking Messages

You do not have to display and search the tracking log to track a message. Microsoft Exchange Server has provided a feature to do this. There are two steps you have to follow:

◆ The Select Message to Track dialog box enables you to select a message through the use of criteria.

◆ The Message Tracking Center dialog box tracks a message through all its paths as it makes its way through the system.

Finding the Message(s) to Track

To begin the tracking process, open the Microsoft Exchange Server Administrator's window, then follow these steps:

1. Choose <u>T</u>rack Message from the <u>T</u>ools menu, then choose the Server that is maintaining the tracking log.

2. When the Select Message to Track dialog box is displayed (see fig. 17.9), enter as much criteria as you can in order to narrow the search.

Figure 17.9

You can use a variety of criteria to set up the search for a message.

You do not have to fill out all the fields in the dialog box, but you should give some thought to the ramifications of leaving fields empty. Here is the way the fields work to make the search:

◆ **F**rom opens the shared address book so you can select an address. No personal address book listings are displayed here. However, you can use personal address listings in the Message Tracking Center window, which is discussed in the next section.

If you leave this field empty, the search will begin on your entry in the Sent **T**o field. You must enter data in either the **F**rom or Sent **T**o fields.

◆ Sent **T**o opens the Select One or More Recipients dialog box so you can choose the recipients you want to include in the search criteria (see fig. 17.10).

◆ **L**ook back is the field in which you enter the number of prior days you want to search. By default, the lookback specification is 0, which means today's log will be searched. The Start date field automatically changes to match your selection.

◆ **S**earch on server lets you change the server you want to search.

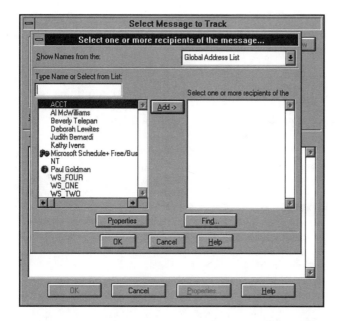

Figure 17.10

Select one more recipient by highlighting the name, then choosing Add (or double-click on the recipient).

When you have specified the information necessary (or the information available to you), choose Find Now.

All the messages that meet the criteria you set are listed. If you do not see the message you need, you can change the criteria and begin the search again.

What to Do when No Messages Are Found

When the search begins, if there is no log for the date(s) you selected, a message to that effect displays.

If the criteria you established doesn't have a match in the log, no messages will be found and the bottom of the dialog box will contain no found messages.

You do have one more chance, however (unless the problem is that there is no log available because message tracking wasn't enabled for the dates you need). Choose Cancel and the Message Tracking Center dialog box will display, and you can specify different criteria. See the section on Tracking the Message later in this chapter.

Choosing the Message to Track

When the list of matching messages is displayed, it may look as if there is duplication. However, the list represents an action, so some messages may be represented in multiple actions (depending on the criteria you set, or on the way the message might have been sent or forwarded or copied). If this occurs, it doesn't matter which message you choose because the tracking process hunts down the message's history, not the action that is listed.

If you need more information before deciding that a particular message is the one you want to track, select it and choose **P**roperties. If there are multiple recipients, you will be able to see all of them here (the list of matching messages does not display more than one recipient). The details available vary, depending upon the type of mail handling the listed message/action used.

Once you decide you have the right message, select it and choose OK.

Tracking the Message

The Message Tracking Center dialog box displays when you select the message you want to track (see fig. 17.11).

Figure 17.11

The message ID, the originator of the message, and the server log on which it was found are displayed in the Message Tracking Center dialog box.

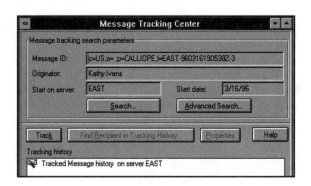

You cannot edit the fields that are displayed in the dialog box, but you can choose **A**dvanced Search if you want to tighten or change criteria (see fig. 17.12).

Figure 17.12

Use Advanced Search to narrow the search by establishing criteria that wasn't available before you found the messages.

In the Advanced Search dialog box, you can make one of these criteria active:

◆ Sent by Microsoft Exchange **S**erver, which searches for messages that came from Microsoft Exchange Server components such as the System Attendant or Directory Services.

◆ Transferred into this **s**ite, which searches for messages that were received through a gateway or connector. Messages that came into the site from any mailbox that doesn't appear in the shared address book also fall into this category.

◆ By **M**essage ID, which is a unique identifier that is placed on every message that travels through your system. To learn the ID, ask the sender or the recipient to find the message listing in the client software Inbox. If the message is listed in the Sent Items or Inbox folder, select it and choose P**r**operties from the **F**ile menu. The message ID will be displayed.

If you want to use one of the Advanced Search criteria, select it, then choose OK. Otherwise, choose Cancel.

Once everything is as good as you can make it, choose Trac**k**.

Viewing and Using the Tracking Information

The results of message tracking are displayed in a hierarchy of the events that occurred, as found in the tracking logs. Each level of the hierarchy represents a step in the path the message took (some steps may be concurrent). You can examine the information in these ways:

◆ Click on the plus or minus buttons to expand and collapse the hierarchy of events.

◆ Highlight an event, then choose **P**roperties to see details about the event.

◆ Choose Find **R**ecipient in Tracking History to search for recipients you specified when you entered your criteria. Then, any events involving those recipients will be displayed in bold type.

To put all this information to use, you have to compare the data produced by the tracking with the report of a problem. If one user sends a message to several addresses and one recipient required the use of a gateway, if receipt of that message cannot be tracked, you need to check the health of the gateway. Perhaps you set size limits on mailboxes—perhaps the tracking process will make you rethink the specifications for size (or explain the rules again).

If there seems to be a serious problem, you should take a look at the Windows NT Application event log (in the Administrative Tools program box). You might also have to think about changing the way particular components are configured.

Viewing and Maintaining Queues

There are queues for all messages waiting for delivery. There is a queue for each server in a site, every installed connector, and every gateway. You can view the queues, see the messages that are in the queues, and manipulate those messages.

 Throughout this section's discussion of viewing queues, remember that when you display the queue's contents you are looking at a display of information as it existed at the moment you asked to see it. Because queues are dynamic (and frequently very busy), every dialog box has a Refresh button. You should invoke it as you work with a queue to make sure you're seeing timely information.

There are actually two types of queues in the system:

◆ Unsecured queues, which are part of the MTA and appear in the queue list. These queues go to components on the MTAs server, to Site Connectors, X.400 Connectors, RAS Connectors, and MTAs of other servers in the site. You can change the priority of messages in unsecured queues.

◆ Secured queues, which are the queues to the Internet Mail Connector and the MS Mail Connector. These queues do not display in the queue list unless they are getting messages from the MTA or sending messages to the MTA. The priority of messages in secured queues cannot be changed.

Viewing the MTA Queues

Viewing a queue is more than just looking at it—there are actions you can take upon the messages in the queue. To begin, you have to see the queue, which is accomplished by following these steps:

1. In the Administrator window, select the server you want to use.

2. Open the Message Transfer Agent object and click on the Queues tab. From the **Q**ueue name box, select the queue you want to view (see fig. 17.13).

Figure 17.13

When you select a queue, the list of messages in that queue is displayed.

Viewing Message Details

Highlight a message and select De*t*ails to view the following information:

◆ The Originator of the message (which includes the host address and sender's name)

◆ The message ID

◆ The time the message was submitted to the queue

◆ The priority given to the message by the sender

◆ The size of the message (in bytes)

Changing Message Priority

In an unsecured queue, you can change the order in which messages are serviced. Highlight the message and choose **P**riority.

Priority is a sort parameter that has no subsorts. All messages with the same priority are delivered in the order in which they entered the queue (you cannot give a high priority to a group of messages and then sort them within that priority by sender or receiver, or any other characteristic).

The priority options are High, Normal, and Low. As you change the priority, messages will move to another part of the queue.

 One of the useful things you can do with rearranging the priorities of messages in a queue is lower the priority of any message you think might block or slow down the queue. Then, at least the rest of the messages get through before any anticipated problem or slowdown.

Deleting Messages

In an unsecured queue, you can delete a message by selecting it, then choosing **D**elete. The message is returned to the sender as non-deliverable.

 You cannot delete the first message in the queue if it has been picked up by the MTA or a receiving service and transport has begun.

If the message is blocking the queue so that you must delete it in order to let the remaining messages through the queue, it's too late to do it from the Queues dialog box. You have to stop the receiving service, using the Services icon in the Windows NT Control Panel. Once the service is stopped, all transport of messages ceases and you will be able to delete the message. Then restart the service.

Viewing the Internet Mail Connector Queues

If you are experiencing problems with Internet mail, you should examine the Internet Mail Connector queues. To see them, follow these steps:

1. In the Administrator window, select the Configuration object, select the Connections object, then open the Internet Mail Connector object.

2. Select the Queues tab (see fig. 17.14).

You can choose any queue that has messages, then you can perform actions on those messages.

The queues for the Internet Mail Connector are the following:

◆ The MTS Out queue, which receives messages from the MTAs Internet Mail Connector. These are messages that local users are sending out to the Internet. The MTS Out queue is in the information store of your Microsoft Exchange Server system.

◆ The OUT queue, which sends the messages on to the Internet recipients.

◆ The IN queue, which receives incoming messages. These messages will be converted and sent to the information store. The MTA will fetch them from the information store and deliver them to users.

Once you select a message, there are several things you can do.

Figure 17.14

You can view the messages in any of the Internet Mail Connector queues.

Viewing Message Details

You can choose Details to see additional information about the selected message. The following data is displayed:

◆ Originator

◆ MTS-ID (an ID that identifies the component that sent the message; available only in the MTS queue)

◆ Message ID

◆ Destination Host (the computer to which the message will be delivered)

◆ Submit Time

◆ Size (in kilobytes)

◆ Next Retry Time (appears if an attempt to send the message failed; the time at which the connector will again try to send the message is displayed in this field)

◆ Retries (the number of times the connector tried to send the message)

◆ Expiration (the time when any effort at retrying will end)

◆ Recipients, which also includes the status of attempts to deliver to each recipient

Deleting a Message

You can delete the selected message if it is interfering with the queue's work. A non-delivery notice is sent to the sender.

Forcing a Retry

If a message is marked for later retry, you can force the connector to try to send it again before the scheduled time. Choose Retry **N**ow to force the connector to attempt to send the message immediately. If it doesn't work, you can leave it there for later retry or delete it.

Viewing the MS Mail Connector Queues

The MS Mail Connectors each have a queue of messages waiting to go out. Messages in the MS Mail Connector queues should be dispatched rather quickly and if you find a particular message hanging around for any length of time, you should take a careful look at it.

To view the queue for each MS Mail Connector, follow these steps:

1. From the Administrator window, select the Connections object, then open an MS Mail Connector.

2. Move to the Connections tab and highlight the connection you want to examine (see fig. 17.15).

 Warning   You cannot view the local queue if it is running. You have to stop the service first.

3. Choose **Q**ueue to see the queue of the selected connection.

The messages in the selected queue are displayed with the following fields:

◆ From, which is the e-mail address of the sender

◆ Subject, which is taken from the subject line of the message

Figure 17.15

*Each MS Mail
Connector has its
own queue, which
can be viewed and
manipulated.*

◆ Message ID, which is its unique identifier

◆ Date/Time, which is the date and time the message was submitted to the queue

You can change the way the list is sorted by clicking on the column heading button for the field on which you want to sort (the current sort field has an arrow on the button).

Once you select one of the messages, you can manipulate it.

Returning a Message

Choose **R**eturn to send the selected message back to the sender. Usually, you perform this task at the request of the sender (who has had a change of mind or a panic attack, depending on the contents or recipient of the message).

Deleting a Message

Choose **D**elete to remove a message that seems to be slowing down the queue. If **S**end Non-Delivery Reports When Messages Deleted has been selected, the originator of the message will receive an NDR. If that option is not selected, the sender is not notified.

Maintaining Permissions

For a variety of reasons, you will probably want to establish user permissions for some of the components in your system:

◆ You might want to give certain users the right to create top-level public folders. This means department heads who need to distribute information, forms, or other files can establish a hierarchy on a case-by-case basis.

◆ You may want to give higher permission levels to individuals who can assist in the administration of the system.

◆ As the system's forms libraries grow, it might be productive to let project leaders administer them.

You can give additional permissions to individuals or groups in the following Microsoft Exchange Server components:

◆ The Directory

◆ The MTA

◆ The Private Information Store

◆ The Public Information Store

◆ The System Attendant

 Remember that the users and groups are Windows NT concepts and definitions. Mailbox names on the Microsoft Exchange Server system have nothing to do with permissions. If users are grouped in a way that makes sense for their NT permissions, but not for the way Microsoft Exchange Server is being administered, you have to use the NT User Manager to modify user rights. Otherwise, you have to add user permissions one person at a time.

When you want to change user or group permissions, Microsoft Exchange Server provides predefined roles. Each of these roles has specific rights attached, so you do not have to enable each of the rights individually. If you want to give some users or groups a combination of rights that is not preconfigured in a role, you can create a custom role.

Accessing Permissions Pages

The process of configuring permissions is similar for each component, although the specific permissions and roles may differ.

Figure 17.16 shows the Permissions tab for the Directory Service component. The Permissions tabs for all the other components look very much the same, and the configuration process is always the same.

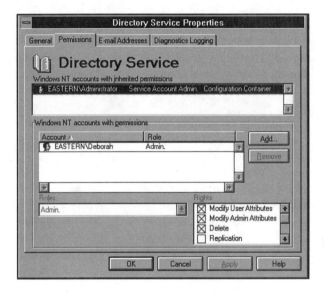

Figure 17.16

The Permissions tab is the property page used to give users and groups additional rights to the components of Microsoft Exchange Server.

The two large boxes in the Permissions tab display the following information:

◆ Windows NT accounts with inherited permissions is a read-only box that shows the Windows NT accounts that have automatic full rights to this object.

◆ Windows NT accounts with permissions displays all the accounts (names or groups) that have been given permissions to this object, along with the Role.

Adding Permissions

To add users and groups to the permissions box, follow these steps:

1. Choose Add to display the Add Users and Groups dialog box (see fig. 17.17), which lists all the groups and users in the domain. Groups are listed first, and individual user names follow the group list.

Figure 17.17

All the Windows NT groups and individual users for the current domain are displayed when you are configuring additional permissions.

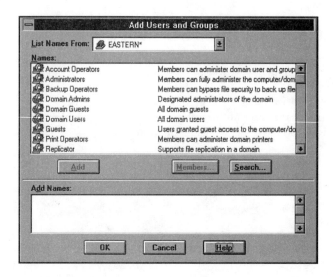

2. Choose <u>L</u>ist Names From if you want to give permissions to a user from another domain. The <u>N</u>ames box will change to display the information from the new domain.

3. If the list of groups and users is large, it might be faster to choose <u>S</u>earch instead of scrolling through the list. The Search tool lets you set parameters such as limiting the group or domain to explore (and also searches for a specific name, of course).

4. If you select a group, you can choose <u>M</u>embers to see a list of users who belong to that group.

 If you know you want to limit the users to whom you will add permissions to those users who are already administrators, replicators, or other high-permission users, choose <u>M</u>embers for that group and select the appropriate users.

5. After you choose a group or a user, select it and choose <u>A</u>dd. The name is added to the Add Names box.

6. Continue to select groups or users. When you are finished, choose OK.

Assigning Roles

The roles for components vary, depending upon the component. However, the process for assigning roles is the same:

1. Select the name, then click on the arrow to the right of the Roles box to see the available roles.

2. Select the appropriate role for this name.

3. If the rights given for this role do not match your intentions, repeat the process to select a different role.

4. If you want to give a specific combination of rights to this name, choose any role, then select and deselect the rights as you choose. If the combination you select matches an existing role, that role will be assigned automatically. If there is no match, the name will display Custom as the role.

Once you configure the components for additional user rights, you should develop and distribute a set of administration guidelines. That way, all the assistant administrators and users will know what their assigned responsibilities are. This should cut down on the number of user calls for help made to the chief administrator.

PART VI

Application Development with MES

CHAPTER 18

Understanding Application Development with Exchange Server

Microsoft Exchange Server is a powerful client-server messaging system that enables you to connect your users and sites easily and reliably. However, much of the power of Exchange Server comes from the application capabilities it brings you. Using these capabilities, you can take e-mail to a new level in your organization and automate many tasks that now require paper forms. Just as basic e-mail has taken the place of paper memos in most offices, the application capabilities in Exchange Server enable you to go much further in impacting how your company does business.

Think for a minute about all the paper that flows in your company. There are purchase requisitions, check requests, payroll time allocation sheets, vacation request forms, work orders for your facilities department, and many others. Chances are that the larger your company is, the more forms there are to manage your increasingly complex business. Unfortunately, paper forms can often be misplaced, need to be stocked for people to use, need to be filled out, and need to be routed, acted on, and filed. If you think about it, you'll probably realize that your company spends a substantial amount of time dealing with it all.

The dream of the paperless office isn't yet here, but with the capabilities you'll learn about in this chapter and section on Microsoft Exchange Server's application development capabilities, you can work to streamline your company. Possible benefits include the following:

◆ **Reduced user confusion.** Because you can store your forms inside Exchange Server folders, you can create a single place for people to look to find critical forms. Although the forms themselves will vary, the procedures for filling them out and sending them can be easier to communicate and follow.

◆ **Better communications.** With Exchange Server's public folders, and the forms you can attach to them, you can ease communications within your company and make forming ad hoc groups (and helping them to communicate with each other) simpler.

◆ **Improved accountability.** With no opportunity for paper forms to be "lost in the cracks," you can help ensure that people are as accountable for the results needed from them as possible.

◆ **Automatic tracking.** Flowing information through Exchange Server can pay off by giving you better ways to track information.

◆ **More accessible information.** By setting up shared databases within public folders (with security restrictions that you control), you can make sure that all the members of a particular project have access not only to current information, but also to historical information.

There are many other imaginable benefits besides these few listed here. The possibilities are entirely up to you.

Reaping all these benefits is not automatic, however. In order to get the most from this area of Exchange Server, you need to delve into the world of Exchange custom applications. There are a number of tools built into Exchange Server to make this job easier, but it will still require work on your part and diligence to design and implement the ideas that will most benefit your company.

Knowing Application Capabilities

Microsoft Exchange Server applications are built out of a combination of forms and folders.

You've already learned about folders earlier in this book. They are repositories of messages, and you can control where each folder is in the hierarchy of folders and who can access each folder. You can even control where different folders are stored, whether they are shared or not, and whether they are available to many sites in your organization or just one site.

Forms are custom message templates that guide a user in filling out the form. Often, forms are just simple fields added to an otherwise normal message. They can also be very complex, however, with rules and intelligence built in that increase their usefulness. Figure 18.1 shows one of the sample Exchange forms, used for tracking help desk requests.

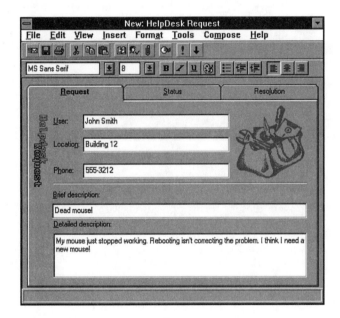

Figure 18.1

The help desk tracking form.

Forms can be used in two ways. The first is called a *form application.* It is a custom form that a user fills out and then sends to one or many recipients. For instance, you may have a form on your system for taking telephone messages. A user fills in the information on the on-screen form, then sends it to the person who was called. The other type of form is used along with a folder and is often part of a *folder application.* These forms are used just like a database entry screen, with the completed form not sent to any particular recipient, but instead posted to a folder in Exchange Server. Other people can then access the form and its data within the folder to which it was posted. An example of this kind of application might be a customer-tracking database folder, into which completed forms are posted. Another example would be the sample Classified Ads application included with Exchange Server and shown in figure 18.2.

Figure 18.2

A Classified Ads sample application.

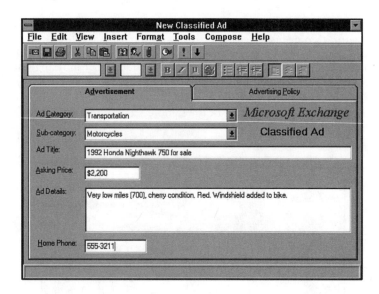

Exploring Form Applications

There are many different possibilities for form applications within your organization. Here are some ideas to start you thinking:

◆ Legal contract or confidentiality agreement request forms

◆ Purchase requisitions or purchase orders

◆ Reports, such as status reports, weekly reports, or monthly reports

◆ Survey forms

◆ Telephone message forms

◆ Travel authorization or travel expense forms

◆ Vacation request forms

◆ Work order forms

A form application is appropriate when you want to replace a paper form that is typically sent to a particular recipient or department.

Understanding Forms

Exchange Client has *built-in forms,* such as the New Message form and the New Post form. You can also use the sample forms included with the product or create your own. These are *custom forms.*

There are two fundamental types of forms in Exchange Server: *send forms* and *post forms.* Send forms are used to send information from one person to another or to multiple recipients. Post forms are used to add information to a folder.

Each form created with the Form Designer is made up of one or two windows. The first window may be used to create new messages, and the second is used to read existing messages. (Messages can also be referred to as *items.*)

All forms also contain fields. These fields may simply hold some text that labels an area of the form or that contains a graphic image. Other fields accept data, such as the To or From fields.

Each form element has associated properties that control how it works. The Form Designer enables you to control these properties so that you can control how the form behaves. For instance, you may set the properties on a particular field so that it accepts only numerical entries.

Forms are held in *form libraries.* There are four libraries available to hold forms:

◆ Folder Forms are held within a particular folder on the Exchange Server and generally contain post forms for use with that folder.

◆ Local Forms are stored on a user's local hard disk and are part of a local program associated with Exchange Client. Schedule+ is an example of this kind of application.

◆ Organization Forms are held in the Exchange Server in a place called the Organization Forms Library. These are libraries of send forms that are used across the company.

◆ Personal Forms are post forms that are stored within a specific mailbox or user folder file. Personal post forms may be used when not connected to the Exchange Server computer.

Exploring Folder Applications

Folder applications are used when broad sharing of information or messages is needed. For example, you can have folder applications that enable groups of people to post messages to a particular topic or that track customer or company information, or even that contain news that would be of interest to many people. Here are some ideas for folder applications:

◆ Discussion folders in which groups of people can read and post messages on a particular topic

◆ Classified ads that employees can use to advertise things they want to sell or make available to other employees

◆ Customer service tracking folders that contain information about service calls and their status

◆ Online employee procedures folders

◆ Document repositories

◆ News folders

◆ Sales lead and follow-up tracking folders

Folder applications are best suited to situations in which many people need to access or add to the accumulated information.

Understanding Folders

Recall that there are three types of folders within Exchange Server. Personal folders are used by individuals to hold items they wish to keep. They are listed under Personal Folders in the Exchange Client.

Public folders hold items that many people need to post to or access. Forms may be associated with public folders, and, in fact, folder applications are made in exactly this way.

Mailbox folders are stored in an individual's mailbox on the Exchange Server computer. They are accessed only by the specific user of the mailbox and are secured.

Investigating Sample Applications

The sample applications included with Exchange Server provide you with a rich set of examples to understand what is possible with these powerful tools. The best way to review them is to install them all at once into your own personal folders. To do this, follow these steps:

1. Locate the \ENG\SAMPAPPS directory. It should be installed on your Exchange Server computer and can also be found on the Exchange Server CD-ROM.

2. Copy the file SAMPAPPS.PST to a directory on your local hard disk. You'll need at least 20 MB of free disk space to do this.

3. Start Exchange Client.

4. Access the **T**ools menu and choose Ser**v**ices. This brings up the Services dialog box shown in figure 18.3.

Figure 18.3

The Services dialog box.

5. Click on the A**d**d button to access the Add Service to Profile dialog box shown in figure 18.4.

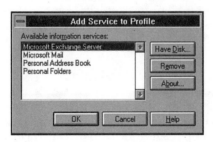

Figure 18.4

The Add Service to Profile dialog box.

6. Choose the Personal Folders entry and click on the OK button. You see the Create/Open Personal Folders File dialog box shown in figure 18.5. (The Windows NT version is shown.)

Figure 18.5

*The Create/Open
Personal Folders
File dialog box.*

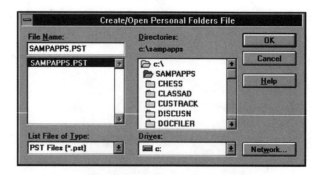

7. Using the dialog box, navigate to the directory in which you copied the
   SAMPAPPS.PST file and select that file. Click on the Open button to proceed.
   You see the Personal Folders dialog box shown in figure 18.6.

Figure 18.6

*The Personal
Folders dialog
box.*

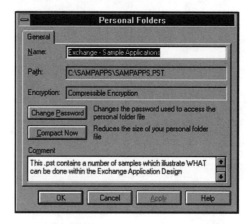

8. Click on the OK button in the Personal Folders dialog box, and then in the
   Services dialog box to finish.

To begin exploring the sample application, access the Exchange Sample Applications
folder in Exchange Client as shown in figure 18.5. To use a particular form, select the
folder and then access the Compose menu. At the bottom of the Compose menu,
you'll see the form entry attached to the selected folder (see fig. 18.7).

Microsoft Exchange Server comes with a number of sample applications that you can
use to learn about Exchange Server development, or use as-is in your company, or
modify for your own use. Table 18.1 lists the sample applications included with
Exchange Server. The entries that are listed as having been created with Visual Basic
are ones that started with the Exchange Server Forms Designer and then had their
functionality extended further with the Visual Basic tools that come with Exchange
Server.

Figure 18.7

Accessing a sample form.

TABLE 18.1
Sample Applications Included with Microsoft Exchange Server

Type	Application	Created with Visual Basic?
Folder	Anonymous Suggestions	X

If you want to create a public folder that enables anonymous postings that encourage the free expression of ideas, you can use this form. It's been modified so that the sender's name is automatically removed from the message when it is posted.

Form	Chess	X

The Chess form supports an e-mail version of Chess, in which you make moves and then send the modified chessboard to the other player as an Exchange message.

continues

TABLE 18.1 CONTINUED
Sample Applications Included with Microsoft Exchange Server

Type	Application	Created with Visual Basic?
Folder	Classified Ads	X

Many company e-mail systems are clogged with ads from employees giving away puppies, selling furniture or cars, and so forth. Using this form along with a public folder designed for this purpose enables you to give people a place to post such ads conveniently.

Folder	Contact Tracking	

A collection of forms that enable you to set up a folder that can hold information about sales contacts, their companies, and actions that have been taken with them.

Folder	Discussion & Response	

Although you can easily post normal messages to a public folder, using these forms enables you to organize the posted messages better within the folder.

Folder	Document Filer	

If your organization uses Word, Excel, or PowerPoint, this form enables your users to store files easily from those programs within an Exchange Server public folder.

Folder	Getting Started Guide	

The Getting Started Guide includes tutorial information about using Microsoft Exchange.

Folder	HelpDesk	

The service organization within your company needs to respond to many requests and needs to follow up on them efficiently. Using the HelpDesk form enables you to set up an easy-to-use system for people to submit requests and a built-in method to follow up on those requests.

Folder	HotTopics	

This form enables users to submit news or information items to a person designated as the News Moderator. The moderator can then allow the item to be posted to the folder or reject the item.

Type	Application	Created with Visual Basic?
Folder	Interpersonal Forms	
	A folder application that enables you to store Send Forms.	
Folder	Survey	X
	Consisting of a Survey and Answer form, this enables you to gather information from people in a number of different ways (for example, multiple choice, yes/no, and so forth).	

Understanding Design Tools

There are a number of tools included with Exchange Server that enable you to create custom applications for your organization. They include the following:

◆ Forms Designer

◆ Form Template Wizard

◆ Form Templates

◆ Sample Applications

◆ Visual Basic for Exchange Server

Combined, these tools offer you the ability to start with simple applications that don't take much effort to create, and move up to more complex applications that make use of the sophisticated capabilities found in Visual Basic.

Learning about the Forms Designer

Forms Designer enables you to design a form quickly. You can add basic messaging fields, such as To, From, and so forth, with a single click of a button. You can also add more complex fields that make use of drop boxes, option buttons, text labels, and so forth. Forms Designer is shown in figure 18.8.

 Learn about designing forms with Form Designer in Chapters 19, "Developing Forms," and 20, "Advanced Development: Exploring Sample Applications."

Figure 18.8

The Exchange Forms Designer.

The menu bar and toolbar control the Forms Designer program.

The tool palette enables you to draw form elements quickly.

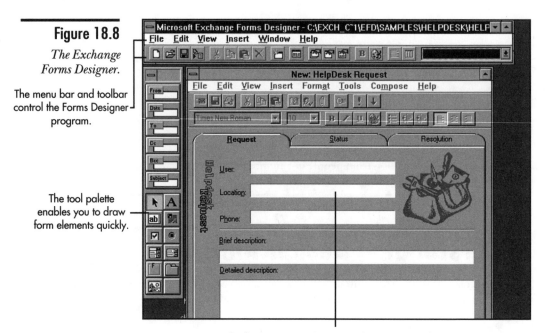

The form you're working on is shown in a window.

Learning about the Template Wizard

The Form Template Wizard walks you through a series of questions designed to help you select a prebuilt form that meets your needs. You can use the selected form as-is, or you can modify it using the Forms Designer. Figure 18.9 shows the Form Template Wizard.

Learning about Visual Basic for Exchange Server

Exchange Server comes with a special version of Visual Basic called Visual Basic for Microsoft Exchange Server.

The Forms Designer has some fundamental limits, because it is designed to be as easy to use as possible and therefore must meet the widest variety of needs without being overly complex or requiring the services of a programmer. However, you may need applications that are more complex than the Form Designer can generate. In cases such as this, you can start your project with the Form Designer and then modify it further with Visual Basic for Microsoft Exchange Server. Using Visual Basic, there are virtually no limits to the complexity of applications you can build. Figure 18.10 shows Visual Basic with a basic form displayed.

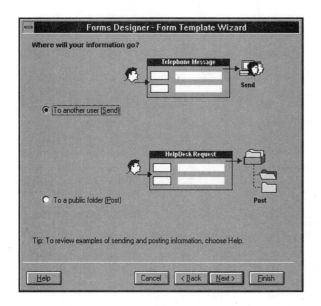

Figure 18.9

The Form Template Wizard.

Note Using Visual Basic for Microsoft Exchange Server is covered in Chapter 21, "Using Visual Basic."

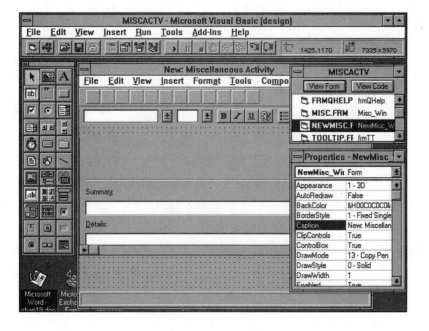

Figure 18.10

Visual Basic for Microsoft Exchange Server.

CHAPTER 19

Developing Forms

As you saw in Chapter 18, "Understanding Application Development with Exchange Server," designing forms for Microsoft Exchange dramatically increases the power the product brings to your organization. Exchange forms can take the place of paper forms in your organization and can add additional capabilities that you don't currently have.

Key to unlocking the benefits of custom forms is the Exchange Forms Designer, a program that enables you to draw and design forms and that is easy to use. However, the form designer has capabilities that may not be immediately apparent. In this chapter, you learn not only how to create a simple form using Forms Designer, but you also learn about its other features that you'll need for more advanced projects.

Designing a Simple Form

In the first part of this chapter, you explore how to create a simple form: a purchasing expedite request form. In many companies, one of the functions of the purchasing department is to expedite orders for goods that are desperately needed or that have not arrived when the vendor promised. An expedite request form requests that someone find out where the shipment is in the process and update the time it will arrive. During that process, the person works to find out whether the order can be expedited so that it arrives sooner than otherwise.

In this example, you create a Send Form. Send Forms are what you use when a form is designed to be sent from an individual to another individual or to a group of individuals.

Overviewing the Forms Designer

Start the Forms Designer from the Exchange client by choosing Application Design from the Tools menu, then selecting Forms Designer. The Forms Designer has several main windows that you use to design and work with your forms. Figure 19.1 shows you the main areas of the Forms Designer screen.

Figure 19.1

Forms Designer windows.

Title bar, menu bar, and toolbar window

Toolbox window —

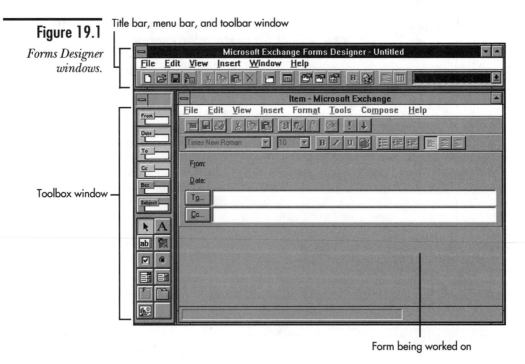

Form being worked on

The top window contains the Forms Designer's title, menu, and toolbars. Table 19.1 shows you the buttons on the toolbar.

TABLE 19.1
Toolbar Buttons

Icon	Name	Description
	New	Starts a new project
	Open	Opens an existing project
	Save	Saves the open project
	Install	Installs the form into Exchange
	Cut	Cuts selection to the clipboard
	Copy	Copies selection to the clipboard
	Paste	Pastes the clipboard to the current form
	Delete	Deletes the selection
	New Window	Creates a new form window
	Insert Field	Adds a field to the form
	Form Properties	Displays the properties for the form
	Window Properties	Displays the properties for the current window
	Field Properties	Displays the properties for the field
	Bold	Bolds the selected field
	Field Appearance	Displays the appearance settings for the selected field
	Align Left	With multiple fields selected, aligns their left edges
	Vertical Spacing	With multiple fields selected, makes their vertical spacing regular
	Field Name	Displays the name of the selected field and enables you to select a field based on its name

The toolbox also contains buttons of crucial importance to you as you use the form designer. Table 19.2 shows you these buttons.

TABLE 19.2
Toolbox Buttons

Icon	Name	Description
From	From Field	Inserts a From field
Date	Date Field	Inserts a Date field
To	To Field	Inserts a To field
Cc	Cc Field	Inserts a Carbon Copy field
Bcc	Bcc Field	Inserts a Blind Carbon Copy field
Subject	Subject Field	Inserts a Subject field
▶	Pointer	Selects the pointer
A	Label Field	Adds a Label field
ab	Entry Field	Adds an Entry field
	RichEntry Field	Adds a RichEntry text field
☑	CheckBox Field	Adds a CheckBox field
◉	OptionButton Field	Adds an OptionButton (radio button) field
	ComboBox Field	Adds a ComboBox field
	ListBox Field	Adds a ListBox field
F	Frame Field	Adds a Frame field
	Tab Field	Adds a Tab field
	PictureBox Field	Adds a PictureBox field

Overviewing the Simple Form

In the Expedite Request form, you need certain fields to guide the user in filling out the form correctly. These include the following:

◆ To field (already filled out with the name of the expediter)

◆ Purchase Order number

◆ Vendor

◆ Product

◆ Original Promise Date

◆ Require Date

◆ Comments

Designing the Form

All forms begin with a template. When you choose **F**ile **N**ew from the Forms Designer menu, you see the screen shown in figure 19.2. This is where you begin the process of building the basic template with which you'll work.

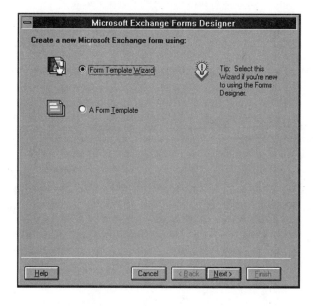

Figure 19.2

The Forms Designer dialog box.

You can choose to select a template by using the Form Template **W**izard or by selecting one of the built-in templates manually. Both yield the same results, but the wizard helps you select which template will work best for you. Table 20.3 contains a list of the templates available to you.

TABLE **20.3**
Form Templates

File Name	Description
PSTN1WND.EFP	Single window Post Form; compose and read items
PSTN2WND.EFP	Double window Post Form; contains compose and read windows
PSTR1WND.EFP	Single window Post Form; reply and read reply
PSTR2WND.EFP	Double window Post Form; contains reply and read windows
SNDN1WND.EFP	Single window Send Form; compose and read items
SNDN2WND.EFP	Double window Send Form; contains compose and read windows
SNDR1WND.EFP	Single window Send Form; reply and read reply
SNDR1WND.EFP	Double window Send Form; contains reply and read windows

For this example, choose A Form **T**emplate in the dialog box. This displays the Select Template dialog box showing the template files available. Choose SNDN1WND.EFP to select a form that enables you to compose items and uses the same form for the recipient to read the item when it's received. You now see your form template on the screen, as shown in figure 19.3.

Select Fields

To select any of the existing fields on the new form, simply click on them with your left mouse button. This shows you the field's handles, like those shown surrounding the Subject field in figure 19.4.

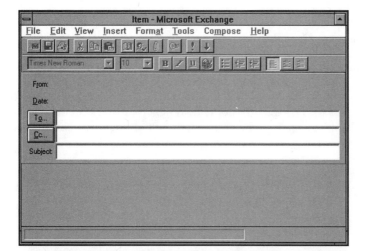

Figure 19.3

The New Form Template ready for modification.

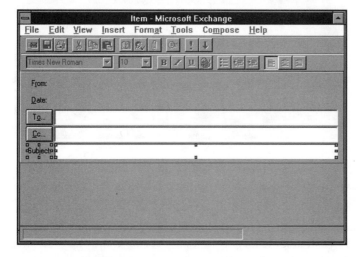

Figure 19.4

Field selection and handles.

Using the handles, you can resize and reposition selected fields. In this example, though, you do not need a subject field. While it's selected, choose **E**dit, then Cle**a**r to remove the field.

Tip You can also press the Del key to remove a selected field.

Add Fields

There are a number of fields that need to be added to this form. In this example, you add Entry fields. Entry fields have a caption and enable the user of the form to enter text or numbers in the field itself.

To add the first field, select the Entry field button in the toolbox. This changes your pointer to a small cross with the picture of the field next to it. Click on the cross right below the **C**c... field, in the open frame at the lower half of the form. This inserts a new Entry field, as shown in figure 19.5.

Figure 19.5

Inserting an Entry field.

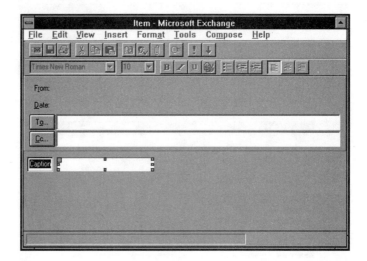

You can move the field by dragging within the field itself. You can also use the handles to resize or move the field. Finally, using the handle in the upper left corner of the caption field enables you to move the caption independently of the field itself.

If the caption isn't yet editable, click on the word Caption with the I-bar pointer. The word Caption should be highlighted, and you'll see a cursor at the end of the word. Replace the word Caption with PO Number: and click outside the field. Resize the field as necessary, as described previously. When finished, the field should appear as shown in figure 19.6.

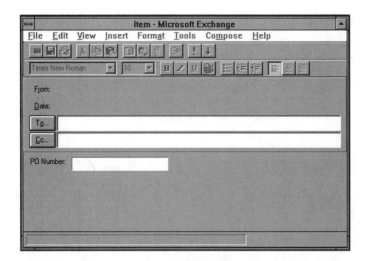

Figure 19.6
The PO Number field.

Now, add the following fields, using figure 19.7 as a guide. Don't worry if you have them positioned just right; you learn about doing that in the next section.

◆ Vendor:

◆ Item:

◆ Promise Date:

◆ Need Date:

◆ Comments:

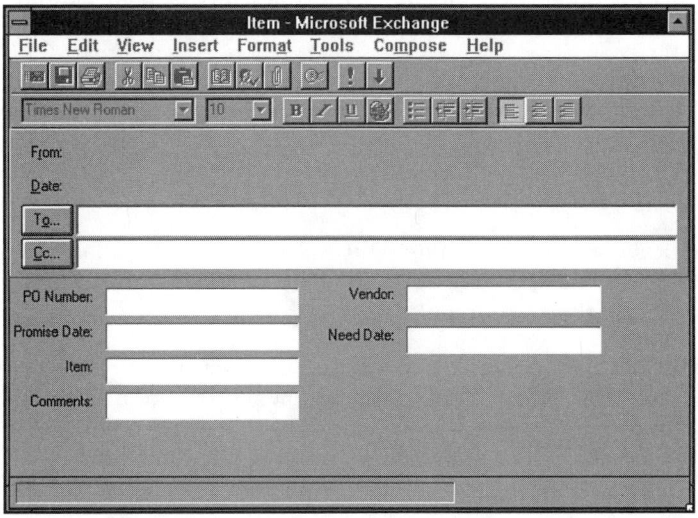

Figure 19.7
Adding fields to the form.

Move and Align Fields

Next, align your fields so that they line up as neatly as possible. The easy way to do this is with the Align Left and Vertical Spacing buttons.

You select multiple fields at once by holding down the Shift or Ctrl field and clicking on each field you want selected. In this way, select the PO Number, Promise Date, Item, and Comments fields. When they're all selected, your screen will look like figure 19.8.

Figure 19.8

Selecting multiple fields.

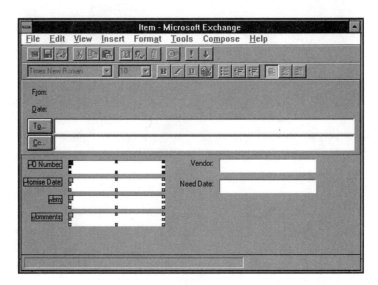

Now click on the Align Left button in the Toolbar to adjust all the fields' positions so that the left side of each entry box lines up with the others.

 Note The leftmost field of the ones selected is used to align the other fields.

Repeat the same operation with the Vendor and Need Date fields.

Next, make the vertical spacing of the fields regular. Start by selecting all the left fields (PO Number, Promise Date, Item, and Comments). Click on the Vertical Spacing button to arrange them with regular vertical spacing.

Because the Vertical Spacing function works only with three or more fields, you can't use it to align the right fields. Instead, carefully move them up or down so that they line up with the appropriate left field. If you accidentally change their horizontal alignments, simply select them both again and click on the Align Left button.

Resize Fields

Notice that the Comments field is pretty small for typed comments. To rectify this, select it, grab the lower right handle, and drag down and to the right until the entire lower frame is taken up. The results should look like figure 19.9.

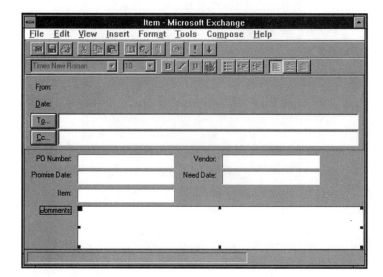

Figure 19.9

Resizing the Comments field.

Change Field Properties

Your next job is to change some of the field properties so that the fields function as you want. Specifically, you want the following properties:

◆ T**o**... field should default to the person who handles expediting.

◆ PO number requires a numeric input with the correct number of digits.

◆ Both date fields require a date entry.

◆ The comments field has vertical scroll bars and allows multiple lines of text.

To access the properties for any field, double-click on the field. This displays the properties notebook for that field.

To begin changing the field properties, double-click on the T**o**... field. You see the notebook shown in figure 19.10.

Figure 19.10

Properties for the To: field.

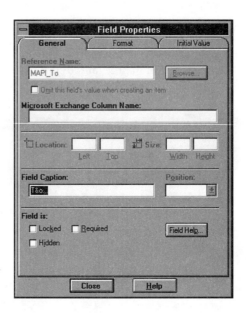

 The To: field is automatic in that you don't need to draw it on the form as you do other fields. Accordingly, the fields for location and size are blank.

Move to the Initial Value tab of the notebook, in which you'll find a T**o**... button. Click on the T**o**... button and select the appropriate recipient for messages using this form. The result looks like figure 19.11. Close the Properties notebook when you're done.

Tip If you'll be designing Send Forms that go to a particular recipient, such as a payroll administrator, an HR administrator, or a buyer, consider setting up a separate mailbox for that person's function. In this example, you would set up a mailbox called Purchasing Expediter. Then, give the person handling that job access to that mailbox. The Exchange Client can then be set to open the Purchasing Expediter's personal mailbox and job mailbox simultaneously. This reduces the chance of needing to modify your form when people change jobs.

Next, access Properties for the PO Number field. Move to the Format page shown in figure 19.12. In this example, the company uses sequential PO numbers that are six digits long. Accordingly, you'll set up the PO Number field to accept only numeric input (as an integer) with a fixed number of digits. Change the **T**ype field to Integer and set the F**o**rmat field to six 0s.

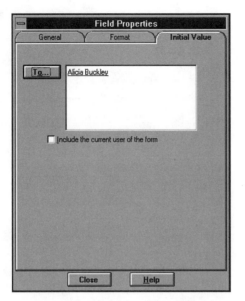

Figure 19.11

Selecting a default recipient.

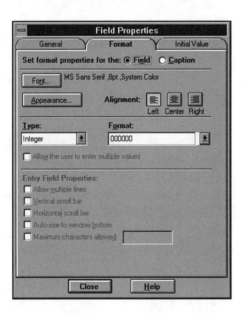

Figure 19.12

Setting the input type.

The PO Number field is also required on this form, because without it the expediter doesn't know which order is being referenced. Move to the General page and select the **R**equired CheckBox, as illustrated in figure 19.13.

Figure 19.13

Setting the field as required.

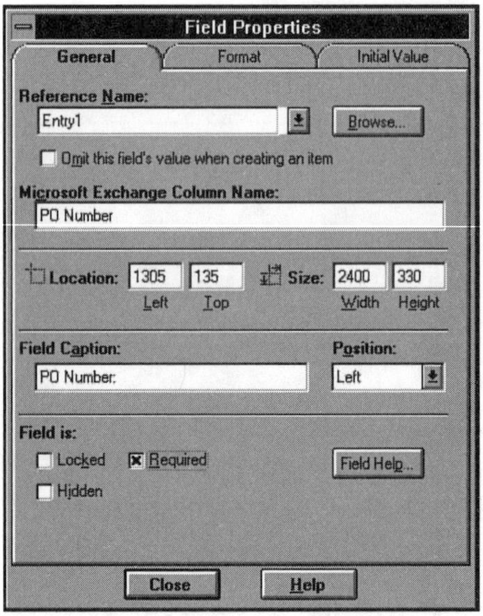

Using a similar procedure, set both the Promise Date and Need Date fields to require date input. Access the Format page of their Properties, and set **T**ype to Date and F**o**rmat to m/d/yy.

Finally, you need to make some changes to the Comments field to allow multiline input. Open its Properties and move to its Format page. Select the CheckBoxes Allow **m**ultiple lines and **V**ertical scroll bar, as shown in figure 19.14.

Figure 19.14

Changing the Comments field.

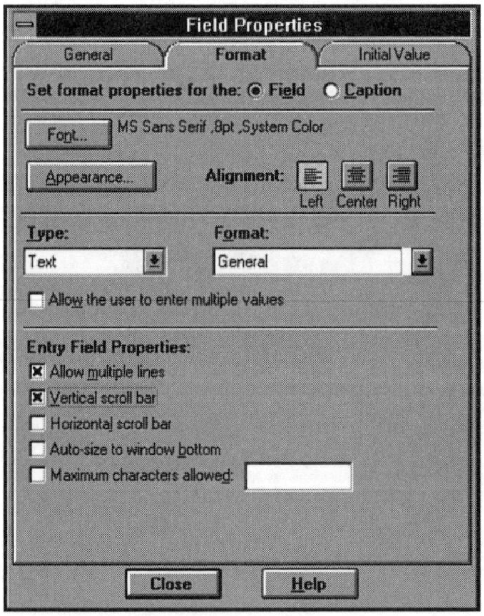

Installing the Form

You're now finished with the example Purchase Order Expedite form. To install and test it, click on the Install button in the toolbar or choose File, Install in the Forms Designer. When you do this, you will see Visual Basic for Microsoft Exchange Server start while it compiles your form and saves the final code. Finally, when that completes, you will see the dialog box shown in figure 19.15 in which you choose where you want to install the form.

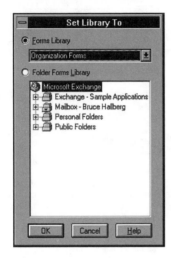

Figure 19.15

Choosing the form install location.

It's often a good idea to install a new form in your personal form library and then test it. Once testing is complete, you can move the form into the Organization Forms Library or reinstall it in the Organization Forms Library. Figure 19.15 shows the form being installed in the Organization Forms Library. After selecting the forms library, click on OK to proceed. This brings up the Form Properties dialog box shown in figure 19.16.

Complete the relevant information in the Form Properties dialog box and click on its OK button to finish installing the form for use.

Figure 19.16

*The Form
Properties dialog
box.*

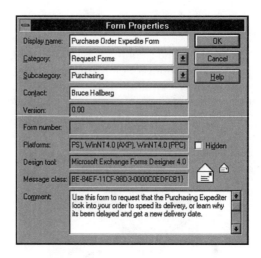

Figure 19.16

*The Form
Properties dialog
box.*

Knowing Form Design

You learned just the basics of form design in the preceding sections. There is a lot of power still untapped in the Forms Designer application that you explore in this section.

Working with Window Properties

When working with a particular window in the Forms Designer, you access the window's properties by accessing the View menu and choosing Window Properties from the menu. You can also press Ctrl+W to access the screen or click on the Window Properties button on the toolbar.

General

Figure 19.17 shows the General page of the Window Properties dialog box. In this page, you can enter the Window Name and its caption, and you can control the tab order of the displayed fields. You can use the Lock Window checkbox to render all the fields in the window read-only (you might use this when creating a form that will only be used to read items).

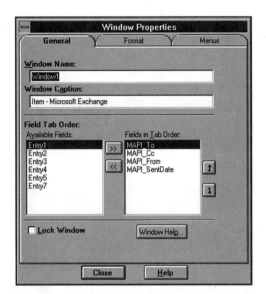

Figure 19.17

General window properties.

Note Good form development practice suggests that you should always choose descriptive names for the elements of your forms. For instance, using the default names of the fields (Entry1, Entry2, and so on) makes it difficult to choose the tab order of the fields, because you can't easily tell which field is which.

The General page is also where you define the help a user receives for the window in question. Access this function by clicking on the Window Help button. This brings up the Window Help for Users dialog box shown in figure 19.18.

Figure 19.18

The Window Help for Users dialog box.

The dialog box shown in figure 19.18 uses basic editing commands and toolbar buttons to enable you to compose the help that users see when they choose Current Window in the form's **H**elp menu.

Format

The Format page of Window Properties (see fig. 19.19) enables you to control what features of the title bar are active, what views are initially active, the appearance of the window when its minimized or active on the screen, and the sizing options for the window.

Figure 19.19

The Window Properties Format page.

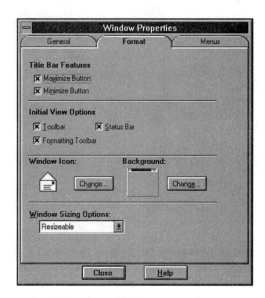

To change the window's icon (displayed when the window is minimized), click on the Ch**a**nge button and select an icon file on the Exchange Server computer. Sample icons can be found in the \EFD\ICONS directory.

Menus

The Menus page of the Window properties enables you to control what menu commands are available for the form. Figure 19.20 shows you this page.

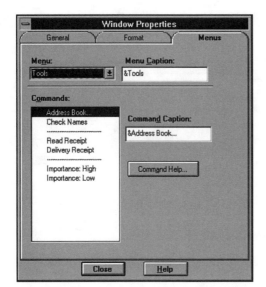

Figure 19.20

The Windows properties Menus page.

To access a particular menu command, first select the menu name in the Me**n**u field. This causes the appropriate menu commands to appear in the C**o**mmands list. You cannot change the menu commands that are present, but you can change their hot keys by changing the location of the ampersand (&); the ampersand should be located immediately before the letter that you want used for the hot key.

 Note If you inadvertently use the same hot-key letter for two menu commands in the same menu, the form still works. Pressing the hot-key letter merely moves the menu highlight bar to the first occurrence, however, and pressing it again moves to the second occurrence. The hot key will not actually make a selection until you click on the menu command or press Enter.

You can also change the help attached to each menu command, its tool tip, and the help displayed in the status bar as the user scrolls through the various commands. QuickHelp can also be defined and is accessed when the user highlights the menu command and presses the F1 key. To access these functions, choose a command in the C**o**mmands list and click on the Comm**a**nd Help button. This causes the Menu Help for Users dialog box, shown in figure 19.21, to appear.

Figure 19.21

The Menu Help for Users dialog box.

Working with Form Properties

Form properties enable you to control the name and version number of the form and set the icon displayed in the Forms Manager and in the user's folder view. You can also set up help for the form and control what actions are taken in response to different form events.

Form Information

The General page of the form's properties (shown in fig. 19.22) enables you to define the name of the form, comments about the form, and the version number and revision of the form.

The Form Display Name is what the user sees when opening the Forms Manager or when using the New Form command in Exchange Client. Version and Number are used by you to keep track of your revisions to the form. Item Type uniquely identifies the form to Exchange; it must be unique from all other forms. It is the entry in Item Type that tells Exchange which form to use when a particular item is opened. You may also change the icons for the form with the displayed Large and Small buttons. The Large icon is used in the New Form display, and the Small icon is used in the folder view of the item.

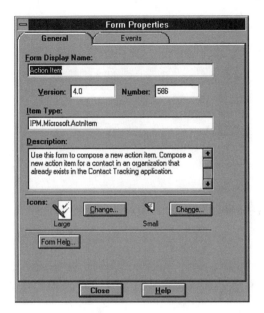

Figure 19.22

*The Form
properties General
page.*

Form Events

The Events page of the Form Properties (see fig. 19.23) enables you to control what action is taken upon certain form events. You can deny certain events by choosing Event Not Supported. Other choices in this dialog should not be changed unless you are developing a more complex form by using Visual Basic.

Working with Fields

There are a plethora of different field types in the Forms Designer to cater to every need you may have. In this section, you learn about each field type and any unique properties it has.

Frame Fields

A Frame field is used to group together other fields logically so that you can move them as a group. Frame fields also serve to group certain fields visually, making the form more understandable to the user. Frame fields are required around OptionButtons, because you need to group together all the buttons so that an exclusive choice can be made among the grouped buttons. In figure 19.24, a frame field is shown surrounding the custom fields in the Expedite form.

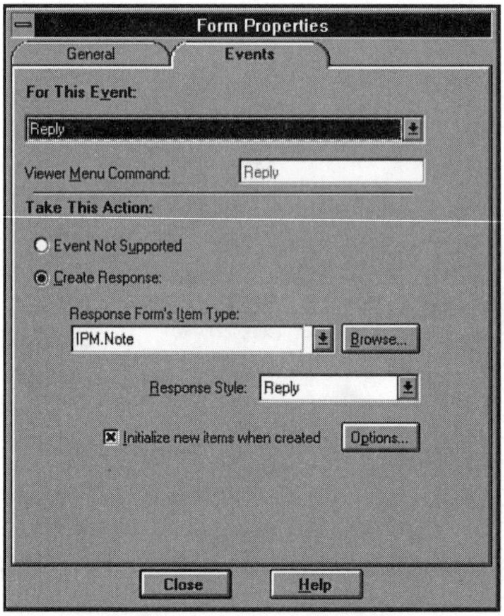

Figure 19.23

*The Form
Properties Events
page.*

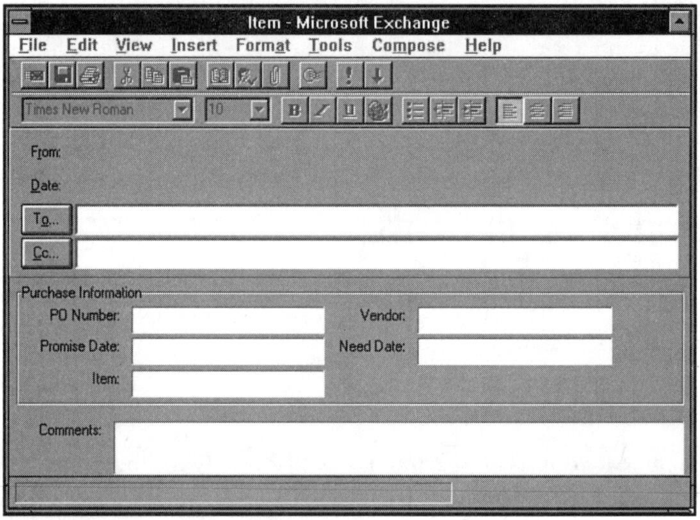

Figure 19.24

*Frame field added
to the Expedite
form.*

To use a frame field, select the field type and drag in the form to draw the box. You can then place other fields within the frame field. You can also access its properties and control its appearance.

List and Combo Boxes

ComboBox and ListBox fields are very similar. Each gives the user a number of predefined choices. The only difference between these two types of fields is in how they display on the screen. You can see examples of each type in figure 19.25.

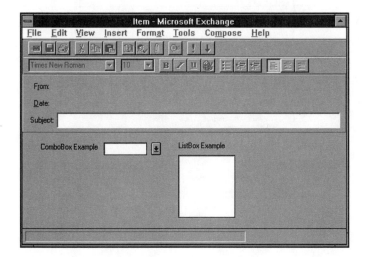

Figure 19.25

ComboBox and ListBox examples.

To define the choices that are seen in these fields at runtime, access their properties notebooks and move to the Initial Value page, shown in figure 19.26. In the list shown, type all the valid choices from which the user can choose. You can use the buttons shown on the page to sort the choices or manually move a choice up or down in the list.

OptionButton Fields

When you need to have a user make a choice that is exclusive from other possible choices, you use OptionButtons. For instance, you might design a survey form to offer the choices `Very satisfied` to `Very unsatisfied`. Figure 19.27 shows an example of an OptionButton field.

OptionButtons must always reside within a frame field so that Exchange knows how to group the buttons (different option buttons within a frame are then mutually exclusive). You can use the OptionButton's properties Initial Value page to choose which OptionButton is initially selected on the form.

Figure 19.26

Initial values for combo and list boxes.

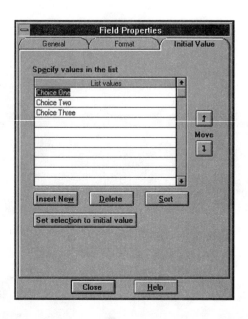

Figure 19.27

An OptionButton field.

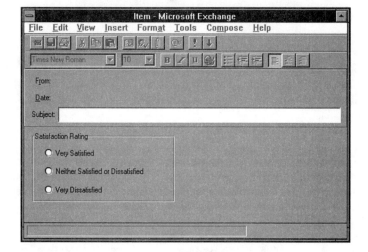

CheckBox Fields

CheckBox fields are used when you need a binary Yes/No answer to a question, and the choices between different CheckBoxes are not mutually exclusive. CheckBoxes can be surrounded by a frame field, or not surrounded; it doesn't matter. Using their Initial Value page, you can decide whether they are initialled checked or unchecked. Figure 19.28 shows a number of CheckBox fields.

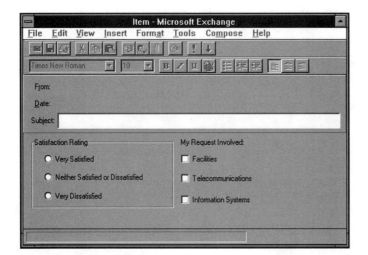

Figure 19.28

CheckBox field examples.

PictureBox Fields

PictureBoxes are used to spice up your forms. For instance, figure 19.29 shows a PictureBox field that includes a piece of clipart from Microsoft Office. PictureBoxes can make your forms more appealing to the people who use them.

When you first create a PictureBox by selecting the PictureBox button and then drawing the box on the form, a File/Open dialog box opens that enables you to select the graphic image to display in the field. Bitmaps, icons, and Windows metafiles can be directly used by the PictureBox field.

Tab Fields

When your forms require more space than can comfortably fit on a screen, you can break them up by using Tab fields, such as the one shown in figure 19.30. Tab fields enable you to have as many tabs as you like and can be broken into rows of tabs easily.

Create tabs by choosing the Tab Field button and clicking in a blank area of the form. You can then resize and move the field (which is a collection of pages with tabs for each page) until you get it arranged as you like.

Accessing the Format page of a Tab field's properties notebook enables you to control how the tabs work. Figure 19.31 shows this page. Add as many tab fields as you wish, and then define an appropriate number of Tabs per row so that the tabs' captions are readable. You can also control the order of the tabs on this page with the two Move buttons.

Figure 19.29

A PictureBox field.

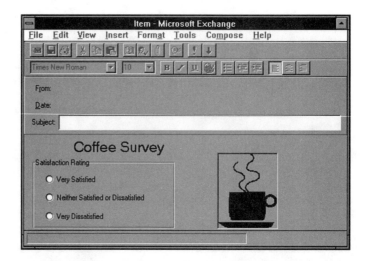

Figure 19.30

Tab fields.

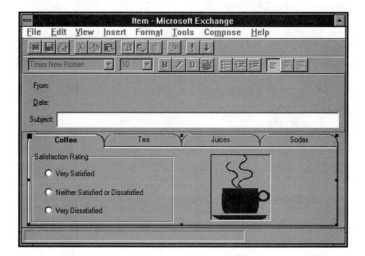

Field Help

Every field on your designed forms can have a help entry associated with it if you want. Access the Field Properties for the field, move to the General page, and use the Field Help button. You see the Field Help for Users dialog box shown in figure 19.32. Simply type in help text in the Help area and save your changes.

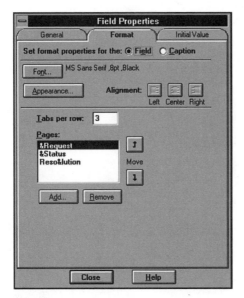

Figure 19.31

The Tab field Format page.

Figure 19.32

The Field Help for Users dialog box.

Tip You can add all your field help at the same time by using the Fiel**d** choice in the Field Help for Users dialog box.

CHAPTER 20

Advanced Development: Exploring Sample Applications

Microsoft Exchange Server includes a number of sample forms that illustrate different ways to implement form and folder applications. One of the best ways to learn more about form and folder design is to understand these included applications thoroughly. Doing so will enable you to understand more about the capabilities of Exchange Server for automating business processes. Because the sample applications are modifiable, they can serve as a basis with which to construct your own organization's applications.

In this chapter, you explore two of the sample applications included with Exchange Server. The first is a Send Form called Charity Donation; it is used for employees to make company-matched donations through a payroll deduction plan. The second is called the Hot Topics folder; it illustrates the use of rules and permissions.

This chapter assumes you have installed the Exchange Server sample applications. If you have not, locate the directory SAMPAPPS on your Exchange Server computer and follow the instructions contained in the README.WRI file that is stored along with the SAMPAPPS.PST file.

Understanding the Charity Donation Application

The Charity Donation form is designed to support company-sponsored donations to charitable organizations. With the form, an employee can choose to make a donation to a specified charity through the use of a payroll deduction. The payroll portion is not part of the application; rather, the employee sends the completed charity donation form to the individual in the company responsible for tracking and accounting for donations. The Charity Donation form is shown in figure 20.1.

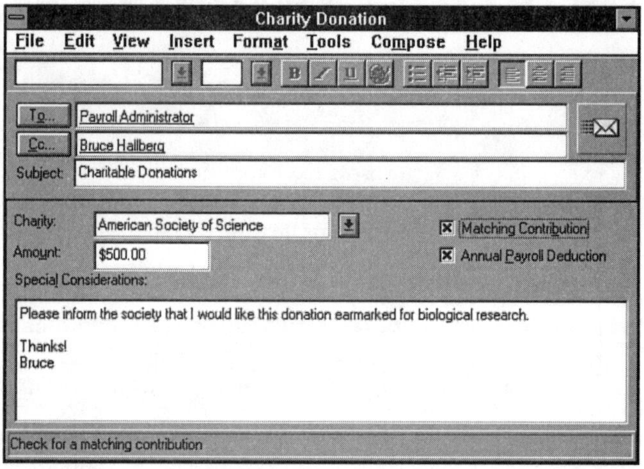

Figure 20.1

The Charity Donation form.

	Charity Donation
File Edit View Insert Format Tools Compose Help	

To... | Payroll Administrator
Cc... | Bruce Hallberg
Subject: | Charitable Donations

Charity: | American Society of Science | ☒ Matching Contribution
Amount: | $500.00 | ☒ Annual Payroll Deduction
Special Considerations:

Please inform the society that I would like this donation earmarked for biological research.

Thanks!
Bruce

Check for a matching contribution

The Charity Donation application is made up of two forms: Create, which is used to submit a new donation request, and Read, which is used by the donation administrator to read submitted items. The Read form is a duplicate of Create, except that all the fields have been changed to have a Locked property so that they cannot be changed by the reader. Figures 20.2 and 20.3 show the Create and Read forms, respectively.

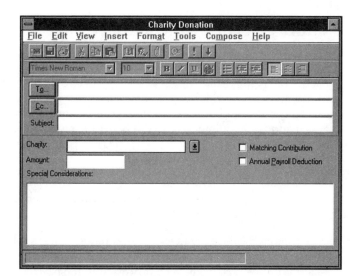

Figure 20.2

The Charity Donation Create form.

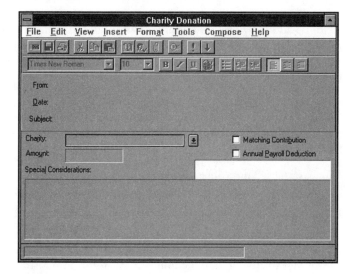

Figure 20.3

The Charity Donation Read form.

Tip

You can quickly create a form to read items by using the form you designed for creating items. For example, the Charity Donation Read form was created by first designing the Create form and then using the **E**dit New **W**indow command in the Forms Designer to copy the form to a new Read form. Finally, all the fields on the Read form were changed to Locked in the field properties, causing the fields to be read-only.

Extending the Charity Form's Functionality

The Charity Donation form is an example of a simple Exchange Server form. Basically, it is just a way for employees to fill out all the relevant information needed when requesting a donation payroll deduction.

For the person administering the deductions, however, much can be done to automate the process further. The donations administrator will benefit from the following additional capabilities:

◆ A filtering rule that tests to ensure that the request meets company policies.

◆ Automated replies that respond to requestors with either error messages or messages letting them know that their requests will be processed.

◆ Filtering rules that automatically place the new donation requests into a folder designed to hold them. This way, the donations administrator can keep all the donations in one place until they are ready to be processed in the payroll system.

All these capabilities can be added by using the Inbox Assistant in the donation administrator's mailbox. You create two rules that take care of the needed capabilities:

◆ The first rule checks to see whether the donation request is for matching funds from the company and exceeds $1000. The example company matches funds only up to $1000, and the rule responds to requestors with a reminder to that effect. It also alerts the donations administrator that an invalid request was made.

◆ For all other requests, the second rule automatically replies to the requestor and moves the request to a folder designed to hold the requests until they are processed into the payroll system.

The following steps and figures illustrate how these rules are created:

1. First, create a new folder for the donation administrator in the administrator's personal mailbox called "Donations to be Processed."

 If the donation administrator's personal folders are stored on the administrator's own computer, consider creating instead a public folder to hold the donation requests and granting access only to the donation administrator. This way, important data in the folder will be part of your normal Exchange Server backups.

2. In the donation administrator's mailbox, pull down the **T**ools menu and choose In**b**ox Assistant. You must be connected to the Exchange Server computer in order to access the Inbox Assistant. You see the screen shown in figure 20.4.

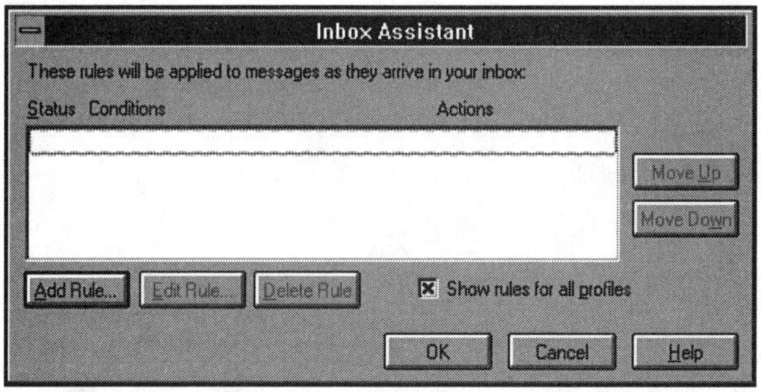

Figure 20.4

The Inbox Assistant dialog box.

3. Choose the **A**dd Rule button. You now see the dialog box shown in figure 20.5.

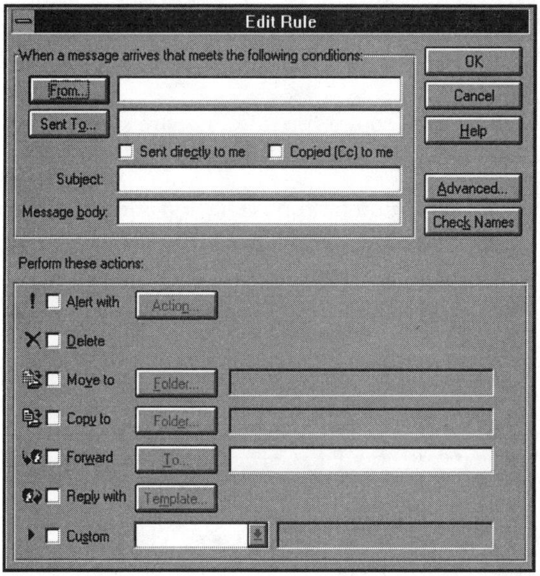

Figure 20.5

The Edit Rule dialog box.

4. Click on the **A**dvanced button to move to the Advanced dialog box, shown in figure 20.6.

Figure 20.6

The Advanced dialog box.

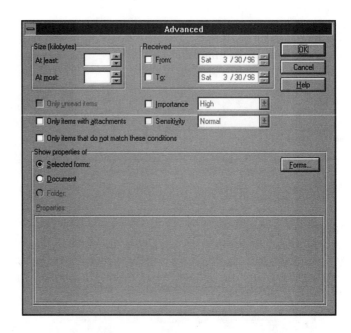

The Advanced dialog box can be used to test for rules that are specific to a particular form type and rely on fields that are included in that form.

5. Make sure the **S**elected forms option button is selected and click on the **F**orms button. This brings up the Select Forms dialog box shown in figure 20.7.

Figure 20.7

The Select Forms dialog box.

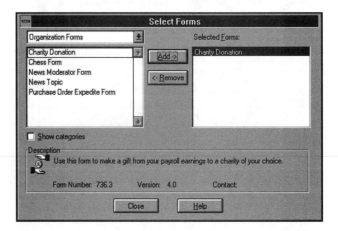

6. Choose Organization Forms from the drop-down list box, choose the Charity Donation form in the left window, and then click on the **A**dd button to add the form to the Selected **F**orms window. Click on the Close button to return to the Advanced dialog box.

In order to access the Organization Forms library, you must first create it in the Exchange Administrator program by using the **F**orms Administrator command in the **T**ools menu. You also need full access to that library in order to install forms to it.

7. In the Advanced dialog box, select the checkboxes next to the $$ and Matching fields. Set the $$ field properties to Greater Than $1000, and the Matching field property to Yes. Figure 20.8 shows the completed screen. Click on the OK button in the Advanced dialog box to return to the Edit Rule dialog box.

<table>
<tr><td colspan="3" align="center">Advanced</td></tr>
<tr><td>Size (kilobytes)
At least:
At most:</td><td>Received
☐ From: Sat   3 / 30 / 96
☐ To: Sat   3 / 30 / 96</td><td>OK
Cancel
Help</td></tr>
</table>

Figure 20.8

The Advanced dialog box with field properties set.

☐ Only unread items   ☐ Importance   High

☐ Only items with attachments   ☐ Sensitivity   Normal

☐ Only items that do not match these conditions

Show properties of
◉ Selected forms: Charity Donation   Forms...
○ Document
○ Folder

Properties:

☐ Cap3		
☐ Charity		
☒ $$	Greater Than	1000
☒ Matching	Yes	
☐ Payroll Ded		

You have now defined an advanced selection that will identify any requests for matching funds that exceed $1000. On the Edit Rule screen, you can now choose how you want to handle those cases. In this example, you decide that you want to reply to the requestor with a message saying that the request cannot be processed. You then want to delete the request, because no further action is required on the part of the donation administrator.

8. Select the **D**elete and Re**p**ly with checkboxes. Then click on the Te**m**plate button next to the Re**p**ly field. You see the Reply Template dialog box. Compose a suitable reply, leaving the T**o** and **C**c fields blank. Figure 20.9 shows the reply template dialog box with an example reply. When you finish typing the reply, close the dialog box and save your changes when prompted.

Figure 20.9

The reply template dialog box.

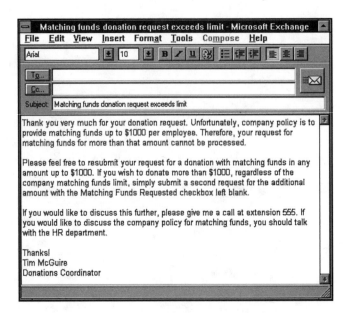

9. In the Edit Rule dialog box, click on the OK button to save your new rule.

After creating the first rule, you can create the second rule dealing with donation requests that do meet the selection criteria. Follow the preceding steps 3 through 9, but substitute these changes:

◆ In the Advanced dialog box, use the same selection criteria that were shown in the preceding step 7, but check the Only items that do **n**ot match these conditions checkbox.

◆ Do not check the **D**elete checkbox in the Edit Rule dialog box. Instead, check the Mo**v**e to checkbox and then click on the **F**older button to select the folder you created in the preceding step 1.

◆ Compose an appropriate reply in the reply template dialog box, such as the one shown in figure 20.10.

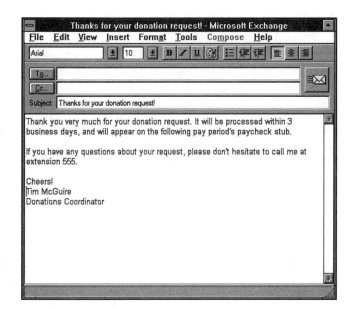

Figure 20.10

Accepted request reply template.

Understanding the Hot Topics Application

As companies become more connected to the Internet and other sources of news and information, people tend to spend more time distributing information that they think is relevant to other people. There are two problems with this:

◆ The information may not actually be relevant.

◆ There is the chance of duplication of effort as the information is distributed.

One of the sample applications, Hot Topics, helps address these problems. You already know how to install a folder to which many people have access, and in which they can create and read new items. The Hot Topics application, though, enables you to build a moderated information folder. The moderators read new items privately and can then approve or decline the new items.

The mechanism for the Hot Topics application can be easily applied to any folder to provide moderation, and special forms are not required (although Hot Topics includes special forms). To create a moderated folder, you create two folders. The first, top-level folder, contains approved items. The second folder is nested inside the first folder, and it contains new items that require approval.

Users post new items to the top-level folder, in which they have create and read access. Users have no access to the nested second folder. Rules attached to the top-level folder automatically move new items to the moderated folder. Once a moderator, who has access to the second folder, approves an item, a rule attached to the second folder moves the item back to the top-level folder, in which the users can read the posted item. To see how this works, walk through the setup for the Hot Topics application in the following steps. Using these steps as a general guide, you can then create your own moderated folders:

1. To begin, copy the folder Hot Topics in the Exchange-Sample Applications folder to your set of public folders. Select the Hot Topics folder and choose the Copy command in the File menu of Exchange Client. This prompts you for a destination. When you finish, you see the new folders, as shown in figure 20.11.

Figure 20.11

Copy of Hot Topics folders.

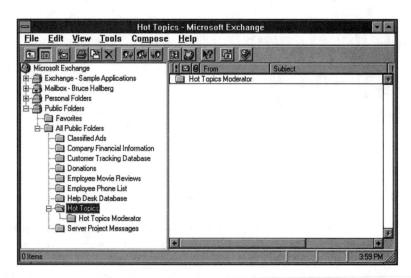

2. You next need to add both folders to your Personal Address Book. Select the Hot Topics folder, pull down the Tools menu, choose Application Design, and then choose Folder Designer. Move to the Administration tab, shown in figure 20.12.

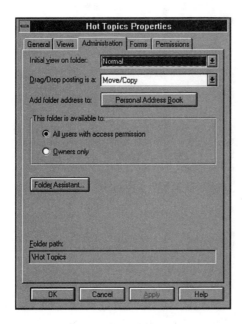

Figure 20.12

The Administration tab in Folder Designer.

3. Click on the Personal Address **B**ook button to add this folder's entry to your personal address book. Click on OK to close the dialog box.

4. Repeat the previous two steps for the Hot Topics Moderated folder.

5. Next, you need to set permissions for the two folders. First, select the Hot Topics folder, and then reaccess the Folder Designer. Pull down the **T**ools menu, choose Application Desig**n**, and then choose F**o**lder Designer. Move to the Permissions tab, shown in figure 20.13.

6. Change the Default role to Reviewer and ensure that you are set as Owner. Add a new permission to the folder for the Hot Topics Moderator folder. Click on the **Ad**d button and choose the Hot Topics Moderator from your personal address book. The Hot Topics Moderator should be given a role of Author. Click on OK to close the dialog box.

 Note You can grant access permissions that enable one folder to post to another folder. This is necessary for the rules that you are creating for Hot Topics to function. For the Hot Topics application, the folders—rather than you or your users—move the messages between the two folders that make up the application.

Figure 20.13

The Permissions tab in Folder Designer.

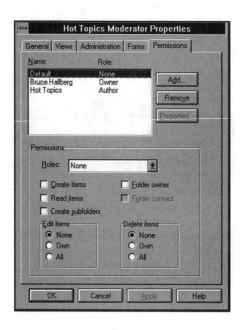

7. Repeat the previous two steps for the Hot Topics Moderator folder, except use these permission roles: the Default role is None, any moderators will be given the Editor role, and you will add the Hot Topics folder to the permissions list with a role of Author. Figure 20.14 shows you the completed Permissions page.

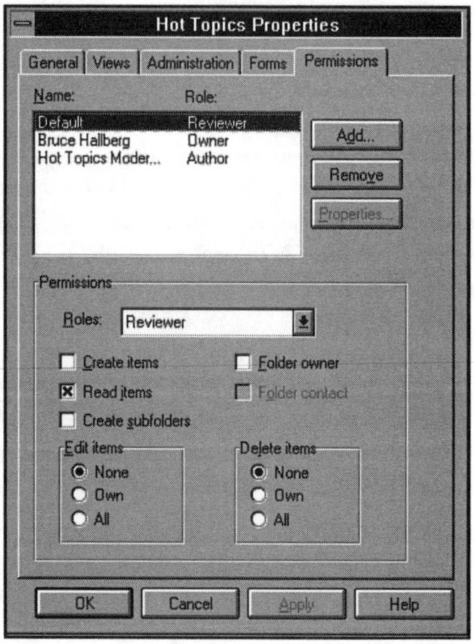

Fig. 20.14

The Hot Topics Moderator Permissions page.

Your next task is to create the rules that make this application work. Rules are already in place in both the Hot Topics and Hot Topics Moderator folders, but they need to be changed so that they refer to the copy of the application that you're working with rather than the original. Follow these steps to create the needed rules:

1. Select the Hot Topics folder and access the Folder Designer notebook. Move to the Administration tab and click on the Folde**r** Assistant button. You see the Folder Assistant dialog box shown in figure 20.15.

Figure 20.15

The Folder Assistant dialog box.

2. Select the top rule, the one with a Reply action, and click on the **E**dit Rule button. You will see the Edit Rule dialog box shown in figure 20.16.

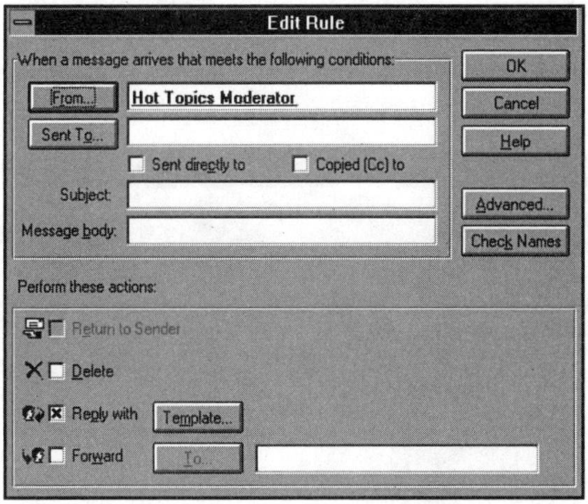

Figure 20.16

The Edit Rule dialog box.

3. In the F**r**om field, delete Hot Topics Moderator from the field. Then, click on the F**r**om button and select Hot Topics Moderator from your Personal Address Book. Click on OK to close the Edit Rule dialog box.

Note The original copy of the Hot Topics application referred to the original copies of the folders in the rules section. When you copied the Hot Topics folders earlier in this example, the rules were not updated and still referred to those original folders. Deleting the folder name from the rules and re-adding it with the steps shown ensures that your working copy uses its own folders.

4. Select the second rule, the one with the FORWARD TO action, and click on the **E**dit Rule button. Replace the **F**rom field and the bottommost **T**o field in the same way as you did in step 3. You are deleting the Hot Topics folder from those fields and re-adding it so that the correct folder will be used. Close the Edit Rule dialog box and then the Folder Assistant dialog box with their respective OK buttons.

5. Select the Hot Topics Moderator folder and access its Folder Assistant as you did for the Hot Topics folder in step 1. You will see only one rule in the Hot Topics Moderator Folder Assistant dialog box. Edit the rule so that you replace Hot Topics in both the **F**rom field and the bottom **T**o field the same as you did in step 4 for the Hot Topics folder.

To test the Hot Topics folder, select the Hot Topics folder in the Folder view of Exchange Client. Access the Co**m**pose menu and choose New News Topic. This brings up the new topic form attached to the Hot Topics folders. Fill out the form and send it. You should see that the item you just sent does not appear in the Hot Topics folder, but instead appears in the Hot Topics Moderator folder. Accessing the item in the Hot Topics Moderator folder brings up the reviewer form shown in figure 20.17.

Figure 20.17

The Hot Topics Moderator review form.

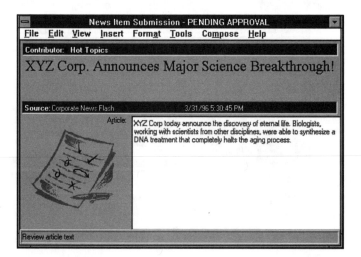

The moderator can read and, if necessary, edit the item in question. Once the item is approved, the moderator accesses the Compose menu and chooses Approve from the menu. Then click on the Post button. Once this is done, the item is automatically posted back to the Hot Topics folder and can be read by anyone with access to the Hot Topics folder (which, by default, is everyone).

The rules that are preset in the Hot Topics and Hot Topics Moderator folders are relatively straightforward, and you should spend time reviewing them before creating your own moderated information folder from scratch. Paraphrased, here are the rules that make this all work:

◆ The Hot Topics folder has two rules. The first one says that any items posted to this folder that are *not* from the Hot Topics Moderator folder should invoke a reply to the person who posted the item with an acknowledgment message template.

◆ The second Hot Topics folder rule states that any items posted to the folder that are *not* sent from the Hot Topics Moderator folder should be forwarded to the Hot Topics Moderator folder and then deleted from the Hot Topics folder.

◆ The Hot Topics Moderator folder has one rule: any items posted to the folder that are *not* from the Hot Topics folder should be forwarded to the Hot Topics folder and should then be deleted.

Items sent to the Hot Topics folder are from one of the users of the system. The Hot Topics folder then forwards them to the Hot Topics Moderator folder, and the sender changes during that process; it is now being sent by Hot Topics and not by the original sender. Then, when the Hot Topics Moderator folder forwards the message back to Hot Topics, the sender name is changed again and is now Hot Topics Moderator. Because of this, there is no risk of causing an endless loop with these rules.

When you approve an item in the Hot Topics Moderator folder, you are actually creating a new post to the Hot Topics Moderator folder that contains your name as the sender. The folder then sees that new posting and uses the rule that checks to see whether the post is from the Hot Topics folder. Because it is not, it is forwarded to the Hot Topics folder, and the sender's name becomes Hot Topics Moderator.

CHAPTER 21

Using Visual Basic

The forms you created using Microsoft Exchange Forms Designer will improve the way information moves throughout your organization, but perhaps you have found that a particular form or group of forms could offer even more benefits if you could add a few more features and capabilities. Exchange Forms Designer is a useful tool to create most forms, but it can run out of steam in some situations. To solve these problems, you can use Visual Basic to expand the functionality of your forms.

The Forms Designer creates Visual Basic code for all your existing forms. Once that is done, you can use Visual Basic for Microsoft Exchange Server 4.0 to embellish your projects further. Visual Basic is a powerful development tool designed for Windows application development.

You can create all the forms for your project with Visual Basic. Why would you use Visual Basic when you can create them faster and easier using Forms Designer? With Forms Designer you can create your forms in an easy-to-use interface and let Forms Designer generate all the Visual Basic code for you. In this chapter, you begin with a form created by using Forms Designer, generate the Visual Basic code by using Forms Designer, then complete your development by using the Visual Basic environment.

 You should be an accomplished Visual Basic programmer if you plan on modifying Exchange Server forms with Visual Basic. For more advanced work on forms in Visual Basic, you should also be familiar with the Messaging API (MAPI).

Understanding Forms and Visual Basic

All forms in Exchange Server are actually Visual Basic programs that use the Messaging API (MAPI) to communicate seamlessly with Exchange Client so that users cannot tell that a separate program is being run when they use a form. In fact, as you have seen if you installed forms from Forms Designer, each form goes through a Visual Basic compilation process that produces the final EXE file for the form. It is this EXE file, along with some other files, that is installed into Exchange and is invoked when forms are used. Each form includes the following component files:

◆ A form EXE file that contains the compiled Visual Basic program

◆ MSRICHED.VBX, a file that provides rich text editing for text fields

◆ MAPIFORM.VBX, which contains the code needed to communicate between Exchange Client and the form through OLE automation

◆ OLE Messaging Resources

◆ The Visual Basic runtime modules

◆ The Visual Basic source code stored in VBP files

When you install a form from the Forms Designer into Exchange, a subdirectory is created beneath the form template called *formname*.vb in which all the Visual Basic files are kept. They are left in place once the form is installed.

The files stored in the *formname*.vb subdirectory are composed of both variant and invariant files. The *variant files* are those that contain code that is specific to the form. *Invariant files*, on the other hand, are produced for each form and do not change from form to form. When you use Visual Basic to modify a form program, you edit the variant files listed in table 21.1.

Table 21.1
Variant Files

File Name	Contents
WINDOW1.FRM	This file contains the main form generated in a one-window project. For a single-window project, you generally only need to modify this form file.
Compose.FRM, *Read*.FRM	In a two-form project, there are individual files for both the read and the compose forms. By default, these files are called COMPOSE.FRM and READ.FRM. However, if you choose other window names for these forms, the files will use the window names for their file names. These are the two main files to modify when extending a form.
VAR.BAS	This program file performs administration for the form, including setting the name of the form window that is activated and evaluating the status of the message.
INVAR.RES	This file contains form-specific information, such as QuickHelp messages, initial field values, and so forth.
Formname.CFG	A key file for every form, this file contains the form specifications; Exchange uses it during form installation. When you add a custom control to a form program and want the custom control to be available as a filtering field in Exchange Client, you modify this file to register your new custom control.

Making Changes to Procedures

Within the WINDOW1.FRM or Read.FRM and Compose.FRM files, there are four key procedures with which you generally work:

- ◆ **Window_Prep.** This procedure handles the user interface of the form.

- ◆ **Window_Init.** You modify this procedure to change initial values for controls found in the form.

- ◆ **Window_Load.** This procedure works with a control's MAPI properties and sets its values.

- ◆ **Window_Store.** This procedure saves a control's MAPI properties.

Starting a Form Project

Open an existing Forms Designer form from the File menu and choose Open. Select the forms project you want to convert and click on OK. Figure 21.1 shows an example of a simple entry form for sending vacation and sick leave information to another person. Although this form may serve its purpose, you can enhance its functionality by using Visual Basic. To begin the conversion process, select the Install command from the File menu. Exchange Forms Designer automatically converts your form to a Visual Basic project, creating all the code necessary for Visual Basic.

Figure 21.1

The Schedule Time Away Forms Designer form.

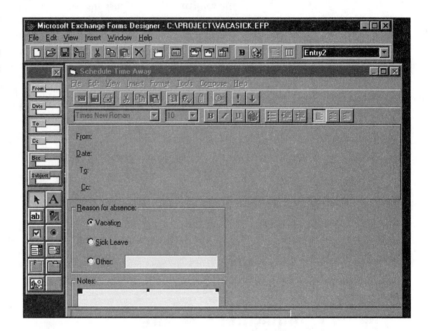

Forms Designer generates the VB code, opening Visual Basic during the process. Once it is completed, you are returned to Forms Designer and Visual Basic is closed. The Forms Designer then opens the Library dialog box (see fig. 21.2) permitting you to choose in which Forms Library you want to install the form. Normally, this is a public folder containing other similar forms. You may choose not to install the form in a Forms Library at this time by clicking on Cancel.

Your new Visual Basic project has been saved in a new folder located in the same directory as your form project and named *\formname*.VB. The folder contains all the components of your new Visual Basic project.

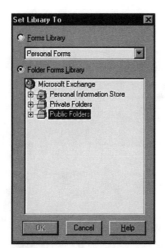

Figure 21.2

*The Set Library
To dialog box.*

Using Visual Basic with Forms

Visual Basic may appear to be similar to Forms Designer at first glance. It has several main windows: a main form with drop-down menus across the top of your screen, a toolbox along the left side, and a central window for working on forms. Do not be fooled, however—it is a powerful development tool used by professional application developers. Figure 21.3 shows you the main windows of a Visual Basic session. On the right side of your screen is the Project window. This is where each of the components of your project are shown.

The program Visual Basic for Microsoft Exchange Server 4.0 is included with the Exchange Forms Designer package. The application file is called VB.EXE and is located in the VB folder in the directory where you installed Exchange Forms Designer; by default, this is \EXCHANGE\EFDFORMS\VB.

 For you programmers who already have Visual Basic installed on your system, you can use your installed software if you prefer. However, you must use a 16-bit version of Visual Basic, version 4.0 or later, to modify forms generated with Forms Designer.

Start Visual Basic and open your converted project by selecting Open Project on the File menu. Remember where the file is? Begin from the folder where your original Forms Designer project was saved. Look for the folder *formname*.VB and you will find the file *formname*.vbp, where *formname* is the name of your form. Figure 21.4 shows your Visual Basic project. Note the Project window on the right of the screen showing all the components of the project.

Figure 21.3

Visual Basic windows.

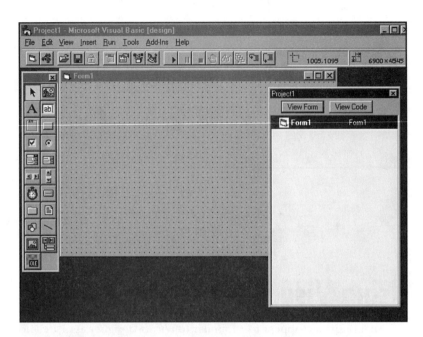

Figure 21.4

New Visual Basic project created by Forms Designer.

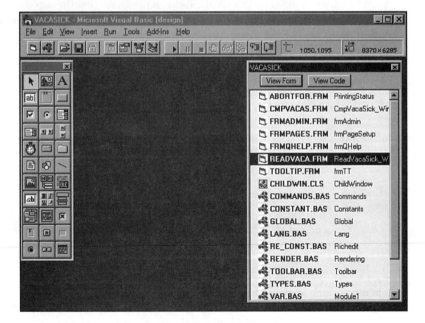

Opening Forms

Forms in Visual Basic are opened from the Project window. Highlight the desired form (with the FRM extension) and click on the View Form button. Figure 21.5 shows the original Forms Designer form in the new VB project.

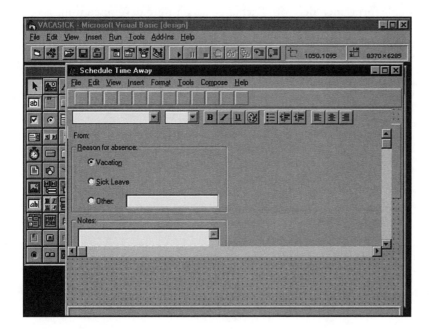

Figure 21.5

Visual Basic representation of Forms Designer.

Installing Visual Basic Forms

Once you finish modifying the form's Visual Basic code, installing the modified form into Exchange Server requires just a few steps:

1. Access the File menu in Visual Basic and choose the Make EXE file command.

2. By default, Visual Basic will choose to make the EXE file using a file name stored in the *formname*.CFG file. Because Exchange Client relies on the EXE file name found in the *formname*.CFG file in order to install the correct program, accept the default EXE name.

   In Exchange Client, access the Forms Manager and use the Install button. Navigate to the directory where your project is stored, using the File/Open dialog box that appears, and select the *formname*.CFG file. Click on OK to complete the form installation.

Visual Basic is a powerful tool with which you can create virtually any type of form that you can imagine. Beginners to this process should rely on the Forms Designer to create the initial code for their project and then use Visual Basic to extend its functionality. Experienced programmers, who clearly understand Visual Basic, MAPI, and how the two work with Exchange, can build forms entirely from scratch.

Many of the sample forms included with Exchange Server were developed using Visual Basic to extend their functionality. The Chess form is an excellent example of the sort of custom form that can be developed with this tool. Although the Chess form really doesn't constitute a serious business tool, it does give you some idea of the capabilities you have with Visual Basic and Exchange.

CHAPTER 22

Developing and Administering Custom Applications

In a complex organization, the process of deploying custom Exchange Server forms requires planning and careful thought. Although the process of deploying forms is relatively simple in practice, you should be familiar with a number of issues before deployment. In this chapter, you learn about these issues and how to handle form and folder implementation.

Application development and deployment should consist, at a minimum, of the following steps:

◆ Application design

◆ Installation to personal folders for testing

◆ Rollout to a limited number of users for further testing

◆ Rollout to all users, including multisite and offline implementation—depending on your company, this last step may be further broken up into smaller chunks (for example, deploy to one site, and then a second, and then the rest of your sites, and finally to offline users)

You also need to plan how you will make changes to forms already in place. Generally, if your changes are limited to permissions changes or view changes, you can make the changes in place to the existing form. However, when you want to modify a form's layout or rules, it is best to make changes to a copy of the implemented form rather than directly to the original. This way, your changes can be tested before you apply them.

Using the Forms Manager

Most of the time, you initially install forms right from the Form Designer application. When you do this, it is best to install the application to your personal folders first so that you can test the application's functionality. After you are satisfied that the application is working according to design, you can then copy the application from your personal folders to either the Organization Form Library (if it is a Send Form) or to an appropriate Public Folder (if it is a Folder Form).

You already learned, in Chapter 19, "Developing Forms," how to install forms to your personal folders. Then, depending on the type of application, you copy it either to the Organization Form library (if you've created one) or to a Public Folder. Use the following steps to copy a form to an Organization Form Library:

1. Access the **T**ools menu and choose **O**ptions. This brings up the Options dialog box. Move to the Exchange Server tab, shown in figure 22.1.

2. Click on the Manage **F**orms button to access the Forms Manager, shown in figure 22.2.

3. By default, the left window should display the Organization Forms library, and the right window should display the Personal Forms library. If this is not the case, or if you want to select a different library, click on the appropriate Set button to open a different library. Clicking on the Set button causes the Set Library To dialog box in figure 22.3 to appear.

4. In this particular example, copy the Purchase Order Expedite form to the Organization Forms library. Select the form in the Personal Forms window and then click on the C**o**py button.

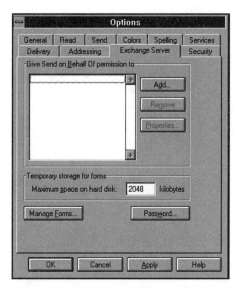

Figure 22.1

*The Options
Exchange Server
tab.*

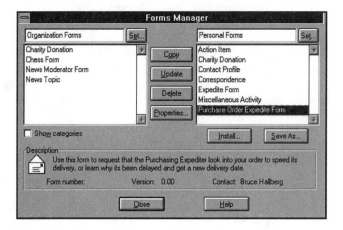

Figure 22.2

*The Forms
Manager.*

> **Note** Remember, in order to install a form into a library, you must have sufficient rights to do so.

You can also update forms in the same way by using the <u>U</u>pdate button in the Forms Manager.

The Forms Manager has two other properties that will be useful to you as you work with your forms. First, you can save a form out to an FDM file by using the <u>S</u>ave As button. An FDM file can be placed onto a disk or otherwise distributed to another person who can then install the form using the <u>I</u>nstall button in the Forms Manager.

Figure 22.3

The Set Library To dialog box.

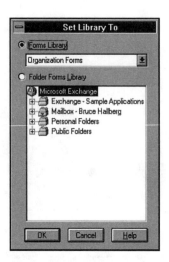

The second property, of course, is the capability of directly installing a form from an FDM file or from the directory in which the form was compiled by using the form's CFG file. Installing forms copies the Visual Basic EXE file into the selected form library (all forms ultimately exist as Visual Basic EXE programs).

 Whenever you install a form using the Forms Designer, a subdirectory is created that holds the necessary Visual Basic files for the form. In this subdirectory is a file that defines the form, and that has an extension of CFG. Chapter 21, "Using Visual Basic," defines this process in more detail.

You can access the Forms Manager, as you have seen, by using the **O**ptions command in Exchange Client's **T**ools menu. You also can select a folder to which you have Owner rights, and access the Forms Manager through the folder's properties, by using the **M**anage button on the Forms tab. Both methods yield the same result, although opening the Forms Manager from a folder automatically opens that folder's associated forms.

Updating Forms

Exchange items that rely on a particular form do so by using a unique identifier for each form. Each item stores that identifier and therefore uses the correct form to display the item.

When you make substantial changes to a form and then install the updated form, you run the risk of making a change that will conflict with existing items (messages) created with the old form. This could happen if you've changed how the fields in the form work—delete fields, for example. You can work around this problem by storing the new, updated form with a new name. You then set the previous form's Hidden property so that users cannot see it in their forms display.

The result is that new items will use the new form, and old items will use the old form (because it is still available, only hidden from normal view). Once sufficient time has passed where you know that old items that rely on the old form no longer exist, you can safely remove the old form.

To mark a form as hidden, select it in the Forms Manager dialog box and click on the **P**roperties button. This displays Form Properties, as shown in figure 22.4. Select the Hi**d**den checkbox to make the form invisible.

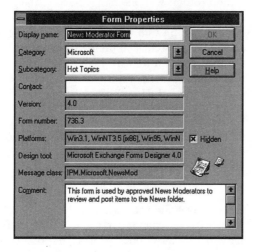

Figure 22.4

Form Properties.

Replicating Form Libraries

Forms attached to a public folder automatically replicate to other sites if replication for the folder is enabled. However, the Organization Forms library is not replicated to other sites automatically. Instead, you need to enable this function.

The Organization Forms library is a folder like any other, except that users cannot view it in their folder displays. Because it is a folder, it is automatically replicated to all other servers in the same site, but it will not automatically replicate to other sites in your organization.

You can view the Organization Forms folder in the Exchange Administrator program, and you can access its properties page to enable replication to other sites. To do this, open the System Folders folder in the Administrator program and then open the EFORMS REGISTRY folder. Inside, you will find the Organization Forms folder. Select it and access the **P**roperties command in the **F**ile menu and then use the Replicas tab to enable replication to other sites. (You can learn more about folder replication in Chapter 9, "Managing Replication and Synchronization.")

Handling Offline Access Issues

There are two issues involved with offline or remote users: form distribution and replication conflicts.

When offline users synchronize their folders with Exchange Server, all forms attached to items in their offline folders are automatically copied to their OST file and are available while they are offline. (The OST files store their offline folders.) This applies to any folders in users' Mailboxes as well as in their Favorites folders. The basic Mailbox folders (Inbox, Outbox, Deleted Items, and Sent Items) are automatically designated as Offline folders. Other folders need to be designated. Users do this with the folder's Properties notebook, using the Synchronization tab.

Individual forms in the Organization Forms library are automatically sent to offline users when they receive an item that makes use of them. However, if offline users want to access other forms for offline use, they need to use the Forms Manager to copy the forms from the Organization Forms libraries to their Personal Forms libraries.

When users modify items in offline folders and then synchronize with Exchange Server, the modified items are automatically changed in the Exchange Server folder. Similarly, modifications in folder views are also updated, assuming that the users are the owners of the public folders.

It is possible for two users to modify the same item offline, or folder view if they are owners, and then synchronize their changes without knowing that another user is doing the same thing. When this happens, the most recent change is the one stored in the folder. Users may need to modify items in a folder. If you are concerned about changes being lost in this way, consider setting up your folders in such a way that changes are posted to another folder, and a single individual reviews the changes and then decides whether they should be applied to the master folder. You also could consider alternatives, such as simply removing security rights to change posted items.

INDEX I

Symbols

A

CHECK OUT THESE RELATED TOPICS OR SEE YOUR LOCAL BOOKSTORE

CAD	As the number one CAD publisher in the world, and as a Registered Publisher of Autodesk, New Riders Publishing provides unequaled content on this complex topic under the flagship *Inside AutoCAD*. Other titles include *AutoCAD for Beginners* and *New Riders' Reference Guide to AutoCAD Release 13*.
Networking	As the leading Novell NetWare publisher, New Riders Publishing delivers cutting-edge products for network professionals. We publish books for all levels of users, from those wanting to gain NetWare Certification, to those administering or installing a network. Leading books in this category include *Inside NetWare 3.12*, *Inside TCP/IP Second Edition*, *NetWare: The Professional Reference*, and *Managing the NetWare 3.x Server*.
Graphics and 3D Studio	New Riders provides readers with the most comprehensive product tutorials and references available for the graphics market. Best-sellers include *Inside Photoshop 3*, *3D Studio IPAS Plug In Reference*, *KPT's Filters and Effects*, and *Inside 3D Studio*.
Internet and Communications	As one of the fastest-growing publishers in the communications market, New Riders provides unparalleled information and detail on this ever-changing topic area. We publish international best-sellers such as *New Riders' Official Internet Yellow Pages, 2nd Edition*, a directory of over 10,000 listings of Internet sites and resources from around the world, as well as *VRML: Browsing and Building Cyberspace, Actually Useful Internet Security Techniques, Internet Firewalls and Network Security*, and *New Riders' Official World Wide Web Yellow Pages*.
Operating Systems	Expanding off our expertise in technical markets, and driven by the needs of the computing and business professional, New Riders offers comprehensive references for experienced and advanced users of today's most popular operating systems, including *Inside Windows 95, Inside Unix, Inside OS/2 Warp Version 3*, and *Building a Unix Internet Server*.

New Riders Publishing   201 West 103rd Street ◆ Indianapolis, Indiana 46290 USA

New Riders has emerged as a premier publisher of computer books for the professional computer user. Focusing on CAD/graphics/multimedia, communications/internetworking, and networking/operating systems, New Riders continues to provide expert advice on high-end topics and software.

Check out the online version of *New Riders' Official World Wide Yellow Pages, 1996 Edition* for the most engaging, entertaining, and informative sites on the Web! You can even add your own site!

Brave our site for the finest collection of CAD and 3D imagery produced today. Professionals from all over the world contribute to our gallery, which features new designs every month.

From Novell to Microsoft, New Riders publishes the training guides you need to attain your certification. Visit our site and try your hand at the CNE Endeavor, a test engine created by VFX Technologies, Inc. that enables you to measure what you know—and what you don't!

http://www.mcp.com/newriders

REGISTRATION CARD

Inside Microsoft Exchange Server

Name _____ Title _____

Company _____ Type of business _____

Address _____

City/State/ZIP _____

Have you used these types of books before? ☐ yes ☐ no

If yes, which ones? _____

_____

How many computer books do you purchase each year? ☐ 1–5 ☐ 6 or more

How did you learn about this book? _____

Where did you purchase this book? _____

Which applications do you currently use? _____

_____

Which computer magazines do you subscribe to? _____

_____

What trade shows do you attend? _____

_____

Comments: _____

_____

_____

Would you like to be placed on our preferred mailing list? ☐ yes ☐ no

☐ **I would like to see my name in print!** You may use my name and quote me in future New Riders products and promotions. My daytime phone number is: _____

New Riders Publishing 201 West 103rd Street ◆ Indianapolis, Indiana 46290 USA

Fax to **317-581-4670**

Fold Here

- -

NEW RIDERS PUBLISHING
201 W. 103RD ST.
INDIANAPOLIS, IN 46290-9058